I0008800

ACCESS 2010 PURE SQL

REAL, POWER-PACKED SOLUTIONS FOR BUSINESS USERS, DEVELOPERS, AND THE REST OF US

Pindaro E. Demertzoglou, Ph.D.

Alpha Press – Albany, New York 2013

© Copyright 2013 by Alpha Press, Albany, NY. All rights reserved.

ISBN-13: 978-0988330023
ISBN-10: 0988330024

Printed in the United States of America

Library of Congress Control Number: 2013932237

No part of this publication or the accompanying software may be reproduced, stored in a retrieval system, or transmitted in any form or by any means – electronic, mechanical, photocopying, recording, or any other means – without the written permission of the publisher.

This publication, its supporting materials and the accompanying database is an information product published for general reference and sold as is. It does not offer legal, accounting, psychological, or tax advice. The publisher and author disclaim any personal responsibility or liability, directly or indirectly, for information presented in this publication. The purchaser or reader of this publication assumes all responsibility for the use of the materials and information contained within. The author and publisher made every effort to prepare this book with care and accuracy. However, they assume no responsibility for errors, inaccuracies, non-working code, or omissions. The material in this book is presented for educational purposes only.

About the Author

Pindaro's relationship with databases started with DBase III back in 1991, continuing with all versions of Access since early 1993, and working with MS SQL Server, MySQL, Oracle, and IBM DB2 for a number of years. From then on, he is still in love with all of them. After twenty years, he still works with data, information processing, integration, and dissemination.

Pindaro is currently a Professor of Information Systems at the business school of Rensselaer Polytechnic Institute in Troy, New York where he is teaching databases for the last thirteen years. Pindaro also completed and collaborated on a myriad of database projects for organizations or in collaborative efforts between the University and various corporations.

Pindaro's interests in information science, transactional systems, and analytics focus on creating more efficient and flexible organizations. The idea is to accomplish more with fewer resources and in less time leaving a small footprint on the environment. Pindaro's education includes a BS from the American College in Thessaloniki Greece, an MS, MBA, and a PhD in the United States. He received national and international distinctions for his work in the field and faculty awards for his teaching methods.

Nevertheless, the majority of the author's experience came from participating in a multitude of industry projects. There, everything has to work efficiently, reliably and above all be acceptable by the people of the corporation. Theoretical knowledge, though useful, takes a second place in these cases. A solid application and strong promotion within the organization are the primary success factors.

Dedication

This book is dedicated to my father Epaminonda Demertzoglou for the continuous and uncompromising support and direction throughout the years.

Acknowledgments

I would like to express my gratitude and say a big thank you to all the teachers around the globe for their effort, patience, and time they devote to their students.

I would like to thank the faculty and staff of the American College of Thessaloniki, Greece who made this college a prestigious and internationally recognized institution. Specifically, I would like to express my deepest appreciation to the former president of the college, Dr. William McGrew and the head librarian Mrs. Pat Kastritsis for their decisive and unrelenting guidance and help to their students. Pat is no longer with us today but the difference she made in my life is propagated to the thousands of students I taught over the last thirteen years in New York. She will live through my own students and the students of my students who receive the same values and attention as the ones I received from Dr. McGrew and Mrs. Kastritsis.

Moreover, I would like to express my deepest appreciation to the staff and faculty of Rensselaer Polytechnic Institute, Troy, NY, United States for the collegiate atmosphere and continuous support in my efforts. I would also like to thank Dr. Shobha Cengalur-Smith, my thesis chair form the State University of New York, Albany United States, who for five and a half years guided me step by step through my research endeavors on databases. I do not know how she did it but she was always there for amazing but lengthy and intricate discussions on databases and their role in organizations.

Finally, I really want to thank my students who with their tens of thousands of questions on databases over the last thirteen years gave me the spark to think and rethink a multitude of points from different perspectives and learn a lot as a result.

BRIEF TABLE OF CONTENTS

DETAILED TABLE OF CONTENTS

PREFACE

The goal of this book is to provide the database professional with knowledge and solutions on everyday database tasks. The rationale has been to reduce needless writing and unnecessary pages and concentrate on providing real learning for the professional setting.

To download the sample database for the book and stay connected with the latest news and updates please go to http://www.databasechannel.com/Products/default.html, and click on the book link to access its resources.

If you need to talk to us for bulk orders or communicate with the author please contact us at alphapress@hotmail.com.

CHAPTER 1
SQL FOUNDATION FOR BUSINESS

1. The origins of SQL

SQL stands for Structured Query Language and it is the standard language for manipulating relational databases. It was developed at IBM in the mid-seventies and at that point it was named SEQUEL standing for Standard English Query Language.

SQL is based on the Relational Database Model officially defined in June 1970 by E. F. Codd in his amazing paper "A Relational Model of Data for Large Shared Data Banks." In his article Dr. Codd explained the need for a new relational model and language for maximum independence from specific programs and system platforms. To this end the goal set more than 40 years ago has been achieved and SQL is used in a multitude of platforms and database servers.

IBM continued its work on SQL throughout the 1970s and introduced SQL/DS in 1981, and DB2 in 1983. The problem was that Oracle was successful in releasing a relational RDBMS in 1979 beating IBM in its own game by two years. Sybase and Microsoft formed a partnership to produce their own RDBMS and they worked together up until version 4 of their

> **A tribute to Dr. Codd**
>
> Dr. Codd joined IBM in 1949 and he worked on numerous projects such the logical design of computers and operating systems. He will be remembered for his creation and work on the relational model of databases in 1970 and relational algebra in 1972. Dr. Codd continued his work on SQL and in 1981 received the extremely prestigious Turing Award for his work on database systems. He is considered the father of modern relational databases.

product. After that, Sybase and Microsoft continued to produce their own databases with Sybase working on their SYSTEM products and Microsoft on their SQL Server versions. Today all commercial vendors face severe competition from open source relational databases like Postgress SQL.

SQL is endorsed by the American National Standards Institute (http://www.ansi.org), and is used by MS SQL Server, dBase for Windows, Paradox, MS Access, INGRES, SYBASE, Oracle,

IBM DB2, and other database software. The American National Standards Institute has the role of maintaining SQL, and periodically publishes update versions of the SQL standard. All major database systems comply with the ANSI standards such as SQL-89 and SQL-92 but the constructs and expressions used in a particular environment might be somewhat different because many of the RDBMS were developed prior to standardization and also commercial vendors introduce proprietary features to gain a competitive edge.

2. What is SQL

SQL is a fourth generation, non-procedural computer programming language. By non-procedural we mean that we are looking at the end result and not the sequence of lines of code. In traditional programming, lines of code execute in sequence, one after the other, to produce the end result. In SQL, a section of code at the end of the SQL statement might execute before a section of code in the beginning of the SQL statement.

The next important characteristic of SQL is that it works to manipulate relational database management systems (RDBMS). These RDBMSs like Access, IBM DB2, Oracle, MS SQL, and PostgressSQL, usually constitute the data layer of the corporation's transaction processing system or at least that should be the case. These transactional databases should be highly normalized which means they consist of a large number of entities with fewer attributes in them or in other words, they consist of many tables with fewer fields in them. It is the job of SQL to manipulate data from multiple tables at the same time. However, in today's working environment transaction processing systems often consist of several relational databases and a host of other heterogeneous data sources (text files, hierarchical files, spreadsheets, etc.) which result in vast amounts of inefficiency for the corporation.

3. SQL in its role as Data Definition Language (DDL)

These SQL statements are further divided into two main categories: In the first category, we have SQL statements we use to create database objects such as tables, indexes, and relationships. In this case we call the SQL code Data Definition Language (DDL). The DDL language supports only three statements which are the CREATE, ALTER, and DROP statements. The ability to use SQL to create database objects does not represent just one additional way to work with a table. By using pure SQL statements, we can understand the inner structure of the objects we are creating. We can also use our knowledge of SQL to enter the realm of other databases like MSSQL Server or MySQL to create objects independent of any design interface, and we can create and delete temporary objects on the fly.

The following is an example of a DDL statement which we use to create a new table with CustomerID as its primary key and two text fields for storing the customer's first and last name.

CREATE TABLE Customer (
[CustomerID] Counter Primary key not null,
[LastName] text(50),
[FirstName] text(50));

The following SQL DDL statement will alter the structure of the existing table "customer" and add one more field called "city". Notice how we can define the data type of the field we are adding as well as its length.

ALTER TABLE Customer
ADD COLUMN City TEXT(25)

Finally, we can delete the table "customer" by using the DROP DDL statement:

DROP TABLE Customer

Now, one might question the practicality of learning how to work with DDL statements since we can do all the above by using the design interface. This is correct but the fact is that we use DDL in many more circumstances than for basic database tasks. Specifically, we use DDL within server side pages in web servers like java server pages or active server pages.net or php to add, delete, and modify tables in the back-end database. The same is true for applications developed with hard-coded languages like C++, Java, or C#. In addition, we use SQL DDL a lot in extraction, transformation, and loading (ETL) packages to move data from one database to another or from a relational database to a data warehouse. Consequently, SQL DDL is a tool that must exist in the belt of any SQL professional and it is part of this book.

4. SQL as data manipulation language

In the second category, we have SQL statements we use to manipulate table data. In this case we call the SQL code Data Manipulation Language (DML). The DML language supports only four statements which are the SELECT, UPDATE, DELETE, and INSERT statements. We use these statements to retrieve, delete, update, and enter new records in the database. The popularity of the statements corresponds with the way they have been presented above. That is, the SELECT statement is the most popular one followed by the UPDATE, and DELETE statements. We rarely use the INSERT statement in SQL per se. Usually, it is used at the application level to insert a multitude of records at once in the database. The conclusion is that for the whole book we will be practically working with the above seven SQL statements; three DDL and four DML ones.

The following is a sample SELECT statement. The SELECT statement identifies which columns or fields of data we would like to retrieve from a table. In this case, we are retrieving four fields from the customers table. The field names must appear identically in the SQL statement as they do in the database table. Many fields can be selected, simply by separating them with commas in the SELECT statement.

```
SELECT state, city, lastname, firstname
FROM Customers
```

We use update statements for two practical reasons: First, we use them to save time by updating multiple records at once. Second, we use them for attaining efficient business operations. The update statement shown below will increase the product price by 10% for all the products coming from a specific supplier. Now, we could go in the table and make the changes manually. That would be ok if we buy only two products from the specific supplier. What if we buy two hundred products? Using an update statement it does not matter if we need to update two, or two hundred, or two thousand records, we can do our job literally in seconds. However, the most important function of update statements is that they let us become more efficient as a business. Specifically, the only constant in business is change. It does not matter if a business expands or contracts, the important thing is to move. A business moves by responding to external or internal stimuli or in other words by responding to initiatives from entities in its external environment like competitors or by initiating actions internally. This means that if a competitor initiates a marketing campaign to obtain market share by reducing their prices, we might respond by reducing prices as well. However, we need to be able to do that quickly at the database level so that the changes in our product catalog are reflected immediately. One way to do that is by using update SQL statements. Then, a couple of days later we might have to change our prices again. We need this agility as a business to be able to stay competitive. The important conclusion is that SQL in general and update statements in particular are not just for the "programming guys" but they can play a central role in any corporation independent of size.

```
UPDATE Products
SET price = price*1.1,
WHERE supplierID = "15"
```

A sample delete statement appears below and its function is to delete from the orders table orders that fall between two specific dates. The main purpose of a delete statement is to save us time and effort by allowing us to delete multiple records at once following very specific criteria. Of course delete statements are used at the application level as well whether we talk about a web application or a hard-coded application like VB.NET or C#.

```
DELETE
FROM Orders
WHERE orderdate BETWEEN #10/15/2014# AND #10/17/2014#
```

We left the INSERT statement for last and though not often used, it is still a very important statement. For example, the INSERT statement below will take all the customers from New York State in the customers table and place them in an archive table. We can achieve this task in seconds using INSERT instead of trying any other alchemies with multiple queries to achieve the same task.

```
INSERT INTO CustomersArchive (firstname, lastname, address, city)
SELECT firstname, lastname, address, city
FROM Customers
WHERE State = 'NY'
```

5. SQL as an ubiquitous standard

If we understand how to work with SQL we have one additional strong advantage. We will, in essence, be able to work with any relational database, commercial or open source, because all of them use SQL. To make an analogy, let us assume that we want to learn how to create web pages. We can buy or download an HTML editor, as there are plenty to choose from. However, what is our strategic goal? Learn how to work with an editor, or understand how to develop web code? The function of HTML editors is always the same: They convert your clicks to HTML code. The same is true for SQL. There are many design interfaces we can use from multiple different vendors or even download open source ones. However, if we know how to work with SQL we will be able to work with any of those interfaces and many times achieve results that would not have been possible to obtain by using a design interface. Therefore, the knowledge of SQL is a must for the database professional, or actually the basis to become one.

6. The position and value of SQL within the enterprise data model

As you can see from Figure 1 below, an organization consists of three hierarchical levels. The strategic level is where the top management of the company sets the strategic objectives of the corporation. Strategic objectives are very specific statements and not just general goals. For example, "we would strive to increase sales of product A by 5% in the State of New York in a period of five years" constitutes a strategic objective. Keep in mind for our purposes that the executives at the strategic level of the corporation need information to be able to make decisions for strategic objectives. This information comes from data at the transactional/operational level of the company where all the action takes place.

The tactical level of the corporation is where managers make sure that the company stays on course to achieve the strategic objectives. For example, if for a period of one or two months sales are not materializing as forecasted, tactical management will take action to bring sales back on track and compensate for lost sales. Keep in mind that tactical management needs information to make these tactical adjustments. This information comes again from the transactional level of the corporation.

The third level of the corporation is the transactional/operational level. This is the place where all the business activity takes place daily. For example, taking an order from a customer is a transaction. Processing a quotation for a customer is a transaction. Updating accounts payable is a transaction. Hiring a new employee and creating a new HR record is a transaction. Preparing a shipment for a customer is a transaction. Fulfilling an order is a transaction. Processing payment for an order is a transaction. All these transactions might aggregate to hundreds or thousands or even hundreds of thousands of transactions every day. That is, we have a lot of data generated every day in various parts of the corporation. This is the fragmented data we need to convert to information and direct it to the tactical and strategic levels for decision. This is exactly the place where SQL comes in to help us generate this data. We also, use SQL to aggregate, summarize, group by, add, update, and subtract data to generate information.

Figure 1: Organizational Hierarchical Levels

In Figure 2, we present a real life corporate transaction system. As you can see, this particular company has a functional design and is divided in four departments: Finance/Accounting, Sales/Marketing, Human Resources, and Production. We also notice that the transactional/operational system has two layers: an application layer and a data layer. The application layer consists of the actual front-end applications corporate employees are using to process transactions. A front-end application is usually made up by a number of forms staff is using to enter, edit, delete, and update data. This front-end is also commonly called the user interface. Notice an additional couple of issues: The various applications do not communicate with each other among departments. Even within the department itself, the departmental units are using different applications. For instance, in the Finance/Accounting department, the accounts receivable, accounts payable, and investment management are all using different applications. This has as a result increased communication times among departments and units which in turn lead to higher cycle times for order processing, fulfillment, accounting debits/credits, and other corporate transactions.

These higher cycle times lead to increased transactional costs and thus in higher operating expenses and a corresponding decrease in our operating margin. Higher operating expenses result in increased risk for the corporation which means that in difficult times we will be the ones to have trouble first. To explain it further, the operational cost of a corporation is not directly related to production. This means that we will incur operational cost regardless of the level of business turnover we have. In times of booming business this is not a problem because the added operational cost we experience becomes lower by unit of output. In times of recession however, that operational cost increases by unit of output and its weight shows in full.

It is exactly in these repressed business and economic conditions that managers make their biggest mistakes as well. Instead of trying to make the corporation more efficient, that is, look at cycle times, transactional cost, operating expenses, and risk, they look at the usual culprit: the employee of the corporation. This trend needs to stop at some point and one of the major ways to do it is for management to understand how data processing, analysis, and dissemination affect their businesses. That is why SQL represents an important technology for our business. We will see how this importance is exhibited when we discuss the data layer of the corporate transaction system.

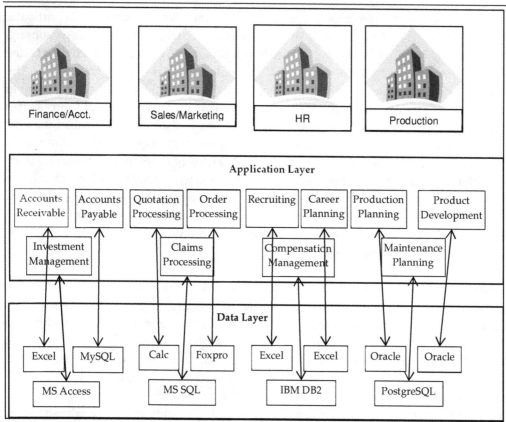

Figure 2: Corporate Transaction Processing System

The second layer we see in Figure 2 is the data layer of the corporation. In the vast majority of cases in the real business world, the corporate data layer consists of many heterogeneous data sources. In theory, in books, and in ERP (Enterprise Resource Planning) package pitches from marketing people an idealized solution is offered where the data layer consists of a single RDBMS (Relational Database Management System). This is very far from the truth and reality. What actually happens is what you see in Figure 2 where not only departments but also individual units within departments use different data sources. For instance, the Career Planning and Compensation Management units in Human Resources use different and separate data sources. Career Planning is using Excel to store and process its data while Compensation Management is using an IBM DB2 relational database and God help the one who will try to get data from the other or will try to integrate the applications or data sources from multiple departments. It is possible, but get ready for the ensuing political conflict that will lead to a quagmire and finally a compromise to a higher or lesser degree. The real situation for us at this point is that for the data layer of the corporate transaction system we have a suite of multiple and heterogeneous data sources. This of course leads to inefficient data exchange. However, what is inefficient? By inefficient we mean we need more time to exchange data and we are more prone to mistakes when we actually do the exchange. This practically means increased cycle times and increased transactional cost which will again lead to high operating costs for the corporation with direct reductions of the operating margin and net profits as well as an increase of perceived risk.

Now, the question is how can we use SQL in the corporation to help in the above situations? We will list specific situations here from the real world on how SQL is actually used throughout the hierarchical levels of the corporation. In addition, we will explore the possibilities of using SQL to get data from other entities in the external environment of the company like corporate customers, suppliers, partners, distributors, and the government. The following list, though not exhaustive, is still comprehensive enough for a very deep understanding of the role of SQL.

7. SQL for Inserts, Updates, and Deletes in the Corporate Transaction Processing System

In Figure 3 we see how SQL is used for transaction processing at the operational/transactional level of the corporation. A business user can conduct transactions such as updating an order, adding a new order, or deleting an order. Business users use applications, usually forms (Access, Oracle, Visual Basic, Java etc.), to be able to work on these transactions. These forms contain "add", "edit", "delete", and other buttons that initiate the requested transaction. However, in most cases, the end user does not see the SQL statements behind these forms but has the expertise to work with the application.

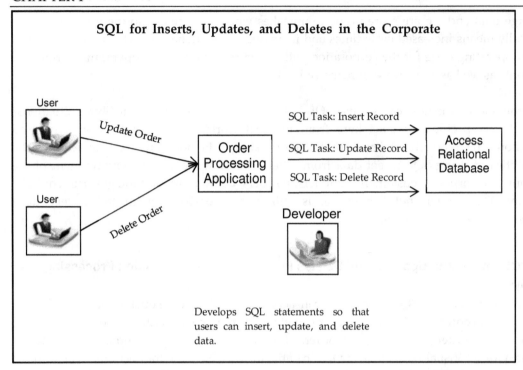

SQL for Inserts, Updates, and Deletes in the Corporate

Figure 3: SQL for inserts, updates, and deletes in the transaction processing system

Behind the scenes however, it is the actual database developer who writes the appropriate SQL statements so that business users can do their job. This developer is needed constantly by the corporation because the SQL statements he or she develops will not stay constant but will change as the business conditions change. That is, as the business engages in activities to acquire market share, to reduce cost, to increase revenue, to increase profit, to launch new products, or respond to competitors, the business requirements, or business logic as we call it, for the application will change. This means that the code of the application needs to change to accommodate the new logic and along with the code the SQL statements for processing the corresponding transactions. Consequently, the role of the SQL developer is ongoing to help the corporation achieve its strategic and tactical objectives. By strategic objectives we mean the long term goals and by tactical objectives we mean we need to stay on course set by the strategic objectives (strategy) of the corporation. The SQL developer in this role is not the technical person who writes code all day long. Actually, most of his or her time will be spent to communicate with users (at any level of the corporation) so that he or she can understand in detail the business expectations behind his or her code. Consequently, it is a big plus if the SQL developer understands how a business works and can integrate his business knowledge in application development.

8. SQL for information generation – from the TPS to tactical and strategic levels.

In this scenario SQL is used to convert data to information. Specifically, instead of using INSERT, UPDATE, and DELETE statements to process transactions, we now use GROUP BY statements, aggregate functions, conditional statements, pivot queries and a multitude of other techniques to generate information out of data in existing transactions. A lot of data is generated at the data layer of the transaction processing system (see Figure 4) as the various departments interact with customers, suppliers, partners, distributors, and the government. For instance, hundreds or thousands of orders and order quotations might be processed every month. All these orders generate data that stays in the data layer of the transaction processing system.

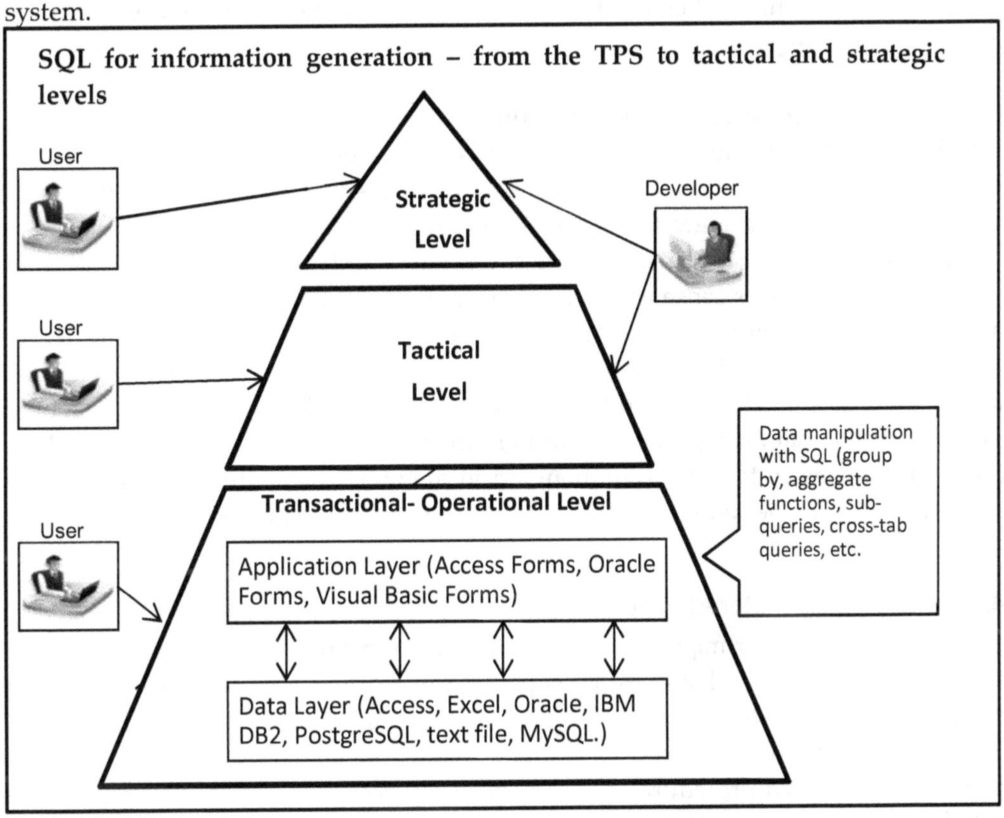

Figure 4: SQL for information generation – from the TPS to tactical and strategic levels

It is the job of the SQL professional to provide intelligence to the tactical and strategic levels of the corporation by using the data stored at the corporate TPS. This process has two tasks. As you can see from Figure 4, not all the data in the data layer of the TPS is in the same format. That is, we have multiple and heterogeneous data sources. Specifically, in this case we need to retrieve data from five different databases, one Excel data source, and one text file. This is because the corporation does not use a single database as the basis for its transaction processing system. Even in the case where corporations engaged in ERP implementations, departmental, unit, and even personal databases emerge like mushrooms. Consequently, we need to accept a degree of heterogeneity of data sources in any corporate environment. The consequence is that the SQL developer needs to do some staging in the first place. That is, he or she needs to import data from various sources such as Excel and text files into the relational database so that he or she can then manipulate this data to extract information. Now, this staging procedure might be something as simple as a simple import or something as intricate as the creation of multiple Extraction Transformation and Loading (ETL) packages. ETL has become an expertise area itself and a whole book can be devoted to it. In any case, a SQL developer who augments his or her portfolio with ETL knowledge becomes a very strong professional.

Once the data is in a common relational format (in relational tables) then the SQL developer can work with SQL statements to convert this data to information. This is actually one of the major goals of this book. Specifically, the SQL developer will use calculated fields, concatenated fields, string and date functions, the group by clause, crosstab queries, union operators, aggregate functions, parameter queries, and other techniques to convert pieces of data to information that makes sense and is needed by the strategic and tactical levels of the corporation. This information is usually provided in the form of web based reports for larger corporations, or at least corporations that have the know-how to work with web servers. If not, usually a reporting capability is provided by the database software itself like in the case of the MS Access. No matter what the reporting platform is, the SQL professional has a central role in the provision of intelligence to the corporation and in many occasions this is a full time job with important responsibilities for the medium and long term planning of the company.

9. SQL for Processing – Stored Procedures

An experienced SQL developer might be surprised to see a topic on stored procedures in this book since Access is a database that does not support stored procedures. However, there are several reasons for which a discussion on stored procedures should take place. First, stored procedures contain SQL code and consequently it is very beneficial to know that a SQL professional can write stored procedures. Second, in many occasions, Access functions as the front-end to back-end databases like MS SQL or MySQL. This happens because it is very easy to develop forms and reports for the user interface in Access while in MS SQL or MySQL front-end development tools are non-existent. See Figure 5 for a schematic representation of this scenario.

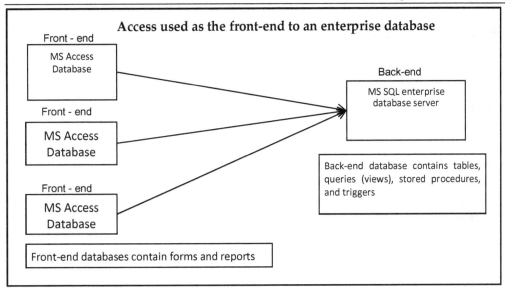

Figure 5: Using Access as the front-end to enterprise databases

However, the most important reason is that stored procedures represent the ultimate implementation of SQL statements and a SQL professional at least needs to know what they are. What are stored procedures anyway? Corporate transaction processing systems process complex business transactions and for this purpose simple SELECT, INSERT, UPDATE, and DELETE SQL statements are not always enough. Often, we need to incorporate in the SQL code conditional processing (if then statements) to process transactions according to the business rules given to us, use dynamic parameters within the SQL code, provide dynamic output according to the input data, automatically update history tables based on user interaction, automatically send emails to administrators and managers, and communicate with other business databases within or outside the organization. The answer to the above are stored procedures, an essential piece in the knowledge portfolio of a SQL professional. Let us explore some examples:

Simple stored procedure

First of all, stored procedures can be simple SQL statements like the simple SELECT statement we see in this example. Some database administrators will use exclusively stored procedures to process select statements instead of queries/views because they are compiled statements and run faster than a simple query. For this example, let us suppose we need a list of customers by city. You see from the code that there is not much difference than writing SQL statements. Only the CREATE PROCEDURE in the beginning and the GO STATEMENT at the end indicate that this is something different from a simple SELECT statement.

Code:
```
CREATE PROCEDURE sp_ContactsByCity
AS
SELECT    City, CompanyName, ContactName, 'Customer' AS Type
FROM      Customers
GO
```

Stored procedure with a parameter

Second, we said that stored procedures accept parameters. Parameters can be simple or complex according to our business logic and the way we want to process transactions (like checking credit, checking inventory quantities, etc.). Also, parameters can be passed around from other applications whether local or remote. Let's say that we would like to pass the city as a parameter in the stored procedure we previously wrote:

Code:
```
CREATE PROCEDURE sp_ContactsByCityParam
@city varchar(20)
AS
SELECT    City, CompanyName, ContactName, 'Customer' AS Type
FROM      Customers where city = @city
GO
```

Stored procedure with control flow

In this stored procedure we use IF THEN statements to process and present information according to our promotion rules. Practically, we ask for a list of products with prices between $10 and $20. If there are any, we will get a list of them. If there are not any, we will get a message that there are no such products and a list of products with a price less than $10. This example is a very simple one but it demonstrates completely the ability of stored procedures to include multiple SQL statements and execute the one according to the logic implemented.

Code:
```
CREATE procedure sp_ProductPromotion
AS
DECLARE @msg varchar(255)
IF (SELECT COUNT(unitprice)
  FROM products
  WHERE unitprice BETWEEN 10 AND 20) > 0

  BEGIN
   SET NOCOUNT ON
```

```
    SET @msg = 'There are several products with values between $10 and $20. These products
are:'
      PRINT @msg
        PRINT ' '
     SELECT productname, unitprice, quantityperunit
     FROM products
     WHERE unitprice BETWEEN 10 AND 20
   END
ELSE
  BEGIN
   SET NOCOUNT ON
   SET @msg = 'There are no products between $10 and $20. You might consider the following
products that are under $10.'
      PRINT @msg
     SELECT productname, unitprice, quantityperunit
     FROM products
     WHERE unitprice < 10
   END
GO
```

You can absolutely write stored procedures in Access

In Figure 6, we see an MS Access 2010 front-end database connected to a back-end MS SQL 2008 enterprise database. As you can see there are no user interface items like forms and reports; only tables that reside in a database server in a remote machine. We can connect an Access database to a back-end database server by creating an *.adp project instead of a *accdb database. The most important item to retain however from this example is that though Access does not support stored procedures by itself, when you connect to a back-end database server, it gives you the tools to create and edit stored procedures! Consequently, we can have a SQL developer in California creating and editing stored procedures on the server in New York City! All that using only Access as the front-end.

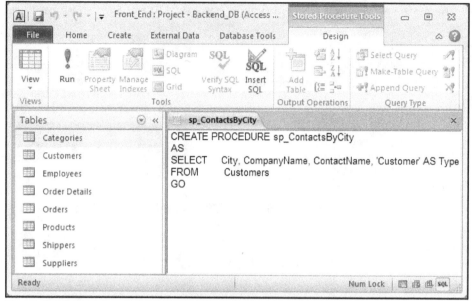

Figure 6: Writing stored procedures in MS Access

10. SQL for automation – Triggers

Triggers are special types of stored procedures that execute automatically when UPDATE, INSERT, or DELETE statements are issued against a table or view. The main characteristic of triggers is that they fire automatically. That is, the SQL statement contained in the trigger will fire automatically when an insert, update, or delete is issued for the table. For example, when an order is deleted from the orders table, we can use triggers to manage this deleted data in many different ways. First, we can use a trigger to move this deleted data to an archive table. Second, we can use a trigger to notify via email a system administrator that an order has been deleted from the orders table. Third, we can use a trigger to beep the sales representative that the customer called in and canceled the order. The main advantage is that the process is automated. In addition, triggers can be setup to fire on inserts, or on updates, or on deletes, or on any combination of these statements. For instance, we can setup a trigger that runs only on updates and another that runs on updates and deletes but not on inserts. This fact gives us great flexibility to manipulate data and channel it to the most appropriate destination for processing.

We can also use triggers to enforce processing rules coming from business requirements. For example, a simple but important business requirement is that the shipping date should be greater than the order date because it is impossible to ship orders which we have not taken. To force this business rule, we can use a trigger that will fire on inserts and updates and which will check to make sure that the shipping date is greater than the order date. Consequently, triggers help us enforce the business logic of the corporation within our relational database. An example of this scenario is the trigger below:

Code:
```
CREATE TRIGGER trg_InsUpd
On orders
for insert, update
As
if update
(shippeddate)
begin
print 'testing shippeddate'
If exists (select * from inserted where shippeddate < orderdate)
begin
raiserror ('shipping date should be greater than order date', 16, 10)
rollback transaction
return
end
end
GO
```

Now, the question is why we need to know about triggers since Access does not support them? The answer, as in the case of stored procedures, is two-fold. First, triggers are practically SQL statements and the professional who knows how to write SQL will be able to write triggers as well. A SQL professional who knows what triggers are and how to write them will definitely position himself or herself better in the market rather than someone who only knows how to create simple queries or views. Second, even though Access does not directly support triggers, it does allow writing them if you connect it to a back-end database server like MS SQL 2008. As you can see from Figure 7, we can actually write triggers within Access when connecting to an MS SQL 2008 database. Consequently, we do not need to work in a MSSQL or Oracle, or IBM DB2 environment to learn about triggers.

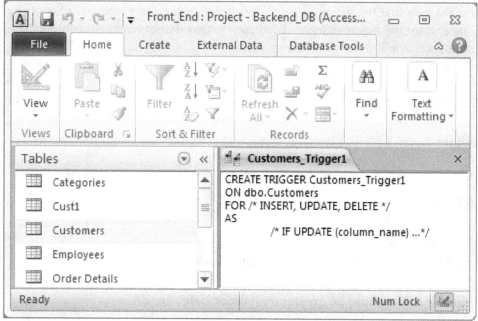

Figure 7: Triggers within the Access environment

11. SQL and its relation to web server side pages technologies

Another area in which you will work as a SQL professional is the web. Specifically, you might be asked to participate in a team for the development of server side web pages like active server pages (asp), still around after more than fifteen years, asp.net, java server pages (jsp), and hypertext preprocessor (php) pages. These pages contain code in languages like java script, vb script, vb.net, c#, and others. They also contain HTML code. However, in many cases they also contain SQL code used to communicate with back-end databases. In these cases, you might be called to write the SQL part of the page since web developers might not have the depth required to write complex SQL statements.

In Figure 8, you can see a scenario of a web site that contains multiple php pages. Specifically, there are four php pages: SubmitOrder.php, UpdateOrder.php, ReviewOrder.php, and DeleteOrder.php. These four pages constitute an application to which customers connect through the web to place and manage orders. Notice that each customer uses a dissimilar browser as the client to connect to the web site on the web server. The beauty of server side pages is that they are browser independent. Consequently, we do not need to worry about the browser used by the customer. In addition, as you can see from Figure 8, the php pages connect to a database on the back-end database server. Now, in most occasions, the web server and the database server are different machines but it might be the case that both the web server software and the relational database software are installed on the same machine. For our purposes, the fundamental point is that php pages use SQL to connect to back-end databases. This in turn means that a SQL professional can find his or her way to the world of web development and this is of the essence for our discussion since it constitutes an additional career path.

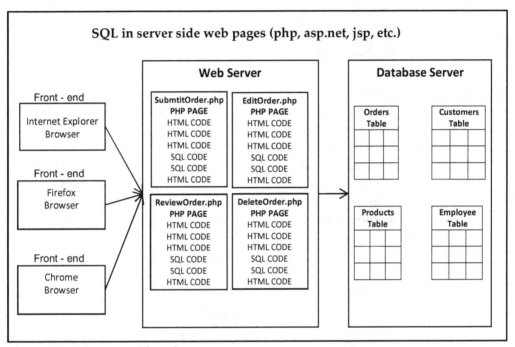

Figure 8: SQL in server side web pages

12. SQL to obtain data from entities in the external environment of the company

An additional area where you can work, shine, and show your true potential as a SQL developer is when connecting client databases like Access to server databases like MS SQL, Oracle, IBM DB2, and MySQL. Actually, you can connect Access to any back-end database provided you can find and download the corresponding Open Database Connectivity Drivers (ODBC). Well, this is too technical already. Let us take a step back and first see why do we want to do this from a business point of view and second, what is in it for us, the SQL developers, so that our motivation stays high.

In today's business environment, when we do business with our customers, suppliers, distributors, and other entities, we practically buy or sell products or services. Those products or services have associated the so called "paperwork" which we need to process for every selling or purchasing transaction. This paperwork is what leads to the development of the purchasing department, accounts payable, accounts receivable, and other places within the corporation where people go around with pieces of papers in their hands for the most part. Now, there are many ways to process this paperwork with corresponding consequences for the well-being of the company. For instance, let us consider the scenario in which we would like to re-order parts from our suppliers, a process we call replenishing. When we replenish our inventories we can communicate, i.e. transact with our supplier, in many different ways. First, we can call them and give our order on the phone. Second, we can send them a fax. Third, we can send them an email with an attached spreadsheet of what we need. Fourth, we can go to their online system and order the materials we need online, right away through the web. Fifth, we can have access to their databases through pre-defined queries so that we can look at the latest products, their descriptions, special pricing for us, and any other piece of information we might need. In this last case, we can also create reports for the tactical management of our company to look at before we make our purchase. We do not imply that the fifth method is always the best method to communicate with external entities but is the best from the four mentioned above. There are other methods to integrate corporate information systems well beyond the scope of this SQL book. However, the SQL developer can make a real difference in the efficiency of transaction processing if he or she has the knowledge to connect and manipulate external databases.

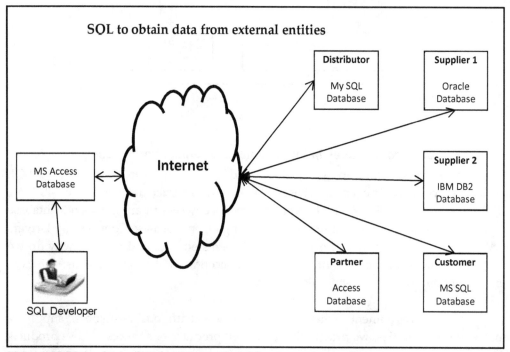

Figure 9: SQL to obtain data from external entities

What is the source of this corporate efficiency? The answer is reducing cycle times and reducing transactional cost. It is one of the primary goals of every corporation to reduce transactional cost and cycle times. That is why banks went from tellers to ATMS and from ATMs to the web. The plain goal was to reduce transaction cost and they got it down to pennies per transaction. However, you need to have the know-how and the technology to do it. That is, you need to have access to database technology and know how to work with it. Going back to our scenario, we would like to do replenishing directly from within the database and without involving any people who would call each other or exchange messages. Some problems might be that the sales person we try to find is out on vacation, the fax machine is not working, the message went to the junk folder, there was a mistake in the order and a multitude of other things that can go wrong. All these situations lead to extended cycle times for replenishing that have multiple consequences all of which lead to increased costs. For example, we might need to keep more inventory which is costly, we lose a customer because we did not have the parts we needed on time, we re-ordered because someone typed in the wrong order amounts or wrong parts, and in general we make our corporation more expensive to operate.

By accessing our supplier databases and doing the work ourselves we avoid all the above and many more tricky situations. As we can see from Figure 9, we can use Access to connect to the databases our customers, partners, and suppliers are using through the Internet. We can literally use the IP address of the database server of the external entity to connect through ODBC drivers or native data providers. ODBC is somewhat slower but nevertheless universal to use with any database and readily available for download through the web. Usually, the supplier or customer will not give us access to their whole database but have some queries available for us to use with the appropriate security setup. From those basic queries then, we can create our own queries and retrieve the data we need exactly the way we would like to retrieve it.

The requirement is that we know how to use ODBC and how above all to use SQL to retrieve the data we need and convert it to information that would be useful to our management. For these purposes a strong SQL developer is needed to work with multiple systems and since in this book we learn how to work with SQL which is the standard for all relational databases, it means that we will be able to write queries against any relational database management system without much difficulty. That is why it is imperative to know how to work with SQL and not just the design interface of Access or any other database.

13. SQL and its relation to XML

The major business goal in this scenario is to outsource replenishing. That is, we want our suppliers to assume the cost of re-supplying us with inventory. Practically, we want to avoid devoting any human or financial resources to this process so that we can reduce our operational costs and decrease our replenishing cycles as well. At the same time the suppliers will be willing to do this since they will be selling more products. Incurring zero cost for inventory replenishing sounds like an excellent idea but how can we achieve this in technical terms and what would be the role of the SQL developer in the process?

As you can see from Figure 10, the SQL developer is working with an MS Access front-end database. He or she should first create an *.adp project so that he can connect to the back-end SQL server and its tables as shown. Now, the SQL developer will write queries that contain all the product related items for inventory purposes. For example, fields included might be the product name, product units per box, unit price, quantity on hand, reorder level, and quantity on order. Then, automation packages will be established in SQL server using integration services so that the result of the SQL statements written by the SQL developer are exported as XML files on the web server. For illustration purposes we named such a file Inventory.xml in Figure 10. Today's database servers support the automated importing and exporting of XML data with easily set procedures. Then, the suppliers can access these XML files through the Internet. They check to see what we need from each product and they replenish our inventory without us getting involved in the process. The basic premise of this process is that it is repeatable. That is, every day, or every three days, or every week we replace the XML files on the web server so that the suppliers have access to all the latest data about the status of our inventory. Though the whole process can run manually once or twice a week we should strive to automate it given the flexibility we have by using today's advanced database software.

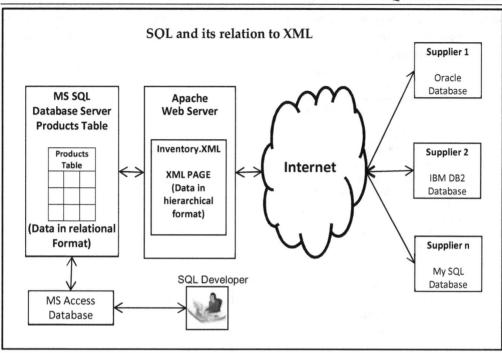

Figure 10: SQL and its relation to XML

On a more technical level, when we export data from a relational database to an XML file there are a couple of items we need to be aware of. First, databases follow the relational data model which means we have a set of related entities (tables) to store data. This for a business task of exchanging data is a problem since the data we need to send to our suppliers might be in four, five or even more related tables and there is no way to send those tables and their relationships across the web. Consequently, what we do is use SQL to get the data we need from those tables in a single query and then we export the result of this query to an XML file which follows the hierarchical model of storing data. But what is an XML file? XML files are practically text documents containing elements. An element can be a book, an employee, a product etc. This single element contains sub-elements and these sub-elements contain additional elements down the hierarchy. Have you noticed the word hierarchy?

In Figure 11, we see a simple XML file. Notice that this file contains information about two employees. In a usual relational database they would represent two records in the employee table. In this XML file we notice that we have a root element called <Employees> which contains two instances of the sub- element <Employee> or in other words information about two employees of ours. We also notice that in the sub-element <Employee> there are additional sub-elements like LastName, FirstName, Title, etc. We see that between the element tags we have the actual name, title, and hiredate for each employee. Consequently, this single XML file contains both the data and the description of this data by means of its tags. When we

41

receive a file like this, it is very easy to make sense of the data it contains. Consequently, when our suppliers connect to a file like this through the Internet, they can read it, they know its meaning, import it into their database for processing, and finally send us the products we need to do our work with no or minimal cost to us.

```
<?xml version="1.0" encoding="UTF-8" ?>
<Employees>
  <Employee>
  <LastName>Smith</LastName>
  <FirstName>George</FirstName>
  <Title>Sales Representative</Title>
  <Address>507 - 20th Ave. E. Apt. 2A</Address>
  <City>Seattle</City>
  <Region>WA</Region>
  <PostalCode>98122</PostalCode>
  <Country>USA</Country>
</Employee>
  <Employee>
  <LastName>Fuller</LastName>
  <FirstName>Andrew</FirstName>
  <Title>Vice President, Sales</Title>
  <Address>908 W. Capital Way</Address>
  <City>Tacoma</City>
  <Region>WA</Region>
  <PostalCode>98401</PostalCode>
  <Country>USA</Country>
  </Employee>
</Employees>
```

Figure 11: Sample XML file

14. SQL and its relation to ETL

Another area with lots of opportunity and work potential for the SQL developer is the area of extraction, transformation, and loading of data (ETL). This area has a lot of potential for work or consulting since all corporate entities, from the business itself down to the departmental unit, need to move data for processing or for intelligence. We can define ETL as the general process of extracting data from one or more data sources, transforming this data to appropriate formats and have the ability to load it in one or more data destinations. An ETL process might involve extracting data from a transaction processing system and load this data to a data warehouse (see Figure 12). This is the most common scenario for which ETL is known but it is not the only one. ETL might involve the exchange of data between two transaction processing databases, an Excel file to an XML file, or an XML file to a data warehouse. The important point is that ETL is a process that needs careful consideration in any data moving scenario.

One of the major differences between ad hoc data moves and rigorous ETL processes is the notion of the timing of data exchanges. A simple import of data from an Excel spreadsheet to an Access database can hardly be described as an ETL process but rather as a data export procedure. However, when we have a process in place that takes data from ten heterogeneous data sources and processes any transformations automatically with workflow and error checking support, and it does this every week, every day, or even every hour, based on a trigger event, then we can say we have an ETL process in place.

Data sources might be homogeneous or heterogeneous in nature. For example, let us suppose that we have an ETL process in place which takes data from ten data sources. These data sources are two Oracle databases, one Access database, one MySQL database, three XML files, an Excel spreadsheet, two text files, and an ODBC connection to our own DB2 database system. The two Oracle databases are considered to be homogeneous data sources but an XML file and the ODBC connection to IBM DB2 are considered to be heterogeneous data sources. In a data warehouse scenario we will usually have to work with a number of heterogeneous data sources so that we can have all the data needed for advanced business analytics.

Such a scenario is shown in Figure 12, where we get data from multiple heterogeneous data sources from our suppliers, partners, and our own transaction processing system. The goal is to integrate all this data into a data warehouse which will function as the basis of our business intelligence system. A data warehouse is practically a historical data repository, or in other words, a repository of completed transactions. We will use this data to come up with information by using tools such as Data Mining, Online Analytical Processing (OLAP), and Multi-dimensional Expressions (MDX).

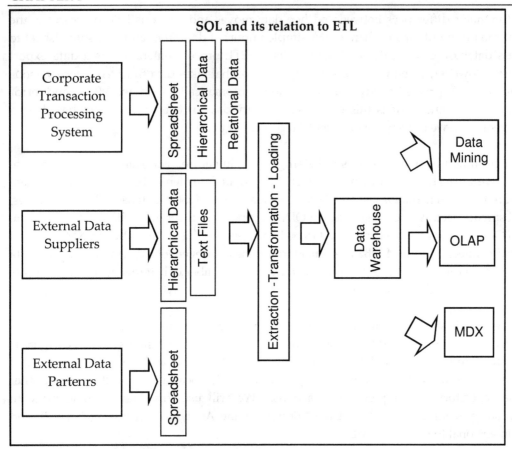

Figure 12: SQL and its relation to ETL

The job of the SQL developer is to provide his or her expertise in designing, developing and implementing the ETL packages. He or she needs to be able to connect to data sources (databases or others), write SQL code, develop queries, concatenate fields, write functions to alter existing data, convert data from text to numeric or other formats, write criteria, and a host of additional tasks that require real command of the SQL language. This is ongoing work as we might have tens or even hundreds of ETL packages setup. Moreover, ETL packages are repetitive and they need editing since business conditions change. For instance, we might need to include a new supplier, delete a partner, include one more data source, delete a field, change scrubbing rules, and a myriad of other tasks. We see at this point how important the role of the SQL developer becomes at any hierarchical level of the company.

15. SQL and its relation to MDX

The power of business analytics comes through the use of multidimensional data stores like data warehouses and OLAP cubes. MDX appeared in commercial products for the first time in 1998 and it was quickly accepted as a fast and efficient way to access multidimensional analytical data. Products that offer MDX capabilities include SAP, SAS, Microsoft, Microstrategy and others.

MDX is a tool designed to unlock the wealth and depth of dimensional data coming from data warehouses, OLAP cubes and dimensional sources in general. If we think about it, MDX is to a dimensional database what SQL is to a relational database. However, this is as close as the two languages come; in terms of syntax MDX is very different from SQL. The case is however that some of the strengths of MDX are SQL's weaknesses and vice versa. In SQL we are working on two dimensions of columns and rows and there is nothing we can do to expand this two dimensional model. In MDX we can practically create and work on multiple dimensions based on the results that we want to have. Moreover, we can define what data goes to each dimension which means that we can manipulate on the fly the content and behavior of each dimension in the multidimensional result.

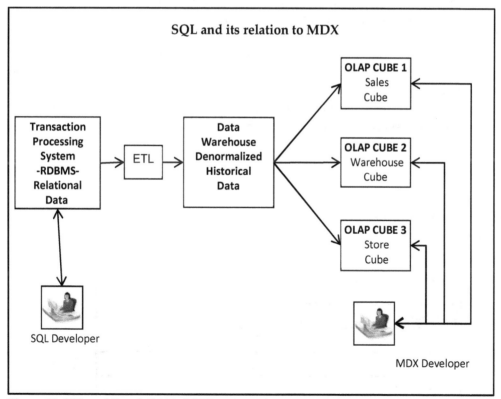

Figure 13: SQL and its relation to MDX

The result of any MDX statement is a virtual cube itself and additional MDX statements can be written against existing MDX statements. It works the same way as SQL queries or views where we can use existing queries as data sources to write more SQL statements and obtain refined results. As you can see from Figure 13, a SQL developer works with relational data in the relational database management system (MySQL, Oracle, DB2) of the company. This RDBMS constitutes the data store of the transaction processing system of the corporation as we examined it in detail in the beginning of this chapter. An MDX developer works with client MDX tools that use OLAP cubes as the data sources. MDX is different in syntax and expressions from SQL. However, a SQL professional who knows how to work with data will be able to make the transition to MDX and add MDX to his or her toolbox. Knowing how to work with MDX statements, opens a whole new stream of career opportunities for the already sought after SQL developer. Below we present some MDX statements for demonstration purposes so that you know how they look like and what kind of information they produce. Our goal in this book is to show you that this road exists. If you decide to follow this path, there are plenty of books focusing on the concepts of OLAP and MDX. Let us have a look at some examples.

The goal in this example is to access a sales cube and provide total cost and sales figures for all stores for the year 2011. Notice that we use two dimensions of the sales cube: time and measures. "Time" is an ordinary dimension and "Measures" is a kind of dimension that contains all the counting and arithmetic (unit sales, store cost, store sales, and sales count) we have previously defined for the cube. Moreover notice that the "on columns" specification means that the time dimension will appear in columns and the "rows" specification means that the "measures" dimension and its members will appear as rows. Practically, this MDX statement contains three specifications: columns, rows, and the cube where the data comes from.

MDX:
SELECT
{[Time].[2011]} on columns,
[Measures].members on rows
FROM Sales

	2011
Unit Sales	266,773.00
Store Cost	225,627.23
Store Sales	$565,238.13
Sales Count	86837

In this example we are looking for total cost and sales figures for all stores for the year 2011 presented by quarter Notice that only the quarters for the year 2011 appear and not the individual months. This is the case since quarters are children to years. Months on the other hand, are children to quarters.

MDX:
SELECT
{[Time].[2011].children} on columns,
[Measures].members on rows
FROM Sales

	Q1	Q2	Q3	Q4
Unit Sales	66,291.00	62,610.00	65,848.00	72,024.00
Store Cost	55,752.24	52,964.22	55,904.87	61,005.90
Store Sales	$139,628.35	$132,666.27	$140,271.89	$152,671.62
Sales Count	21588	20368	21453	23428
Store Sales Net	83,876.11	79,702.05	84,367.02	91,665.72

In this example we are looking for total cost and sales figures for the year 2011 as well as the quarterly figures. Notice that we provide analytics for the whole year and by quarter in the same result pane and those familiar with SQL code will start realizing the power of MDX in that in one short line of code we get such useful results. Also, notice that we can specify exactly the amount of detail that we want by including or excluding parameters in the DESCENDANTS function.

MDX:
SELECT
{[Time].[2011], DESCENDANTS ([Time].[2011], [Time].[Quarter])} on columns,
[Measures].members on rows
FROM Sales

	2011	Q1	Q2	Q3	Q4
Unit Sales	266,773.00	66,291.00	62,610.00	65,848.00	72,024.00
Store Cost	225,627.23	55,752.24	52,964.22	55,904.87	61,005.90

Store Sales	$565,238.13	$139,628.35	$132,666.27	$140,271.89	$152,671.62
Sales Count	86837	21588	20368	21453	23428
Store Sales Net	339,610.90	83,876.11	79,702.05	84,367.02	91,665.72

As you can see from the MDX statements above, we can obtain information from a multidimensional data store which we cannot acquire using SQL statements from the transactional database. The opposite is true as well: We can get data at a very refined level (highly normalized) from the relational database using SQL which we cannot get from the denormalized data in a data warehouse. In addition, it is imperative to keep in mind that transactional data are current data. That is, the transactional database contains data referring to current orders, quotations, invoices, and other current work. In the data warehouse, we keep only historical data, or in other words, data from completed transactions. Consequently, we use SQL for current, highly normalized data while we use MDX for historical, denormalized data.

CHAPTER 2
CREATE, EDIT, AND DELETE TABLES USING SQL

In this chapter, we will work with three DDL statements: CREATE TABLE, ALTER TABLE, and DROP TABLE. We use the CREATE statement to create new tables, the ALTER statement to modify existing ones, and the DROP statement to delete existing tables. The basic structures of the three statements appear below:

CREATE TABLE "tablename" (
fieldname1 datatype (size),
fieldname2 datatype (size),
fieldname3 datatype (size)
)

ALTER TABLE "tablename"
[ADD] [ALTER] [DROP] COLUMN fieldname datatype(size)

DROP TABLE "tablename"

16. Create a simple table using SQL
Create a customer table using pure SQL
Discussion:
This is a simple example of creating a table using SQL in Access 2010. The Access help file says that we need to use data definition queries to create objects. Actually, we can enter this code in SQL view of any query, and it will work. The table in this example contains only six text fields. The table is bare without any primary keys defined, NULLs handling, or indexes.

Code:

```
CREATE TABLE Customer1 (
[LastName] text(50),
[MiddleName] text(50),
[FirstName] text(50),
[Address] text(100),
[State] text(2),
[Zip] text(5));
```

Result:

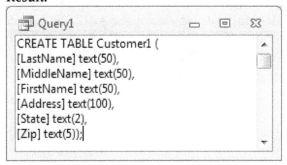

17. Create a table defining its primary key

Create a customer table, and assign CustomerID as the primary key

Discussion:

In this scenario, we create a table with a primary key of data type "Number" and two simple text fields. Notice the primary key picture on the left of the CustomerID field in the table design view in the picture below:

Code:

```
CREATE TABLE Customer1 (
[CustomerID] number Primary key not null,
[LastName] text(50),
[FirstName] text(50));
```

Result:

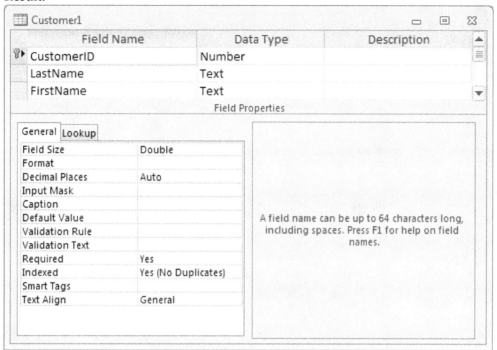

18. Create a table defining the primary key as autonumber

Create a customer table, and assign the PK CustomerID as an autonumber

Discussion:

In this scenario, we create a table with the primary key of data type "AutoNumber" and two simple text fields.

Code:

```
CREATE TABLE Customer1 (
[CustomerID] Counter Primary key not null,
[LastName] text(50),
[FirstName] text(50));
```

Result:

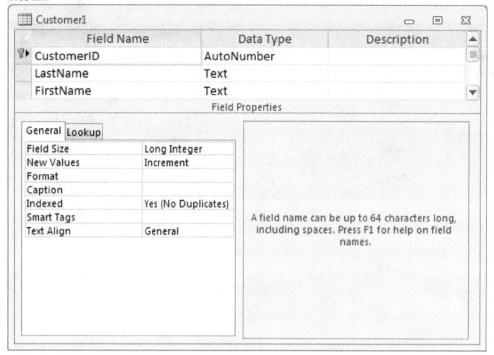

19. Create table with a field that does not accept nulls

Discussion:

On some occasions, we might want to create a table with a field that will not accept null values. Null values are different from zero-length strings or zeros. (Check chapter 24 for a full discussion of null values). To avoid nulls for a field, we simply make the field required. In other words, we force users to enter a value, or they will not be able to save the record in the database. We can do this with the following code, which makes the lastname field required.

Code:

```
CREATE TABLE Customer1 (
[CustomerID] Counter PRIMARY KEY NOT NULL,
[LastName] text(50) NOT NULL,
[FirstName] text(50),
[Address] text(50));
```

Result:

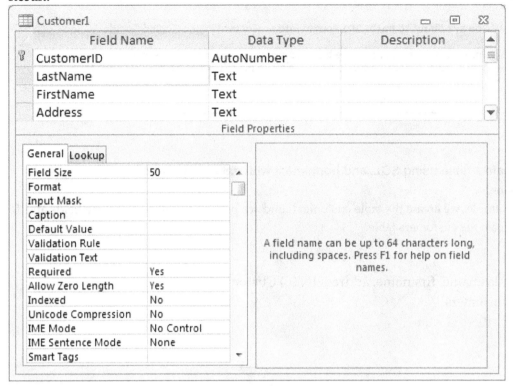

20. Create a table using SQL, and populate it with data on the fly

Discussion:

In most of our work tasks, we do not just need to create a table. We also need to put some data in it on the fly. Creating a table and populating it on the fly is possible using the SELECT INTO statement in Access 2010. In this example, we create the table customer1, and we populate it with data from the customers table.

Code:

```
SELECT * INTO Customer1
FROM customers
```

Result:

The table customer1 will be created and populated with all of the records from the customers table. Of course, you can modify the SQL statement above to move specific fields and records.

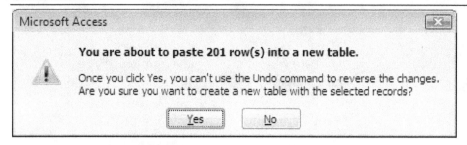

21. Create a table using SQL, and populate it with data in one step

Discussion:

In this example, we create the table customer1 and we populate it with only three fields and 14 records from the customers table.

Code:

```
SELECT lastname, firstname, address INTO Customer1
FROM customers
WHERE city = "Boston"
```

Result:

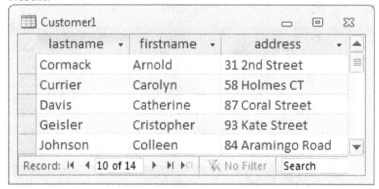

22. ALTER table: add a field

Add a city field in the customer table

Discussion:

On most occasions, we need to modify the design of existing tables instead of creating new ones. We can alter table designs almost at will using pure SQL. In this example, we add the city field to the customer1 table.

Code:
ALTER TABLE Customer1
ADD COLUMN City TEXT(25)

or if you would like to make it a required field:

ALTER TABLE Customer1
ADD COLUMN City TEXT(25) NOT NULL

Result:

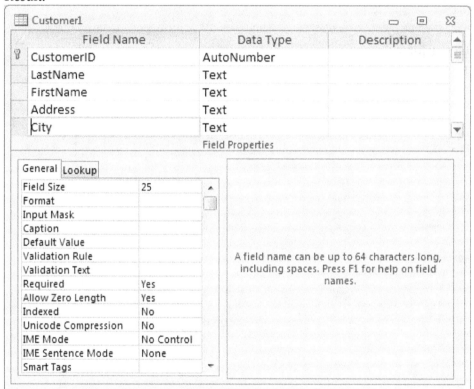

23. ALTER table: delete a field

Delete the city field from the customer table

Discussion:

We can easily delete a field from a table using the ALTER and DROP statements in combination. For instance, in this case, we delete the "city" field from the customer1 table.

Code:

ALTER TABLE Customer1
DROP COLUMN City

24. ALTER table: modify the size of an existing text column

Change the size of the lastname field from 50 to 80 characters

Discussion:

Let us say that we want to modify the size of the lastname field from 50 characters to 80. Notice that the data type of the lastname field is already text. We can also change the data type or the name of the field, if we wish, using the ALTER COLUMN statement.

Code:

ALTER TABLE Customer1
ALTER COLUMN LastName TEXT(80)

Result:

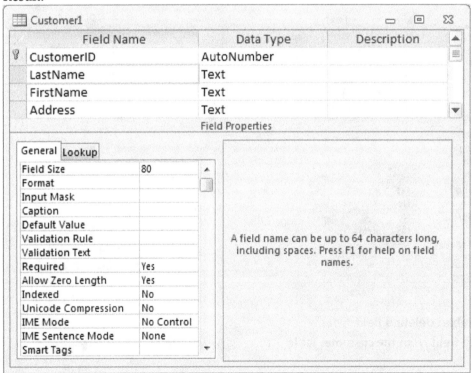

25. Delete Table

Delete the table customer1 from the database

Discussion:

We can use SQL to delete tables using the DROP statement. In this example, we delete the customer1 table. We must pay attention, however, when we delete tables using the DROP statement because there is no warning or undo action for it. The table will be deleted permanently from the database.

Code:

DROP TABLE Customer1

Result:

The table customer1 has been deleted from the database.

CHAPTER 3
CREATE, EDIT, AND DELETE INDEXES USING SQL

The use of indexes is another low-lighted topic in the world of databases. It is common knowledge that indexes are useful, but the guidelines to use them are obscure at best. First, indexes will speed up searching operations. They work great with WHERE and ORDER BY clauses. However, they will slow down INSERT and UPDATE statements since every insert or update needs to be saved in both the table and the index. Third, they should be avoided in small tables with few records. They work better in large tables with thousands of records. Fourth, it is a good idea to create indexes for fields used a lot in searching operations. If we have a form in Access or a web form that we use as the front-end in which we provide the users with the option to search customers by first and last name fields, then we need to index those two fields.

In addition, indexes can be set up as unique or non-unique. In this case, the indexes accept unique or non-unique values and they can function as constraints disallowing duplicate values for the indexed field or fields. For example, if we set up a unique index on a last name field, all of the last names in the table will have to have unique values. Furthermore, primary key columns in Access 2010 tables are automatically indexed when created, and these indexes are set up as unique.

We can also use indexes as constraints to disallow null values for fields in Access tables. If we want to make the last name field a required field, we can use an index to assign a field as required. In this case, we force the users to make an entry for this field.

Finally, we can create multi-field indexes that will index the combination of values of multiple fields instead of just indexing the values of each individual field. For example, if we create a unique index on last name and a unique index on first name, what we practically told the database is not to accept duplicate values for last names and not to accept duplicate values for first names. In other words, we cannot have two Smiths or two Johns in the database, which is, of course, impractical. However, we can create a multi-field unique index on both the last and first name fields that will accept duplicate values for the individual last and first name fields but will not accept duplicate values for their combinations. Let's go through some examples to demonstrate the points we mentioned above in practice.

26. Create a table and set a unique index for one of its fields

Optimize customer searches on the last name field

Discussion:

Since we expect heavy searching activity on the LastName field, we need to create an index to accelerate these searches. In this scenario, we create a new table and a unique index (no duplicates values allowed) on the LastName field. That is, we do not allow two customers to have the same last name in the tblCustomers2 table.

Code:

```
CREATE TABLE tblCustomer2 (
[CustomerID] Counter Primary key not null,
[LastName] text(50),
[FirstName] text(50),
[Address] text(50),
CONSTRAINT indLastName UNIQUE (LastName));
```

Result:

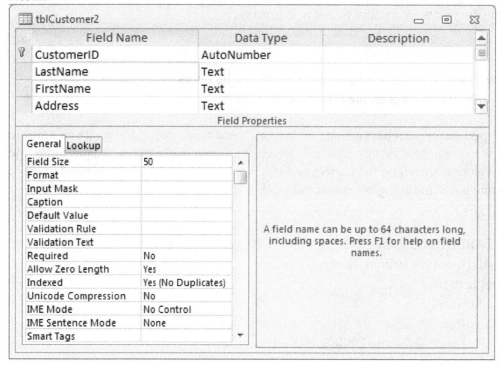

In the figure above, the LastName field is indexed and, at the same time, does not accept duplicates. This is because we created a unique index on this field with the SQL code in this example.

HINT: After a lot of trial and error I realized that trying to create a non-unique index within the CREATE TABLE statement is not working. Just a hint so that you do not waste your time.

27. Create a non-unique index for an existing table

Add a non-unique index for the first name field in the customer table

Discussion:

Let us assume we have a table with data in it. Later on we decide we would like to add an index using SQL. We can easily do this by using the following code. Notice in the figure below that the indFirstName is non-unique. This means that we allow duplicate values for the FirstName field. In other words, we can have two "Johns" or two "Marys" in the table, but they definitely have to have different last names as defined by the indLastName, which is a unique index.

Code:

CREATE INDEX indFirstName ON tblCustomer2 (FirstName);

Result:

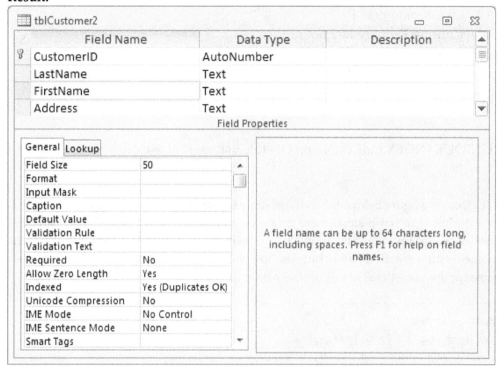

28. Create a unique index for an existing table

Add a unique index for the last name field in the existing customer table

Discussion:

As we can see from the figure in the previous example, the indFirstName index is non-unique, and it does not ignore nulls. What is the exact meaning of a unique index? What is the meaning of an index ignoring or not ignoring nulls?

First, by a unique index, we mean that no duplicate values are allowed for that field. We know very well that unique values are not allowed for fields that have been designated as primary keys. However, by defining a unique index, we can disallow duplicate values for a field that is not the primary key of the table. For example, if we are working with the LastName field, and we create a unique index on it, we cannot have two customers in our table with the same last name. If we try to enter two customers with the same last name, the database will not allow their entry. The SQL code below will create a unique index on a field other than the primary key for an existing table. Let us create the table first:

Code:
CREATE TABLE tblCustomer1 (
[CustomerID] Counter Primary key not null,
[LastName] text(50),
[FirstName] text(50),
[Address] text(50));

Code:
CREATE UNIQUE INDEX indLastName ON tblCustomer1 (LastName);

Result:
As we can see from the figure below, the indLastName is a unique index now. However, this is not always a desirable scenario since there might be multiple customers with the same last name. How can we set up index constraints so that we allow multiple customers to have the same last name or the same first name, but disallow multiple customers to have the same last and first names at the same time? Let us see the next example with multiple-field indexes.

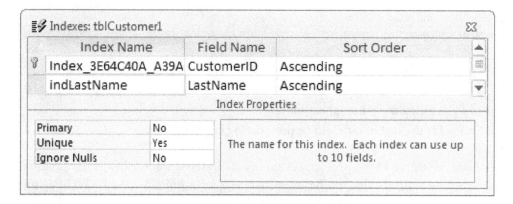

29. Create multiple-field indexes to avoid duplicates
Add a unique multi-field index for the last and first name fields
Discussion:
When working with customers, we would like to make sure that no duplicate customer records exist in our database. At the same time, it is logical that many customers might have the same last name, and many of them will have the same first name.

With a multi-field unique index, our database will accept values such as Smith John and Smith Tracy. However, if we try to enter another Smith John in the database, we will get a message that such an entry violates existing index rules and will not be accepted. Multi-field indexes are extremely useful to keep our data in a good state.

Code:

CREATE UNIQUE INDEX indLastFirst ON tblCustomer1 (LastName, FirstName);

Result:

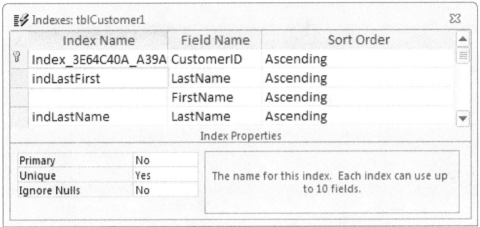

30. Create an index on a field that will not accept nulls.

Add a unique index for the last name field that will not allow null values

Discussion:

In this scenario, we would like a field to be indexed, not accept duplicate values, accept zero-length strings, and not accept null values at the same time.

Code:

CREATE UNIQUE INDEX indLastName2 ON tblCustomer1 (LastName) WITH DISALLOW NULL;

Result:

As we can see, the LastName field is indexed, accepts no duplicates (UNIQUE), and it will require an entry (DISALLOW NULL). Pay close attention because Access 2010 does not indicate a field as required in the table design view when we use an index constraint. In the picture of the table design view below, we see that the field last name looks like it is not required when it is actually required. Try to go to data view to add an entry for first name, while leaving the last name field empty. We will get a constraint violation error.

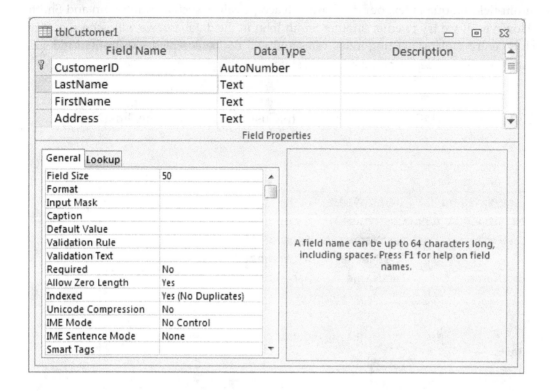

31. Create an index that ignores nulls

Create an index on lastname that ignores null last name values

Discussion:

By default when we create an index for a field, this index will include the field's null values in the indexed entries. We might, however, want nulls to be excluded from our index and only entries with data in the field to be included. Note that this is not the same as setting a field to not accept nulls. Our index will simply not include any null values from this field.

Code:

```
CREATE UNIQUE INDEX indLastName3 ON tblCustomer1 (LastName) WITH
IGNORE NULL;
```

Result:

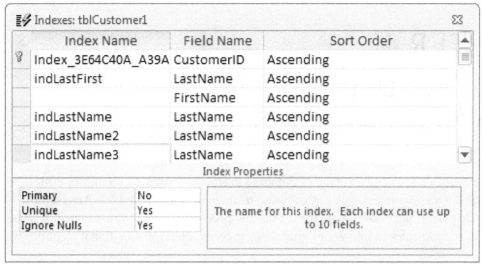

32. Delete Index

Delete the "indLastName" index from the customer table using SQL

Discussion:

In our previous examples, we have created an index on the LastName field for the tblCustomer1 table and we named it indLastName. In this example, we write a DROP statement to delete the index from our tbl1Customer1 table.

Code:

DROP INDEX indLastName ON tblCustomer1

Result:

The index "indLastName" will be deleted from the tblCustomer1 table.

CHAPTER 4
CREATE, EDIT, DELETE
RELATIONSHIPS USING SQL

Our manager asked us to create a customer database to store information about our customers and their orders. One of our tasks will be to create relationships among tables. After almost 20 years of working with databases, I can attest that this process is much more art than science. There are neither rigid rules to follow nor guidelines to cover all of the situational scenarios we might encounter.

However, we have two great tools at our disposal: First, we should have a total and complete understanding of the meaning of relationships and their related topics like primary keys, foreign keys, referential integrity, cascade updates, cascade deletes, and join types. Second, we can use our logic to achieve a well-built relationship resulting in a solid database. The purpose of this chapter is to completely demystify the obscure area of relationships not only with respect to building them but, most importantly, with respect to their interpretation and usage.

33. Why and how to create a one-to-many relationship
Create a one-to-many relationship between customers and orders

Our first task is to create a relationship between the customers and orders tables. The logic here is that each customer can have multiple orders while one order definitely belongs to one customer only. This is the case for a one-to-many relationship. This one-to-many relationship is depicted graphically in the figure below. I have included data values on purpose to actually show how records from one table relate to records in the other table. This is because when we talk about relationships among tables, we are actually talking about record relations.

CUSTOMERS		ORDERS		
CustID	Name	OrderID	CustID	OrderDate
1	John	1	2	9/10/2012
2	Mary	2	2	10/10/2012
3	George	3	1	11/10/2012
4	Stacy	4	3	11/11/2012

Primary Key	Primary Key	Foreign Key

The steps for creating a one-to-many relationship between two database tables (customers and orders in this case) are the following:

1. Assign a primary key to both tables if they do not already have one. In this example, the primary key for the Customers table is "CustID", and the primary key for the Orders table is "OrderID".

2. Make sure your primary key is not a "natural" key like a social security number, or driver's license number. The data types for the primary keys in both tables should be of the "Auto Number" data type.

3. Create a field in the Orders table, which we will name "CustID." The "CustID" field in the Orders table is the "Foreign key" of the table. The data type of the "CustID" field in the Orders table should be of the number data type so that it can be joined with the CustID in the Customers table.

4. In Access 2010, click on the "Database Tools" tab on the ribbon. In the "Relationships" group, click on the relationships button. In the "relationships" group again click on the "Show Table" button." The "Show Table" dialog box opens. Add the tables we would like to join.

5. The relationships window in Access 2010 shows the entity relationship diagram (ERD) of the database. In the ERD, all related tables appear along with the field names and the primary and foreign keys. The ERD allows us to understand the structure and design of the database, and it constitutes the place in which we can create, edit, and delete relationships. In this case, we will create a new relationship between customers and orders.

6. Click on the CustomerID field in the Customer table, and drag it on the CustomerID field on the Orders table. The "Edit Relationships" window will come up.

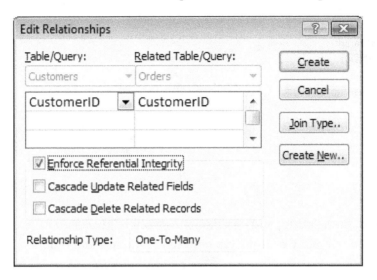

7. We can just click "Create", and our relationship is ready. However, in this case, we will also click on "Enforce Referential Integrity" so that our database remains sound when inserting new records and deleting existing ones. For example, with referential integrity on, we will not be able to add an order in the orders table without an existing customer in the customers table. In addition, we will not be able to delete a customer from the customers table for whom there are orders in the orders table. We will have to first delete the orders for that customer and then delete the customer. For a full and detailed understanding of referential integrity and its important implications, read the corresponding section in this chapter.

8. Finally, our Entity Relationship Diagram (ERD) will look like this:

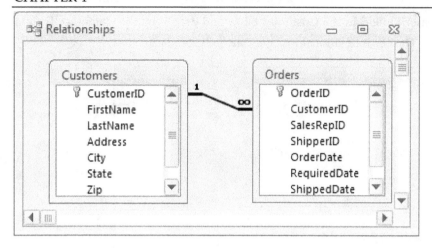

34. How to read, understand, and use a one-to-many relationship

The meaning of one-to-many relationship between customers and orders

Learning how to create a one-to-many relationship is really a minimal goal in itself. The essential objective is to actually understand its meaning, be able to apply it, and take advantage of its many powers and possibilities. In this respect, let us try to read what is happening in our two related tables of customers and orders.

First, when looking at the foreign key values in the orders table (the values of the CustID field in the Orders table), we notice that only John, Mary, and George have orders. Second, we see that John and George have one order each, while Mary has two orders. Third, we see that Stacy does not have any orders at all, so we might want to initiate a marketing effort for her. Fourth, when we look at the orders table and examine order number 3 (with OrderID = 3), we immediately understand that this order belongs to John because the corresponding foreign key value is 1. If we look up this value in the customer table, we find that the corresponding customer name is John. This is the way relational databases work and are able to retrieve related records from two or more tables.

CUSTOMERS		ORDERS		
CustID	Name	OrderID	CustID	OrderDate
1	John	1	2	9/10/2009
2	Mary	2	2	10/10/2010
3	George	3	1	11/10/2010
4	Stacy	4	3	11/11/2010

Primary Key	Primary Key	Foreign Key

35. Why and how to create a many-to-many-relationship

Create a many-to-many relationship between orders and products

Our task this time is to create a database to keep track of customers, orders, and products. We already know how to create a one-to-many relationship between customers and orders. Now, we need to create a relationship between orders and products. Whenever we design a database, the setup of relationships is the cornerstone of the design process. We do have an ally in this process, which is our logic.

In this respect, we examine and make conclusions on the relation of each table to the other or of relations among entities because this is how we refer to tables in database parlance. From the orders point of view, we conclude that each order in the orders table can contain more than one product. It is only logical that a customer can order multiple products in one order. From the products point of view, we conclude that each product can participate in more than one order. It is logical that we can sell the same product to multiple customers through their orders. When this is the case, we need to establish a many-to-many relationship between Orders and Products.

To create a many-to-many relationship between the Orders and Products tables, we need to create a join table between them like the Products_Orders table in this example. The primary key of the join table is the combination of the primary keys of the tables that we would like to join in a many-to-many relationship. In other words, the primary key of any join table in a many-to-many relationship is a composite key consisting of two fields. As we know already, the values of a primary key in a relational table must always be unique, and this uniqueness is expressed in this case by the combination of the values of OrderID and ProductID. For example, in Figure 14 the value (1,2) of the first record in the Products_Orders table is different from the value (2,2) in the second record. This is how we obtain uniqueness of primary key values of join tables in many-to-many relationships.

CUSTOMER	
CustID	Name
1	John
2	Mary
3	George
4	Stacy

ORDERS		
OrderID	CustID	OrderDate
1	2	9/10/2009
2	2	10/10/2010
3	1	11/10/2010
4	3	11/11/2010

Products_Orders		
OrderID	ProductID	Quantity
1	2	2
2	2	5
3	1	3
4	2	4

Products	
ProductID	ProductName
1	A
2	B
3	C
4	D

Figure 14: A many-to-many relationship

To create a many-to-many relationship in Access 2010, we follow these steps:

1.   Make sure that the two tables that you are about to join in a many-to-many relationship already have primary keys. These primary keys should be of the autonumber data type.

2.   Create a new table whose name is the combination of the names of the two tables that you would like to join—in this case "Products_Orders." You can follow any other naming convention you prefer as long as you can remember in the future that this is a join table between Orders and Products.

3.   In the join table "Products_Orders", create two fields whose names are: ProductID and OrderID. The data types of both OrderID and ProductID should be "Number". This is because we need to join these fields with the corresponding keys in the Orders and Products tables, and we cannot join two fields with dissimilar data types. Your table should look like this:

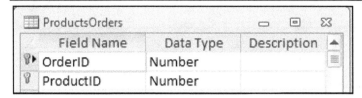

4. We are not finished yet, however. Let us assume that a customer orders two units of product (A) and three units of product (B). This customer is ordering multiple quantities of the same product in the same order. In addition, we might want to give discounts on particular products in the same order while extending no discounts for other products. How do we accomplish this? The answer is to include additional fields in the Products_Orders table so that we can enter this information. Our final table will look like this:

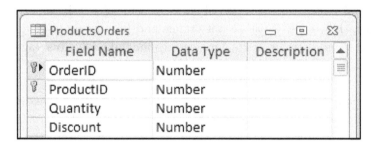

5. The next step is to join the Orders table to the ProductsOrders table by dragging the OrderID field from the Orders table on the OrderID field in the ProductsOrders table. We do the same by dragging the ProductID field from the Products table on the ProductID field in the ProductsOrders table. Our relationships window will now look like the figure below:

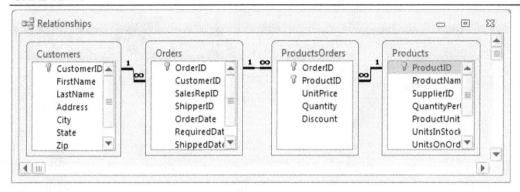

36. How to "read", understand, and use a many-to-many relationship

The meaning of many-to-many relationship between orders and products

The important goal in any database work is to understand what we are doing and not so much the process of doing it. If we do not remember the series of clicks to achieve a task, we can always resort to a handy reference. However, if we do not understand how many-to-many relationships work, we are reluctant to use them or, at the very least, cannot take full advantage of them.

Let us examine the meaning of a many-to-many relationship from A to Z. The figure below depicts a many-to-many relationship between the Orders and Products tables. Let us try to answer a couple of questions:

What specific products were included in John's order?
To answer this question, we should go to John's record in the customer table. There, we see that John's primary key value is 1 (PK=1). Then, we proceed to the Orders table, which is joined with the customer table through a one-to-many relationship. There, we see that John appears in the third record of the table where CustID = 1. In database parlance, this translates to foreign key value = 1 or FK=1. Next, we see that the corresponding OrderID value for FK=1 is 3 (OrderID =3). From there, we are looking for OrderID = 3 in the ProductsOrders table. We see that we have one OrderID with the value of 3 in the ProductsOrders table. The corresponding ProductID value is 1. Next, we go to the Products table and see that ProductID = 1 corresponds to product A. Since the quantity for the pair (3,1) in the Products_Orders table is 3, we can finally answer that John ordered three units of product (A). This is exactly how relational databases use associations (relationships) to store and retrieve information.

CUSTOMER	
CustID	Name
1	John
2	Mary
3	George
4	Stacy

ORDERS		
OrderID	CustID	OrderDate
1	2	9/10/2009
2	2	10/10/2010
3	1	11/10/2010
4	3	11/11/2010

Products_Orders		
OrderID	ProductID	Quantity
1	2	2
2	2	5
3	1	3
4	2	4

Products	
ProductID	ProductName
1	A
2	B
3	C
4	D

Figure 15: Understanding a many-to-many relationship

What specific products were included in Mary's orders?

Mary's PK is 2. For FK=2 in the orders table, the corresponding PK values are 1 and 2. We now know that Mary placed two orders. For OrderID 1 and 2 in the ProductsOrders table, the corresponding ProductIDs are 2 and 2. The quantities are 2 and 5. Therefore, we know right away that Mary ordered seven product Bs in two separate orders. We also note that Mary has a pattern of ordering only product Bs, which allows us to direct our marketing efforts.

37. Create a one-to-many relationship using pure SQL

Use SQL to create a one-to-many relationship between customers and orders
Discussion:
In this scenario, we create a one-to-many relationship between the tblCustomer1 and tblOrders1tables using CustomerID as the joining field. First, let us create the tables:

Create the customer table
Code:
CREATE TABLE tblCustomer1 (
[CustomerID] Counter Primary key not null,
[LastName] text(50),
[FirstName] text(50));

Create the orders table

Code:

```
CREATE TABLE tblOrders1 (
[OrderID] Counter Primary key not null,
[CustomerID] integer,
[OrderDate] datetime);
```

Code:

```
ALTER TABLE tblOrders1
ADD CONSTRAINT C_OrdersRelationship
FOREIGN KEY (CustomerID)
REFERENCES tblCustomer1 (CustomerID);
```

Result:

Go to "Database Tools", and click on "Relationships" in the "Relationships" group. Click on "Relationships" and then the "Show Table" button and make the two tables show in the relationships pane. The two tables will appear with a one-to-many relationship established already. In addition, you will notice that referential integrity is already set as well. This is really cool, isn't it?

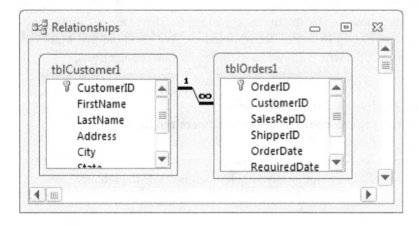

38. What is referential integrity, how to apply it, and what it means
The meaning and implications of referential integrity in table relationships

Referential Integrity is a concept misunderstood and underused in the database professional world. Some developers will turn this option on in Access because it is a good "thing" to do even though they do not fully understand its implications. Let us take it one step at a time and explain the ins and outs of referential integrity.

Referential integrity in relational databases means that relationships among joined tables remain consistent. Of course, as is the case with all definitions, we do not understand much. Let us try to approach it from a more practical perspective. First, we set referential integrity on table relationships (not tables themselves), and we have the choice to apply it when we create those relationships.

Let's first see how we do it before we discuss what it means. Let's say that we would like to create a one-to-many relationship between customers and orders. To achieve this, we drag the CustomerID field (PK in the Customer table) on the CustomerID field in the Orders table (FK in the orders table). The relationships window then opens up as we can see below:

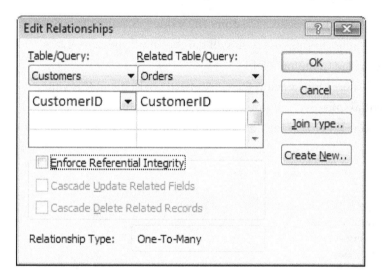

The only thing we need to do is to click on the Referential Integrity check box. In some cases, you might find that the database does not allow you to apply referential integrity. If this is the case, then you should immediately look for orphaned records in the table at the many part of the relationship. In this particular example, it means that we have orders with CustomerID (FK) values without corresponding CustomerID values (PKs) in the customers table. In short, we have orders without corresponding customers. Check chapter 23 for a full explanation of orphaned records. I have devoted a whole chapter on orphaned and unrelated records because this topic is crucial in any database work.

Once referential integrity is on, we have several consequences: First, the database will not allow us to enter an order in the orders table without a corresponding customer. If we have an order from a new customer, we have to enter that customer's data in the Customers table first and then, the orders in the Orders table. Actually, this is what you will see if you try to enter an order without an existing customer.

In Access 2010 pay attention with this aspect of referential integrity because there is a dual scenario:

1. You enter an order in the orders table with a CustomerID value (FK value) that does not exist in the Customers table. In this case, you will get the above message that a related record is required in the Customers table.

2. You enter an order in the orders table leaving the CustomerID field blank (FK value null). In this case, referential integrity will not be enforced. The solution to this is to make the CustomerID field (FK field) in the orders table required as shown in the figure below:

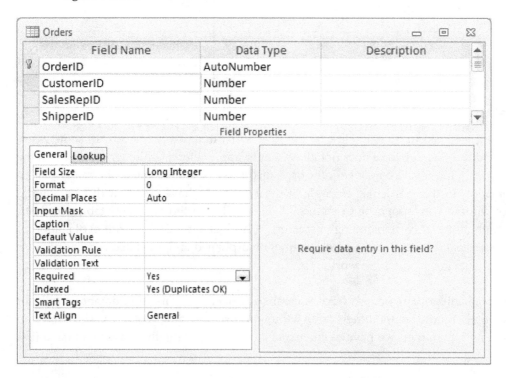

The next major consequence of referential integrity is that the database will not allow us to delete a customer who has orders in the database. First, we need to delete all of the orders for that customer and try to delete the customer. If we try to delete a customer with existing orders, the following message will appear.

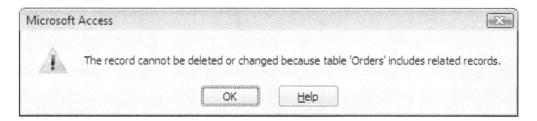

If we want to delete a customer with existing orders in one step, we can also click on "Cascade Deletes". This option helps the professional delete all related information about a customer in the database, but it is very dangerous to leave on because end users might delete customers and their related information by mistake. Check chapters 28 and 29 on "Cascade Updates" and "Cascade Deletes" for full details on their use since they are an important productivity tool for developers and power users.

CHAPTER 5
THE SELECT STATEMENT

The SELECT statement is the most widely used keyword in any relational database, and it constitutes the basis for a multitude of Structured Query Language (SQL) code statements. We will go through examples of how to use the SELECT statement alone or in combination with its various clauses like WHERE, GROUP BY, HAVING, and ORDER BY. However, we will devote whole chapters to some of its clauses since there are many ways and tricks in using them to achieve the intricate results we need in our daily business tasks. In this chapter, we will focus on the SELECT statement in detail, and you will be surprised to see that SELECT can be used in many more ways than simply selecting records. The general structure of the SELECT statement in Access 2010 appears below:

SELECT field1, field2, field3
FROM table
[WHERE]
[GROUP BY]
[HAVING]
[ORDER BY]

39. SELECT with * to retrieve all columns and rows from a table
Create a quick report selecting all columns and rows from the customer table
Discussion:
We can use the * wildcard character to quickly retrieve all of the columns and records from a table. Note that a SELECT statement used this way will retrieve records in the order they are stored in the table.

Code:
SELECT *
FROM Customers

Result:

CustomerID ▾	FirstName ▾	LastName ▾	Address ▲
1	John	Demarco	11 Lark Street
2	Mary	Demania	12 Madison Ave
3	George	Demers	23 New Scotlan A'
4	Phillip	Demetriou	22 Academy Road ▾

Query4 — ▢ ⊠

Record: ◄ ◄ 10 of 201 ► ►I ►⊞   No Filter   Search   ◄   ►

40. SELECT to retrieve only field names

Provide documentation for the Orders table by retrieving a list of its fields

Discussion:

There are occasions when we would like to retrieve only the field names and not any records. This is usually for documentation purposes or for just having a look at the field names before we write a query. We can easily do this by using the following code, which will result in no records because there is no way for 0 to equal 1.

Code:

```
SELECT *
FROM Orders
WHERE 0=1;
```

Result:

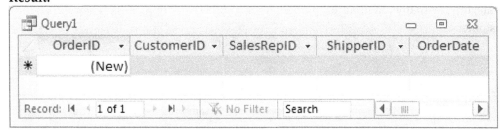

OrderID ▾	CustomerID ▾	SalesRepID ▾	ShipperID ▾	OrderDate
* (New)				

Query1 — ▢ ⊠

Record: I◄ ◄ 1 of 1 ► ►I ►   No Filter   Search   ◄ IIII   ►

41. SELECT to retrieve specific columns from a table

Create a quick customer list for mailing labels

Discussion:

Experience indicates that in the vast majority of cases, we need to retrieve only a subset of columns from a table. We can define exactly what columns to get using the SELECT statement.

In this particular example, we need to send out letters to our customers, and we only need to retrieve address related fields.

Code:
SELECT lastname, firstname, address, city, state, zip
FROM Customers

Result:

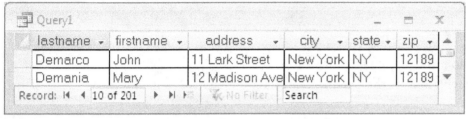

42. SELECT to retrieve columns in the order you prefer

Retrieve a customer list arranging the columns in a specific order
Discussion:
We can specify the order in which we would like to see columns in the query output. In this case, we would like to see the state field first, followed by the last and first names of our customers. When rearranging columns in SQL statements, pay attention to your commas. It is prohibited to have a comma after the last field before the FROM clause.

Code:
SELECT state, city, lastname, firstname
FROM Customers

Result:

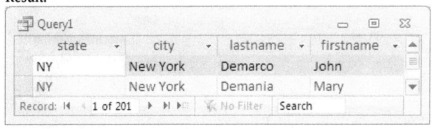

43. SELECT to retrieve specific records from a table

Create a report of customers in Boston

Discussion:

SQL statements provide great flexibility for retrieving records. For instance, we can retrieve all columns from a table, all rows, some columns and all rows, some rows and all columns, or some rows and some columns. In this example, we are retrieving all of the columns from the customer table but limiting the rows by selecting customers who reside in Boston. Notice from the result set that the database returned only 14 customers.

Code:

```
SELECT *
FROM Customers
WHERE city = "Boston"
```

Result:

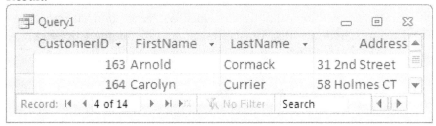

44. SELECT to retrieve specific columns and specific rows

Create a list of suppliers from NY but do not display the state

Discussion:

Sometimes, we need to retrieve specific columns and specific rows from a table. When in this situation, always work with the process of getting the columns first and then, apply the appropriate clauses (WHERE) and criteria ("Houston", "Texas") to get the rows that you need. In this example, we are retrieving only the company name and the contact name of suppliers who operate in New York. In addition, notice that although we use the state as a criterion field, the state itself will not appear in the result set.

Code:

```
SELECT companyname, contactname
FROM suppliers
WHERE (state = "NY")
```

Result:

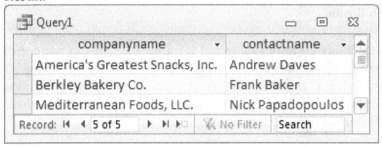

45. SELECT AS: column aliases

Retrieve data from the suppliers table but change the column titles

Discussion:

In many cases, table fields have names that make sense to the database developer but not the end user. For example, Cust_LN and Cust_FN might make sense to the database developer because they represent naming conventions for the customer last name and customer first name fields. However, if we use them as titles for queries or reports, no one will be able to discern their meaning.

In these cases, we use the SELECT AS statement to assign field aliases or column titles that make sense for all of us. We can do this on the fly in a SELECT statement. In the example below, we change the titles of the fields for two columns in the suppliers table. Notice we enclose the second alias [Supplier Contact] in brackets because we have a space between the two words. If we forget the brackets, the SQL statement will not run.

Code:

SELECT companyname AS Company, contactname AS [Supplier Contact]
FROM suppliers

Result:

46. SELECT combined with plain text

Create a quick letter to customers

Discussion:

SQL allows us to mingle field data with plain text, which results in the creation of some interesting results. In this example, we are writing a quick letter to customers. Notice that we enclose plain text in double quotes (" "). In addition, note that the characters (+ ' ' +) add spaces between fields and plain text. Finally, the whole statement in the code below is just one concatenated field named "CustomerLetter." For a full understanding of concatenated fields, refer to chapter 16 where you will find many tips and tricks working with them.

Code:

SELECT "Dear" + ' ' + [firstname] + ' ' + "We would like you to know that our full product catalog is on sale in the city of" + ' ' +[city] + ' ' + "Please visit our website at: http://www.company.com" As CustomerLetter
FROM customers

Result:

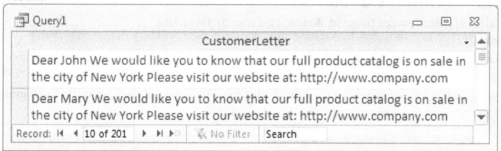

47. SELECT with ORDER BY

Sort a customer list by last name

Discussion:

In this example, we use the * wildcard character to retrieve all of the columns and rows in the customers table and then, sort the data on last name. To sort data in SQL, we use the ORDER BY clause. Specifically, to sort in ascending order, we use ORDER BY ASC, and to sort in descending order, we use ORDER BY DESC. In this example, the ORDER BY clause is not followed by the ASC or DESC keywords. This is fine since when we use the ORDER BY clause alone, it will sort in ascending order by default.

Code:
SELECT *
FROM Customers
ORDER BY lastname

Result:

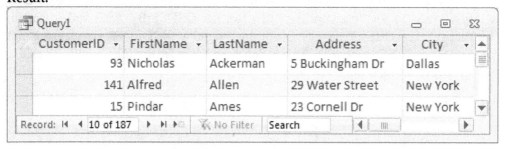

48. SELECT with WHERE and ORDER BY

Retrieve all customers except those in Boston and sort by last name
Discussion:
In this example, we use the * wildcard character to retrieve all columns in the customers table. For rows, we filter the result set by using the WHERE clause with the inequality predicate "<>" to select all customers except those in the city of Boston. Then, we sort ascending on lastname. Note that there are 187 customer records returned out of 201.

Code:
SELECT *
FROM Customers
WHERE city <> "Boston"
ORDER BY lastname

Result:

CustomerID	FirstName	LastName	Address	City
93	Nicholas	Ackerman	5 Buckingham Dr	Dallas
141	Alfred	Allen	29 Water Street	New York
15	Pindar	Ames	23 Cornell Dr	New York

Record: 10 of 187 — No Filter — Search

49. SELECT with WHERE, GROUP BY, HAVING and ORDER BY

Calculate the number of customers in all states except NY and show states with more than ten customers

Discussion:

Our business manager asked us to calculate the number of customers in each state. In addition, she asked us to exclude New York State from the results. From the remaining states, she also asked us to exclude states with less than ten customers. Finally, states with bigger numbers of customers should appear first in the result set.

To comply with the above requirements, we need to use SELECT, WHERE, GROUP BY, HAVING, and ORDER BY in combination. Let us examine the purpose of each statement: First, we use the SELECT statement to select two fields from the customers table. Specifically, we select the state field as it is and the CustomerID field on which we apply the Count() function to calculate the number of occurrences of CustomerID in the table. Since CustomerID is the primary key of the table, we know that Count() will produce reliable results because there is no way to have null values in a primary key field.

Then, we use the WHERE clause with the inequality operator "<>" to exclude from the calculations customers in New York State. Practically, "<>" means retrieve everything else except 'NY'. Next, we use the GROUP BY clause to aggregate calculations by state. The database will calculate the number of customers and produce results by state since we group on that field.

The next point is a bit tricky if not understood well. The WHERE and HAVING clauses are both filtering statements. We use them both to obtain a subset of records. They do, however, have their specific roles in SQL statements, and they can be used individually or in combination. In this specific example, we use the WHERE clause to exclude customers from the state of New York from the result set. The WHERE clause will run before any groupings and calculations by the GROUP BY clause. In this particular example, the WHERE clause will exclude customers from NY, and the GROUP BY clause will produce groups and count customers for the remaining records. After the groups of customers by state are generated from the GROUP BY clause, and the customer numbers are calculated by the count() function, the HAVING clause takes effect. It will exclude from the final result any states with less than ten customers. Therefore, the HAVING clause will wait until the groupings and calculations are complete before it takes effect. This is logical since the numbers produced by the count() function are not known in advance.

Finally, the ORDER BY clause takes effect, and it will sort results by the highest number of customers. What you need to remember in one sentence is that when using the WHERE and HAVING clauses in combination, the WHERE clause always takes effect first, while the HAVING clause takes effect after the groups by the GROUP BY clause have been established. The ORDER BY clause will take effect last.

Code:

```
SELECT State, Count(CustomerID) As NumberOfCustomers
FROM Customers
WHERE State <> "NY"
GROUP BY State
HAVING Count(CustomerID) >10
ORDER BY Count(CustomerID) DESC
```

Result:

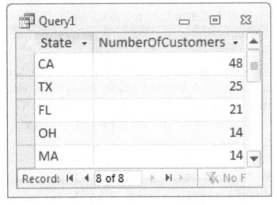

50. SELECT with INSERT INTO to append records in an existing table

Append records from the customer table to a historical customer table

Discussion:

Our goal in this example is to copy (append) a number of records from our customer table to another table in which we keep historical customer data. This scenario applies in situations where we no longer do business with some customers, but we do not want to delete them from the database. At the same time, we do not want these old customers to clutter our operational customer table, slow it down, or interfere with our calculations. We can easily copy them to a historical table by using the INSERT INTO statement. The general structure of the INSERT INTO statement appears below:

```
INSERT INTO TargetTable (field1, field2, field3…)
```

SELECT (field1, field2, field3…)
FROM SourceTable

In this particular example, we copy records from the customers table to the customer2 table. Since customer2 does not exist, we create it with the CREATE statement below. Then, we use the INSERT INTO statement to append three fields with 201 records (all records in the customer table) in the customer2 table.

Code:
CREATE TABLE Customer2 (
[CustomerID] Counter Primary key not null,
[LastName] text(50),
[FirstName] text(50),
[Address] text(100),
[City] text(50));

INSERT INTO Customer2 (firstname, lastname, address, city)
SELECT firstname, lastname, address, city
FROM customers

Result:

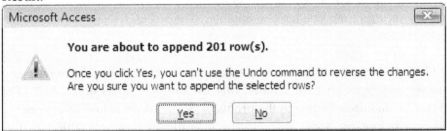

51. SELECT with INSERT INTO to append specific records in a table
Append selected customer records to a historical table
Discussion:
In some occasions, we might want to copy only a subset of records in one table into another table. We can easily achieve this by using the INSERT TO statement and the WHERE clause in combination. In this specific example, we append customer records from NY only.

Code:
INSERT INTO Customer2 (firstname, lastname, address, city)
SELECT firstname, lastname, address, city
FROM customers
WHERE State = 'NY'

Result:

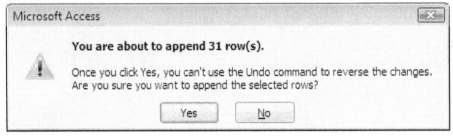

52. SELECT INTO to create a backup or temp table
Create a quick backup copy of the products table
Discussion:
The SELECT INTO statement accomplishes two tasks simultaneously. First, it can create a new table, and second, it can populate this table with records from another table. We do not need to use the CREATE statement to create a new table. In addition, we do not need the INSERT INTO statement to copy records from one table to another. The SELECT INTO statement can accomplish both tasks at once.

We can use the SELECT INTO statement to create quick backup copies of tables, or we can create temporary tables and work on their data leaving the original tables untouched. For instance, we might want to manipulate data in the products table, but we would like to see the results of the edits first before we apply them in the operational products table. In this particular example, we create a backup copy of the products table, and we name it Products_Backup.

Code:
SELECT *
INTO Products_Backup
FROM Products

Result:

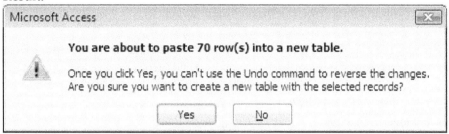

53. SELECT INTO to create a backup table with a subset of data from the original table

Create a temporary table that contains a subset of data from the products table

Discussion:

We can use the SELECT INTO statement and the WHERE clause in combination to create a new table that will contain a subset of data from the original table. The choice of the word "data" is not accidental. In fact, using the SELECT INTO statement in combination with the WHERE clause, we can transfer any fields and records we wish. In this particular example, we create a new table named "Products_Subset" which will contain only three fields and product records from suppliers with supplier ID 1, 2, 3, and 4 only.

Code:
```
SELECT ProductName, UnitsInStock, UnitsOnOrder
INTO Products_Subset
FROM Products
WHERE SupplierID IN (1,2,3,4)
```

Result:

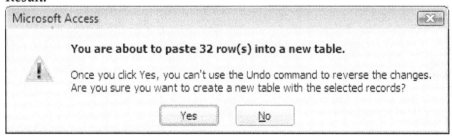

54. SELECT INTO to create a new table with a subset of data from three joined tables

Create a new table that contains data from the three joined tables

Discussion:

The SELECT INTO statement can create a new table that contains data from multiple joined tables. In this example, we create a new table that contains fields from the customers, orders, and productsorders tables. In addition, we restrict the number of records it will contain by using the WHERE clause for customers in NY only. Why do we need to create a new table since we can easily retrieve the same records using a query? Actually, a move like this one serves multiple purposes. First, we might want to give access to this data to other people and not worry if they edit or change it any way they want. If we provide them with a query, they could affect the data in the underlying tables. Another scenario might be that we would like to hide the complexities of the joins to the people working with this data. It is much easier to work with one table than with two inner joins from three tables. Finally, we might be in a business scenario in which this table is the data source for XML or PHP or ASP.Net or other server side pages on our website, and we generate this table every week. Those pages will return results much faster working out of a table data source instead of multiple joins and WHERE clauses.

Code:

```
SELECT customers.lastname, customers.firstName, Orders.OrderDate,
ProductsOrders.UnitPrice, ProductsOrders.Quantity
INTO TempCustomersOrders
FROM (customers INNER JOIN Orders ON customers.CustomerID =
Orders.CustomerID) INNER JOIN ProductsOrders ON Orders.OrderID =
ProductsOrders.OrderID
WHERE (((customers.State)="NY"));
```

Result:

> **Microsoft Access** [X]
>
> ⚠ **You are about to paste 375 row(s) into a new table.**
>
> Once you click Yes, you can't use the Undo command to reverse the changes. Are you sure you want to create a new table with the selected records?
>
> [Yes]   [No]

55. SELECT INTO to create a new table with the structure of an existing table but without the data

Discussion:

Using the code below, we will create a new table named "Products1" which will be identical to the Products table but without any data. Field names and corresponding data types transfer wonderfully but remember to define the primary key and any indexes in your new table.

Code:

```
SELECT * INTO Products1
FROM Products
WHERE 1=2
```

Result:

56. SELECT INTO to create a new table with part of the structure of an existing table

Discussion:

As a continuation from the previous example, you can transfer part of the structure of an existing table to a new one as in the code below. Remember, no data will be moved to the new table.

Code:

```
SELECT ProductID, ProductName, QuantityPerUnit, ProductUnitPrice INTO
Products2
FROM Products
WHERE 1=2
```

Result:

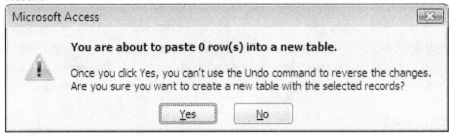

57. SELECT to retrieve a list of user tables in the database

Discussion:

Sometimes, we might want to obtain a simple list of the user tables in our Access database. We can achieve this goal using the code below.

Code:

```
SELECT Name, Type
FROM MSysObjects
WHERE Type =1 and left(name,4) <> "msys"
```

Result:

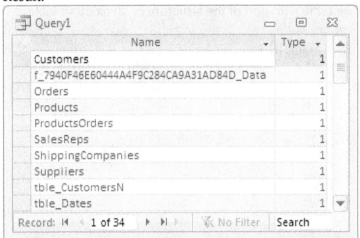

Notice we assign type=1 because this is the number that MSysObjects is using for tables. If we had assigned type = 5, then we would have retrieved queries. In addition, we use the left function to extract the first four characters out of the name of the table and make it different than "msys" (<>"msys") so that we retrieve user tables only. If we leave out the expression left(name,4) <> "msys", then we would retrieve system tables as well:

Code:
SELECT Name, Type
FROM MSysObjects
WHERE Type =1

Result:

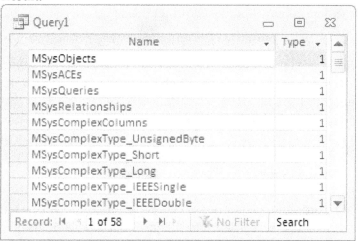

CHAPTER 6
THE OR AND AND OPERATORS

The OR and AND operators are widely used in relational databases. There are four points you need to remember about them: First, their task is to produce a subset of records from the total records in a table or query. Second, they have no effect on the columns we retrieve from that table or query. Third, they are always used with other operators such as LIKE, with equality and inequality predicates, or with wildcard characters. They cannot be used by themselves in SQL statements. Fourth, the OR and AND operators can be used individually or in combination with varying results as we shall see in the following examples.

The OR operator is inclusive so that records will be returned for every OR condition satisfied in our query. For example, if we want to retrieve invoice information from suppliers in three different cities (New York, Texas, or Houston), we will use the OR operator twice. The AND operator is exclusive, and it will produce results only when all of the multicolumn conditions are met.

58. Using OR on the same column
Create a quick report with customers in New York or Houston
Discussion:
Let us suppose we have a request to create a list of all customers who reside in New York or Houston. In this case, we need to use the OR operator on the city field with two equality predicates. Note that since we used the SELECT statement with *, the database will return all columns in the table. However, when it comes to records, only 43 out of 201 will be returned. This is because we filtered the recordset to include customers in the cities of New York or Houston only.

We can use the OR operator on the same column multiple times as in this example to retrieve customers from multiple cities. However, we cannot use the AND operator multiple times on the same column because we would ask the impossible: that is, having a customer who resides in many cities simultaneously.

Code:

```
SELECT *
FROM customers
WHERE (city = "New York") OR (city = "Houston")
```

Result:

59. Use the IN operator to replace multiple OR operators

Produce a report of customers from four cities

Discussion:

The OR operator works fine with two cities as we have seen in the previous example. What if we need to use OR on the city field but use five or six cities as criteria? We have two problems in this case: First, we need to write a long SQL statement using multiple OR operators. Second, if we have a big number of records in the table, the query will be slow to return results. In cases like this one, we can use the IN operator that produces much cleaner code. It is easy to modify and maintain as you can see below:

Code:

```
SELECT lastname, firstname, city, state
FROM customers
WHERE city IN ("Albany", "Denver", "Houston", "Phoenix")
ORDER BY lastname ASC
```

Result:

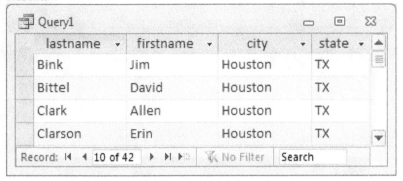

60. Using OR on multiple columns

Create an inventory report listing product quantities for units in stock and units on order

Discussion:

A very efficient way to use the OR operator is to apply it on multiple columns. For instance, we might have a business request to create an inventory report that lists products for which we have more than 10 units in stock or products for which we have more than 10 units on order. As you can see from the result set, we obtained a total number of 70 products. This means that 70 records satisfied at least one condition. This is because any record that satisfies at least one of the conditions will appear in the result set.

In addition, this is why the second record in the result set with 32 units in stock and 0 on order appears as well. We asked for units in stock >10 or units on order >10. This particular record satisfies only the first condition, and this is enough to appear in the result set. The outcome will be very different when we use the AND operator as we will see presently.

Code:

```
SELECT productname, unitsinstock, unitsonorder
FROM products
WHERE (UnitsInStock > 10)
OR (UnitsOnOrder > 10)
```

Result:

productname ▾	unitsinstock ▾	unitsonorder ▾
Almonds, Hickory Smoke	40	5
Almonds, Roasted and S	32	0
Banana Chips - 20 oz. Ba	25	0
Berry Cherry in 8 oz. Bag	50	0

Record: ⏮ ◀ 10 of 70 ▶ ⏭ ▶ No Filter Search

61. Use UNION instead of OR to speed up results

Create an inventory report using UNION instead of OR operators

Discussion:

We can use the UNION statement instead of multiple OR operators to speed up the response time of the database engine. This is a trick used in databases, and the difference in response time is enormous. The SQL statement below with the UNION operation achieves the exact same results as the SQL code in the previous example. However, the response is instant using UNION, while it takes quite a few seconds using the OR operators.

Response times deteriorate as the number of records or the number of OR operators increase. Consequently, if you have statements with multiple OR operators that you use often, you might consider replacing them with UNION statements. The only difference is the order in which the retrieved records appear since in this case, the results of the first SELECT statement in the UNION operation will appear first. The results of the second SELECT will follow and so on. You can easily reorder the recordset using the ORDER BY clause with a UNION statement. For a full understanding of UNION operations, plus related tips and tricks refer to chapter 22.

Code:

```
SELECT productname, unitsinstock, unitsonorder
FROM products
WHERE (UnitsInStock > 10)
UNION
SELECT productname, unitsinstock, unitsonorder
FROM products
WHERE (UnitsOnOrder > 10)
```

Result:

productname ▾	unitsinstock ▾	unitsonorder ▾
All-Purpose Marinade I	27	15
All-Purpose Marinade II	26	15
Almonds, Hickory Smok(	40	5

Record: I◄ ◄ 10 of 70 ► ►I ► No Filter Search

62. Using AND on multiple columns

Produce a report of customers from a specific state and a specific city

Discussion:

This time, we have a business request to produce a report of customers who reside in the state of NY and, in particular, the city of Albany. In this case, we need to use the AND operator to isolate records which satisfy both criteria at the same time. Note that if we use the OR operator, we will get all of the customers in the state of NY irrespective of city and all the customers from all of the cities named "Albany" around the country. This is a problem because there are 28 cities in the U.S. named Albany! If we do business worldwide, there are six additional cities named Albany. An experienced database user will always use AND to isolate the customers only for Albany, New York. As you can see from the result set, we have only four customers that satisfy both criteria.

Code:
```
SELECT lastname, firstname, city, state
FROM customers
WHERE (state = "NY")
AND (city = "Albany")
```

Result:

lastname ▾	firstname ▾	city ▾	state ▾
Vanton	Kenneth	Albany	NY
Trindan	Luis	Albany	NY
Riegert	Joanne	Albany	NY

Record: I◄ ◄ 4 of 4 ► ►I ► No Filter Search

63. Using OR and AND in combination

Produce a report of customers from one state and two cities

Discussion:

Our objective in this scenario is to produce a report that will list customers from the cities of Albany and New York in NY State. In this case, we need to use the AND operator twice and the OR operator once as it appears in the code below:

Code:
```
SELECT lastname, firstname, city, state
FROM customers
WHERE
state = "NY" AND city = "Albany"
OR
state = "NY" AND city = "New York"
ORDER BY lastname
```

Result:

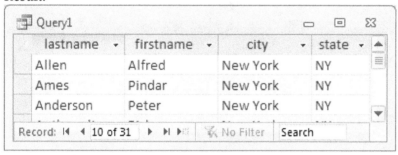

64. Using multiple OR and multiple AND operators in combination

Produce a report of customers from three states and three cities

Discussion:

This time, we have a request to create a customer report that will list customers in the cities of Houston, Albany, and Phoenix from the states of Texas, New York, and Arizona respectively. In this case, we need to use the AND operator three times and the OR operator twice as it appears in the code below. The database returned 29 records.

Code:

SELECT lastname, firstname, city, state
FROM customers
WHERE
state = "NY" AND city = "Albany"
OR
state = "TX" AND city = "Houston"
OR
state = "AZ" AND city = "Phoenix"
ORDER BY lastname

Result:

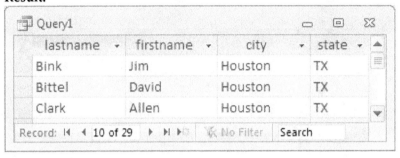

CHAPTER 7
SORTING RECORDS: THE ORDER BY CLAUSE

The ORDER BY clause, with the ASC or DESC keywords, allows the sorting of records in ascending or descending order respectively. The ORDER BY clause is much stronger than what is generally assumed and it allows for some cool tricks with our data.

65. Sorting ascending on one column
Create a list of customers sorting by last name in ascending order
Discussion:
This is a basic example of how to sort our customers by last name and in ascending order. Customers whose last names start with an "A" will appear first. The keyword "ASC" is not required to sort records in ascending order. If we leave the keyword "ASC" out, the ORDER BY clause will sort ascending by default.

Code:
```
SELECT *
FROM Customers
ORDER BY lastname ASC
```

Result:

CustomerID ▾	FirstName ▾	LastName ▾	Address ▾
93	Nicholas	Ackerman	5 Buckingham Dr
141	Alfred	Allen	29 Water Street
15	Pindar	Ames	23 Cornell Dr

Record: I◀ ◀ 10 of 201 ▶ ▶I ▶ No Filter Search

66. Sorting descending on one column

Create a list of customers sorting by last name in descending order

Discussion:

Sometimes, we want to see names in reverse alphabetical order—names that start with Z, Y, or X first. In this case, we add the DESC keyword to our SQL statement. Note that if we want to sort descending, the DESC keyword is required.

Code:

```
SELECT *
FROM Customers
ORDER BY lastname DESC
```

Result:

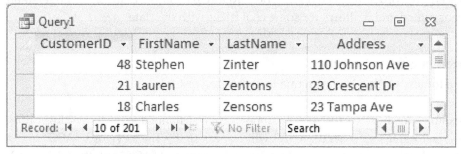

67. Use the ORDER BY clause to sort multiple columns

Create a customer list sorting by city and last name simultaneously

Discussion:

We can sort records on the values of multiple columns. For example, we might want to obtain a report which will include a list of customers sorted first by city and then, by last name.

Let's say we have some customers in Albany and some customers in Boston. Sorting ascending on both city and last name fields will create the following result: The records with the city of Albany will appear first in the result set, followed by the records with the city of Boston. Now, within the Albany records, customers will be sorted alphabetically and in ascending order. Within the city of Boston records, customers will again be sorted alphabetically and in ascending order. We should not be surprised to see a customer from Boston whose last name starts with an "A" being listed after a customer in Albany whose last name starts with a "Z".

Code:

SELECT city, lastname, firstname
FROM Customers
ORDER BY city, lastname ASC

Result:

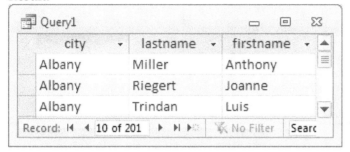

68. Use the ORDER BY clause to sort multiple columns with different sorting directions

Create a customer list sorting by city ascending and customer name descending

Discussion:

We also have the ability to sort on multiple columns forcing a different sorting direction for each column. In this example we sort ascending on the city and then for each city we sort descending on the last name.

Code:

SELECT city, lastname, firstname
FROM Customers
ORDER BY city ASC, lastname DESC

Result:

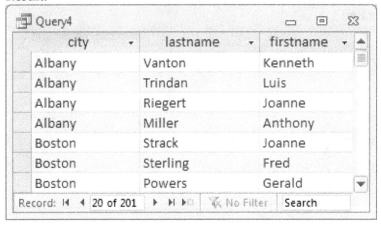

69. Use ORDER BY clause with null values

Find customers who do not have a first name registered in the database

Discussion:

Let us suppose that we have a suspicion that some first name values are missing from our records. How can we quickly find out which ones they are? We can simply create a query that includes the fields we would like to check and sort ascending on the field we suspect includes blank entries. In this instance, we sort ascending on the first name field from our customers table. As you can see from the result set, we immediately found one customer without a first name.

Code:

SELECT lastname, firstname
FROM Customers
ORDER BY firstname ASC

Result:

70. Use the ORDER BY clause with numbers

Create an inventory report sorting products by quantity on hand

Discussion:

In this scenario, we would like to list products from our inventory with the biggest quantities on hand. We can easily achieve this task using the DESC keyword with numbers. When sorting numbers, the DESC keyword will cause the biggest ones to show first, while the ASC keyword will cause the smallest numbers to show first.

Code:

```
SELECT productname, unitsinstock
FROM products
ORDER BY unitsinstock DESC
```

Result:

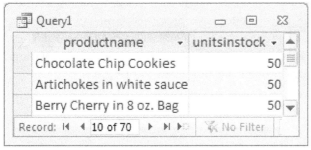

71. The ORDER BY clause with dates

Create a list with the latest orders on top

Discussion:

The ORDER BY clause works with dates the same way it works with numbers. So, to list the latest dates first, we use the DESC keyword. If we would like to show the oldest dates first, we use the ASC keyword.

Code:

```
SELECT orderid, orderdate, shippeddate
FROM ORDERS
ORDER BY orderdate DESC
```

Result:

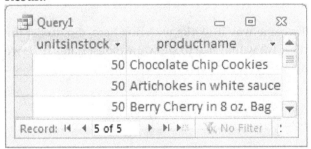

orderid	orderdate	shippeddate
4	12/19/2014	12/19/2014
874	12/16/2014	12/16/2014
165	12/14/2014	12/14/2014

Record: ◄ ◄ 10 of 1000 ► ►► No Filter Search

72. TIP: Combine the ORDER BY and TOP clauses to control the result set

List the top five products in the inventory with the biggest quantities on hand

Discussion:

The ORDER BY clause produces very meaningful results when used in combination with the TOP clause. For instance, what if we want to list the top five products in our inventory with the biggest quantities on hand? We can achieve this task by combining the ORDER BY and TOP clauses. Notice the number of records in the result set. Only five products appear, and these five products have the largest unit quantities in stock in our inventory.

Code:

```
SELECT TOP 5 unitsinstock, productname
FROM products
ORDER BY unitsinstock DESC
```

Result:

unitsinstock	productname
50	Chocolate Chip Cookies
50	Artichokes in white sauce
50	Berry Cherry in 8 oz. Bag

Record: ◄ ◄ 5 of 5 ► ►► No Filter

You need to pay attention to the results of the TOP clause however. It will provide consistent results as soon as there are distinct values in the field on which we are using it. If there are identical values, then all of them will appear in the result set if the first one appears. For example, let us say we have four products with quantity per unit at 50 units and ten products with quantity per unit at 49 units. If we use TOP 5 to get the top five quantities per unit, we will actually get fourteen records.

73. Determine your own sort order using the SWITCH function

Discussion:

Now, we have an odd request from the marketing department. They want a list of customers sorted by state but they want to determine the sort order themselves, that is, which state will appear first, which second, etc. In this case, they want the customers from New York to appear first, those from California next, and those from Texas last. This is impossible to achieve by using the simple ascending and descending qualifiers of the ORDER BY clause. However, it is possible by using the SWITCH function as in the code below. This is a very flexible way to order records in any way we like. Notice also that we exclude other states from the result set for simplicity.

Code:

```
SELECT *
FROM Qry_Conditions
WHERE STATE in ("NY","CA","TX")
ORDER BY
SWITCH(
[state]= 'NY',      1,
[state]= 'CA',      2,
[state] = 'TX',     3
)
```

Result:

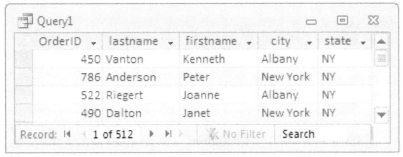

Discussion:

Just in case you wanted to include all the other states in the result set, you could assign them the number 4 for all of them to appear after Texas. The records containing other states will be included in the result set but they will be unsorted. The code below does exactly that.

Code:
```
SELECT *
FROM Qry_Conditions
ORDER BY
SWITCH(
[state]= 'NY',        1,
[state]= 'CA',        2,
[state] = 'TX',       3,
state] <> 'NY' Or 'CA' Or 'TX',      4


)
```

74. Determine your own sort order using lookup tables

Discussion:

We have seen in a previous example how we can force our own sort order using the switch function. There is a second way to achieve the same result by using lookup tables. The benefit is we can update the lookup table at will without the need of changing SQL code in the switch() function. Let us use the same example we used during the switch() function results. From the marketing department they want a list of customers sorted by state where the customers from New York will appear first, those from California next, and those from Texas last. We can create a sort table, in this case tbls_State, which contains the states in the order we want them sorted. This table will look like the tblS_State below:

Result:

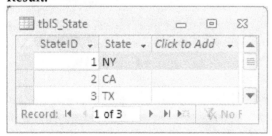

Then, we will join the table tbls_State with the Qry_Conditions with an inner join on the State field as in the code below:

Code:
```
SELECT * FROM Qry_Conditions
INNER JOIN tblS_State ON Qry_Conditions.state = tblS_State.State
```

The result set is now sorted based on the order of the state entries in the tbls_State table. If we change the order of the states in the tbls_state table, or we add new ones, the result set will change accordingly. Notice that the sorting results of cities and last names might not be exactly the same as with those when using the switch function but the sort direction on the state field works perfect.

Result:

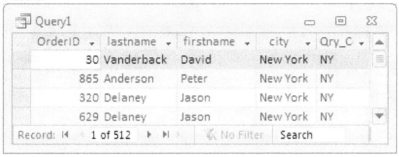

CHAPTER 8
WORKING WITH WILDCARD CHARACTERS

Wildcard characters like (*, ?, !, [], -, #) provide essential functionality and power in databases. They are used in combination with operators such as (LIKE, OR, AND, BETWEEN, IN, etc.) and predicates like (<, >, <>, =, >=). They allow for the formulation of very sophisticated search criteria on text and number data.

75. The * wildcard character

Create a list of customers whose last name starts with D

Discussion:

The * is the wildest of the wildcard characters, and it will match any number and type (letters or numbers) of characters whether we put it in the beginning, middle, or end of a search condition. For example, we can search for all of the customer last names that start with the letter D. As we can see in this example, every customer whose last name starts with a D will appear in the result set. Notice in the code the * is positioned after the letter D. This means that entries such as Dem, D1a, d123, or Dzo will appear in the result set.

Code:

```
SELECT *
FROM customers
WHERE lastname Like "D*"
```

Result:

CustomerID	FirstName	LastName	Address
1	John	Demarco	11 Lark Street
2	Mary	Demania	12 Madison Ave
3	George	Demers	23 New Scotland Ave
4	Phillip	Demetriou	22 Academy Road

Record: 10 of 21 — No Filter — Search

76. The ? wildcard character in combination with *

Create a customer list using ? and * to create intricate search patterns

Discussion:

The ? character matches any single character. Though not used as much as the *, it can still make the difference and enable us to get exactly the results we want in certain cases. Usually, we use it in combination with other wildcard characters. For instance, let's say we want to find names starting with "Da", have any character after the "Da" pattern, and the next letter is "e" followed by any number of characters—"Da?e*". This will give us results such as Darec, Datek, Dale, and Daleney.

Code:
```
SELECT *
FROM customers
WHERE ((lastname) Like "Da?e*")
```

Result:

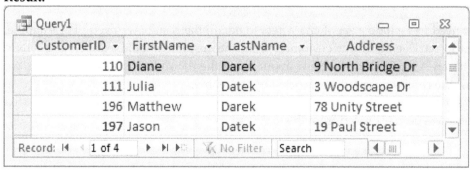

CustomerID	FirstName	LastName	Address
110	Diane	Darek	9 North Bridge Dr
111	Julia	Datek	3 Woodscape Dr
196	Matthew	Darek	78 Unity Street
197	Jason	Datek	19 Paul Street

Record: 1 of 4 — No Filter — Search

CHAPTER 8

77. Create multi-character search strings with [ ]
Create a customer list using multi-character search patterns
Discussion:

Let us assume we would like to search for a number of specific characters within a character string such as a name field. We can do this by using the brackets [ ]. Any character or characters that we include within the brackets will be included in our search. For example, C[ru]* will find Croney, Culey, but not Colonie. Note that we use the * in this example to allow any characters to be included after the brackets.

Code:
SELECT *
FROM customers
WHERE ((lastname) Like "C[ru]*")

Result:

CustomerID	FirstName	LastName	Address
99	Kenneth	Crondos	158 West Lawrence A'
100	Pindar	Crooney	16 Warren Street
101	Joseph	Crandil	192 Tampa Ave
107	Mary	Crawford	21 Aegean Dr

Record: I◀ ◀ 1 of 8 ▶ ▶I ▶※ No Filter Search

78. Use the ! and [ ] wildcard characters to create exclusion patterns
Create a customer list using specific characters as exclusion search patterns
Discussion:

Sometimes, we need to exclude a set of characters to obtain the results we need. For example, we might want to retrieve all of our customers from the customers table except those whose names start with an A, B, C, D, or E. How about using the [!] wildcard to get the results we want? Note that the returned recordset is sorted by last name, and the first customer record to appear has a last name value starting with "F". All of the customers whose names start with a letter before that have been excluded from the recordset.

114

Code:
```
SELECT *
FROM customers
WHERE ((lastname) Like "[!abcde]*")
ORDER BY lastname
```

Result:

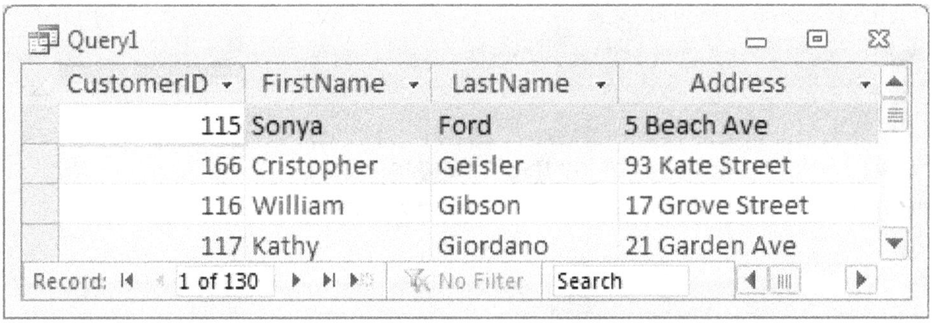

CustomerID ▾	FirstName ▾	LastName ▾	Address ▾
115	Sonya	Ford	5 Beach Ave
166	Cristopher	Geisler	93 Kate Street
116	William	Gibson	17 Grove Street
117	Kathy	Giordano	21 Garden Ave

Query1

Record: I◄ ◄ 1 of 130 ► ►I ►⊞   No Filter   Search

79. Use the ! and [ ] and - wildcards to create exclusion ranges

Create a customer list using sets of characters as exclusion ranges

Discussion:

What if we continue from the previous example using ! and [], but instead of typing in all of the characters, we use ranges? For example, we might want to obtain a recordset of customers whose names do not start with a letter in the range A-P. We can do this by using the "[!a-p]*" exclusion pattern. As you can see from the figure below, the customers who appear in the list have names starting with an "R", which is the one immediately following "P" that was included in our exclusion range.

Code:
```
SELECT *
FROM customers
WHERE ((lastname) Like "[!a-p]*")
ORDER BY lastname
```

Result:

CustomerID	FirstName	LastName	Address
61	Richard	Ramirez	48 Mereline Ave
184	Lisa	Read	12 Madison Ave
17	Allen	Restad	72 Providence Dr
139	Joanne	Riegert	31 Arizona Ave

Record: 1 of 59 — No Filter — Search

80. Use the - and [ ] wildcards to create inclusion ranges

Create a customer list using sets of characters as inclusion ranges

Discussion:

We can continue from the previous example and use [] and - to obtain a recordset of customers whose names do start with a letter between A and P. Simply put, we need to take out the exclamation mark.

Code:
```
SELECT *
FROM customers
WHERE ((lastname) Like "[a-p]*")
ORDER BY lastname
```

Result:

CustomerID	FirstName	LastName	Address
93	Nicholas	Ackerman	5 Buckingham Dr
141	Alfred	Allen	29 Water Street
15	Pindar	Ames	23 Cornell Dr
50	Thomas	Andersen	52 Betwood Street

Record: 1 of 142 — No Filter — Search

CHAPTER 9
THE LIKE OPERATOR

The major aspect of the LIKE operator is its flexibility in creating search expressions. In other words, it has the flexibility to work on text, number, and date data types using intricate expressions to produce results. In addition, its usefulness is greatly enhanced when used in combination with wildcard characters like (*, ?, !, [], -) for the creation of elaborate search expressions.

However, we need to remember two points when using the LIKE operator. First, to supply this flexibility and functionality, it consumes resources, so it should not be the first operator that we resort to for all of our search expressions. Second, we should really know how to use it to get the results we need since it might not always return the expected results.

In this chapter, we approach the usage of the LIKE operator from all perspectives, and we point out tips for using it optimally. To demonstrate the cool functionality of the LIKE operator, all of the examples in this chapter use the table called tbls_CustomerOrders. The records of this table are edited with special values to show how LIKE applies to various circumstances in our working environment.

KIND OF MATCH	PATTERN	MATCH (RETURNS TRUE)	NO MATCH (RETURNS FALSE)
Multiple characters	a*a	aa, aBa, aBBBa	aBC
	ab	abc, AABB, Xab	aZb, bac
Special character	a[*]a	a*a	aaa
Multiple characters	ab*	abcdefg, abc	cab, aab
Single character	a?a	aaa, a3a, aBa	aBBBa
Single digit	a#a	a0a, a1a, a2a	aaa, a10a
Range of characters	[a-z]	f, p, j	2, &

Outside a range	[!a-z]	9, &, %	b, a
Not a digit	[!0-9]	A, a, &, ~	0, 1, 9
Combined	a[!b-m]#	An9, az0, a99	abc, aj0

Figure 16: List of wildcard characters

Source: http://office.microsoft.com/en-us/access-help/like-operator-HP001032253.aspx

81. The LIKE operator with the * wildcard character

Create a list of customers whose last name starts with M

Discussion:

This simple example uses the LIKE operator to find customers whose last names start with an "M". The LIKE operator is used within the WHERE clause, and we enclose the search expression in double quotes. In addition, we use the * wildcard to obtain the result we need.

Code:

```
SELECT *
FROM tbls_CustomerOrders
WHERE (lastname like "M*")
```

Result:

82. The LIKE operator with [ ] and * to search for ranges

Find customers whose zip code starts with a number between 1 and 4

Discussion:

This time, we have a request to prepare a customer report showing customers whose zip codes start with numbers between 1 and 4, such as 12189, 26890, 34123, or 41289 (as opposed to 58659, which would not be included). To obtain the report, we use the LIKE operator with the [ ] and * wildcard characters—LIKE with two wildcard characters simultaneously. The [ ] wildcard will identify all zip codes starting with 1, 2, 3, and 4. The * will then allow for the retrieval of any number of characters after 1, 2, 3, and 4. So, even if we had to work with zip codes comprising of ten characters like 23546-1295, the SQL code in this example would work the same. Of course, we could modify the search condition as "[1-4]????" to only look for five digit zip codes.

Code:
SELECT lastname, firstname, city, zip
FROM tbls_CustomerOrders
WHERE (zip like "[1-4]*")

Result:

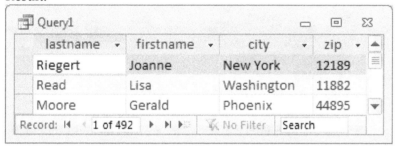

83. The LIKE operator with date fields
Create a report of orders for the month of April for all years
Discussion:
The LIKE operator can produce very useful pieces of information when used with date fields. In this particular example, we look for orders in the month of April irrespective of the day or year they were placed. To achieve what we need, we use the LIKE operator with the * wildcard character. Notice how we use the * twice for days and years, while we fix the month at 4 (April). I know from experience that in your own working environment, dates might not be in the format of "Month number/Day number/Year" (1/1/2012), but perhaps like January 12 2012, for example. This is not a problem at all since we can manipulate dates and change their format on the fly any way we need. I have devoted a whole chapter (chapter 27) on date manipulation for your reference. In addition, using LIKE, we can fix the day, the year, or any combination of month, day, and year and retrieve the corresponding results.

Code:

SELECT lastname, firstname, orderdate
FROM tbls_CustomerOrders
WHERE (OrderDate Like "4/*/*")

Result:

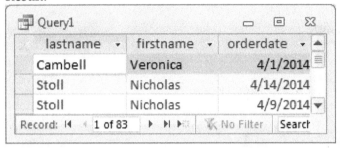

84. The LIKE operator with number fields

Create a report of customer orders with order totals of $200

Discussion:

The LIKE operator can as easily be used with number fields as it can with text and date data. In this example, we have a request to find all customer orders with a total of $200. When we use LIKE with numbers, we do not enclose the numbers in quotes.

Code:

SELECT lastname, firstname, orderdate, OrderTotal
FROM tbls_CustomerOrders
WHERE (OrderTotal Like 200)

Result:

Although we can use LIKE to search for numbers, it is a much better practice to use equality and inequality predicates such as (<, >, <>, =, >=). The above example could be written with the equality predicate "=", and it will produce the same results.

Code:
SELECT lastname, firstname, orderdate, OrderTotal
FROM tbls_CustomerOrders
WHERE (OrderTotal = 200)

Result:

lastname	firstname	orderdate	OrderTotal
Tinons	Matthew	4/18/2012	200
Demaico	Nicholas	5/8/2014	200
Martini	Stephen	4/29/2014	200
Trindan	Luis	4/12/2013	200

Record: 1 of 5   No Filter   Search

85. Compare LIKE, BETWEEN, and "<=" "=>" for number ranges

Create a report of customer orders with order totals between $200 and $400

Discussion:

In this scenario, we have a request from management to prepare a report showing customer orders with order totals between $200 and $400. To achieve this goal, we have three alternatives: We can use the LIKE operator, the BETWEEN operator, and the "<=" "=>" predicates. Which one is the best solution? Let us explore the three cases before we make a decision. In the first case, we use the LIKE operator with the [ ] wildcard for ranges and the "?" to establish the number of characters to be returned at 3. In other words, we are looking for numbers such as 234, 345, or 385. If we have used * after the [ ], we will also get numbers such as 26, 30, and 35, which is not what we want. The result set includes 230 records starting with order totals at $200 and going all the way up to the order total of $393. Attention, here. The LIKE operator is not able to include order totals that are exactly $400. It can go as far up as $399. Consequently, if we have any order totals at exactly $400 they will not be included.

Code:

```
SELECT lastname, firstname, orderdate, OrderTotal
FROM tbls_CustomerOrders
WHERE (OrderTotal LIKE "[2-3]??")
ORDER BY OrderTotal ASC
```

Result:

Discussion:

We use the BETWEEN operator to achieve the same task. We must know about the BETWEEN operator that it is inclusive. For ranges of order totals between $200 and $400, it will include the order totals of exactly $200 and exactly $400 if they are available.

Code:

```
SELECT lastname, firstname, orderdate, OrderTotal
FROM tbls_CustomerOrders
WHERE (OrderTotal BETWEEN 200 AND 400)
ORDER BY OrderTotal ASC
```

Result:

lastname ▾	firstname ▾	orderdate ▾	OrderTotal ▾
Platt	Colleen	9/26/2014	200
Demaico	Nicholas	5/8/2014	200
Trindan	Luis	4/12/2013	200
Tinons	Matthew	4/18/2012	200

Record: I◀ ◀ 1 of 230 ▶ ▶I ▶ No Filter Search

Discussion:

In this case, we are using the "<=" "=>" predicates to achieve the same goal of finding orders between $200 and $400. When it comes to numbers, the "<=" "=>" predicates are the most flexible and trusted to work with. For example, we can use the "<" ">" to exclude lower and upper limits. In addition, predicates will produce consistent results, while operators have issues with result accuracy and performance.

Code:

```
SELECT lastname, firstname, orderdate, OrderTotal
FROM tbls_CustomerOrders
WHERE (OrderTotal >= 200 AND OrderTotal <=  400)
ORDER BY OrderTotal ASC
```

Result:

lastname	firstname	orderdate	OrderTotal
Platt	Colleen	9/26/2014	200
Demaico	Nicholas	5/8/2014	200
Trindan	Luis	4/12/2013	200
Tinons	Matthew	4/18/2012	200

Record: 1 of 230   No Filter   Search

86. The NOT LIKE operator

Find customer orders with order totals different than $200

Discussion:

We can use the negation keyword "NOT" to completely change the result set of an operation using LIKE. In this particular example, we are looking for order totals different from $200. Though we can use LIKE to achieve this, we will be better off using the inequality predicate "<>" for which we include the code below as well. Both pieces of code will produce the same result but prefer to use the predicate instead of the operator.

Code1:

```
SELECT lastname, firstname, orderdate, OrderTotal
FROM tbls_CustomerOrders
WHERE (OrderTotal NOT Like 200)
```

Code2:

SELECT lastname, firstname, orderdate, OrderTotal

FROM tbls_CustomerOrders

WHERE (OrderTotal <> 200)

Result:

lastname	firstname	orderdate	OrderTotal
Riegert	Joanne	11/6/2013	30
Read	Lisa	7/25/2013	210
Moore	Gerald	6/29/2013	231
Davis	Catherine	12/14/2014	45

Record: ◄ ◄ 1 of 914 ► ►► No Filter Search

87. TIP: Use LIKE with the trim() function to get the right results

Filter customer names effectively by eliminating blank spaces

Discussion:

We have a request from our manager to find all orders for which the first name is Mary so that she can have a look and send them a card for their name day. We know how to use the LIKE operator, so we write a statement like the one below and get 20 records. We provide the report to our manager, and two weeks later, she comes back and says we missed three customers. What happened? Well, for three Marys, there were spaces in front of their first names and the LIKE operator did not pick them up. When it comes to LIKE, the statement (LIKE " Mary") is different from (LIKE "Mary"). Consequently, if there are any spaces, the two LIKE statements above will produce different results. What can we do about it? Let us look at the trim() function in the SQL statement after the one shown below:

Code:

SELECT lastname, firstname, orderdate, OrderTotal

FROM tbls_CustomerOrders

WHERE (firstname LIKE "Mary")

Result:

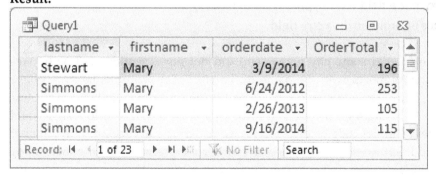

lastname	firstname	orderdate	OrderTotal
Stewart	Mary	3/9/2014	196
Simmons	Mary	6/24/2012	253
Simmons	Mary	2/26/2013	105
Simmons	Mary	9/16/2014	115

Record: ◄ ‹ 1 of 20 › ►I ►⊞   No Filter   Search

Discussion:

The trim() function will eliminate any spaces before or after a string in a field, and this will allow the LIKE operator to function properly. We can use the trim() function in the WHERE clause together with the LIKE operator as you can see in the code below. Notice that this time, the database returned 23 records instead of 20. For a full understanding of string functions and their cool functionality, please refer to chapter 26 where we list multiple examples.

Code:

```
SELECT lastname, firstname, orderdate, OrderTotal
FROM tbls_CustomerOrders
WHERE (trim(firstname) LIKE "Mary")
```

Result:

lastname	firstname	orderdate	OrderTotal
Stewart	Mary	3/9/2014	196
Simmons	Mary	6/24/2012	253
Simmons	Mary	2/26/2013	105
Simmons	Mary	9/16/2014	115

Record: ◄ ‹ 1 of 23 › ►I ►⊞   No Filter   Search

88. TIP: Use LIKE to test a field for the presence of spaces

Check for the presence of blank spaces in a city field

Discussion:

The same supervisor comes back and says she needs a report of customers from certain cities. This time, we are wise enough to know that to get the right results, we need to check for spaces first. Then, however, we reason that some city names do contain spaces. For example, New York contains a space, and Los Angeles contains a space. In addition, we realize that the trim() function is good enough for leading and trailing spaces. What if we have a space right in the middle of the word, however? We can actually look for spaces using the LIKE operator with the * wildcard character. In this example, we are looking for two spaces in any part of the field value. To achieve this, we use the * three times. We can test for one space using two asterisks ("* *"). The cool thing is that we have found two city names with two blank spaces as you can see in the figure below:

Code:
```
SELECT lastname, firstname, city, orderdate
FROM tbls_CustomerOrders
WHERE (city LIKE "* * *")
```

Result:

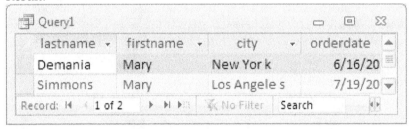

89. TIP: Use LIKE to test a field for the presence of numbers

Check for the presence of numbers in a city field

Discussion:

Now, what if someone entered some city names and did not pay attention, and as he was typing, he mingled some numbers with the name of the city? For example, he might have entered "New 9York". How can we check a field for the presence of numbers within text strings? The answer is by using the LIKE operator, the [ ] wildcard character for ranges, and the * wildcard character as in the code below. Notice we use the [ ] to check for any number between 0 and 9. In addition, we use the * twice to look for the presence of a number at any part of the field, including the end and the beginning of its value. We actually caught two records with numbers mistyped in them.

Code:
SELECT lastname, firstname, city, orderdate
FROM tbls_CustomerOrders
WHERE (city LIKE "*[0-9]*")

Result:

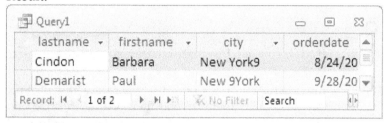

90. TIP: Create an index on a field used often with LIKE

Create an index on the city field

Discussion:

In chapter two, we discussed indexing in detail. Specifically, we mentioned that if a field is often used in searches, we need to create an index on it. We can easily create an index on the city field using the code below. This SQL statement will create a non-unique index because we want to be able to store two cities with the same name in the field "city".

Code:
CREATE INDEX indCity ON tbls_CustomerOrders (city)

Result:

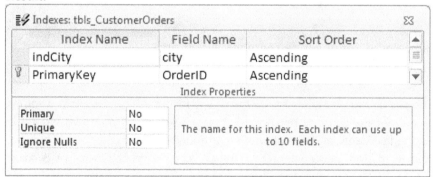

CHAPTER 10
EQUALITY AND INEQUALITY PREDICATES

The primary goal of equality and inequality predicates in search expressions is to find absolute matches. They are more flexible than using the LIKE operator, and their results are solid and unquestionable. They are used in the WHERE clause of a SQL statement, and they can be used by themselves to construct a search condition without the need of any wildcard characters. For instance, the statement (WHERE lastname = "Smith") is valid. They should be given preference over operators such as LIKE, BETWEEN, and TOP.

Access 2010 equality and inequality predicates reference

Meaning	Predicate
Equal to	=
Not equal to	<>
Less than	<
Less than or equal to	<=
Greater than	>
Greater than or equal to	=>

91. The equality predicate "=" for absolute searches in text data
Find a specific customer record searching on last name
Discussion:
In this example, we use the equality predicate to retrieve the record of a particular customer. What we need to know about the equality predicate is that we search for a known value. In other words, we know the last name of the customer we are looking for in advance. Then, we use the equality predicate to find that customer. This is very different when we conduct approximate searches using the LIKE operator where we might know the customer last name starts with "Ma", but we are not certain about the rest of it. That is why we use the expression (LIKE "Ma*") to find all of the customers whose last names start with "Ma" and then, select the one we need to work with. The point to remember is that whenever we can, we should give

preference to the equality predicate over the LIKE operator because it will retrieve exactly what we need, faster, with less overhead for the database, and less clutter in the results.

Code:
```
SELECT *
FROM Customers
WHERE (lastname = "Delaney")
```

Result:

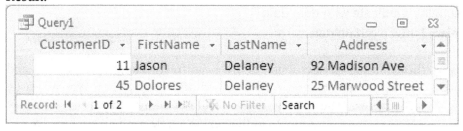

CustomerID ▾	FirstName ▾	LastName ▾	Address ▾
11	Jason	Delaney	92 Madison Ave
45	Dolores	Delaney	25 Marwood Street

Record: 1 of 2   No Filter   Search

92. The equality predicate "=" for absolute searches in number data

Find a specific customer record searching on CustomerID

Discussion:

The equality predicate is very efficient with numbers as well. Actually, it should be preferred and used in multiple working scenarios involving numbers and especially primary keys. For example, let us assume we need to use an UPDATE statement to change the record of a customer. We should unequivocally identify the customer using the equality predicate on the primary key of the table so that we are certain we are updating the right customer. The same logic is valid with DELETE statements where we should use the equality predicate to identify the correct customer for deletion. Another scenario is for those who work with server side pages like ASP.Net, PHP, ASP, JSP, etc. and who need to connect back to the database server to get customer records. Obviously, they would want to transfer as little data as possible between the database server and web server, so the equality predicate is the one of choice. In this example, we retrieve all of the information on a particular order searching on the OrderID, which is the primary key of the Orders table.

Code:
```
SELECT *
FROM Orders
WHERE OrderID = 972
```

Result:

93. The ">" inequality predicate with date data

Retrieve orders placed after a certain date

Discussion:

The ">" inequality predicate means "greater than", and we can freely use it with numbers and dates. For instance, we might want to find orders placed after June 2013. We can easily achieve this using the code below. The last day of June will not be included in the result set because we are using a "greater than" argument. In the next example, we will see how we can include the last day of June as well. In addition, we sort by orderdate ascending so that older orders appear first. We can sort descending (DESC) to get the latest orders. When sorting ascending, the ASC keyword is not needed in Access 2010. The ORDER BY clause defaults to ascending order when no ordering keyword is used (ASC, DESC).

Code:

```
SELECT OrderID, OrderDate, ShippedDate, ShippingCost
FROM Orders
WHERE OrderDate > #6/30/2013#
ORDER BY OrderDate
```

Result:

94. The "=>" inequality predicate with date data

Retrieve orders placed after a certain date including the date specified

Discussion:

The ">=" inequality predicate means "greater than or equal to", and we can use it with numbers and dates as well. In this example, we want to find orders placed after June 2013 including the last day of June. In addition, we sort by orderdate ascending so that older orders appear first.

Code:

```
SELECT OrderID, OrderDate, ShippedDate, ShippingCost
FROM Orders
WHERE OrderDate >= #6/30/2013#
ORDER BY OrderDate
```

Result:

OrderID	OrderDate	ShippedDate	ShippingCost
661	6/30/2013	7/5/2013	50
479	7/1/2013	7/6/2013	52
99	7/2/2013	7/7/2013	36

Record: 7 of 544 — No Filter — Search

95. The "<" inequality predicate with number data

Find orders for which the shipping cost was less than $35

Discussion:

The "<" inequality predicate means "less than", and, in this example, we use it to find shipping costs lower than $35 per order regardless of the date placed. Notice that we do not use quotes or other symbols to enclose numerical data in criteria expressions. We simply type the number. In addition, the first number appearing in the result set is 34 because we specifically asked for "less than 35".

Code:

```
SELECT OrderID, OrderDate, ShippedDate, ShippingCost
FROM Orders
WHERE ShippingCost < 35
ORDER BY ShippingCost DESC
```

Result:

OrderID ▾	OrderDate ▾	ShippedDate ▾	ShippingCost ▾
541	1/26/2012	1/26/2012	34
288	5/5/2014	5/5/2014	34
838	10/3/2013	10/3/2013	34

Record: I◄ ◄ 1 of 180 ► ►I ►☶ 🖙 No Filter | Search

96. The "<=" inequality predicate with number data

Find orders for which the shipping cost was less than or equal to $35

Discussion:

The "<=" inequality predicate means "less than or equal to", and we can use it with numbers and dates. In this example, we want to find shipping costs of less than 35 per order, including those orders with a shipping cost of exactly 35.

Code:

```
SELECT OrderID, OrderDate, ShippedDate, ShippingCost
FROM Orders
WHERE ShippingCost <= 35
ORDER BY ShippingCost DESC
```

Result:

OrderID ▾	OrderDate ▾	ShippedDate ▾	ShippingCost ▾
462	11/9/2013	11/9/2013	35
893	10/12/2012	10/12/2012	35
892	3/24/2014	3/24/2014	35

Record: I◄ ◄ 1 of 219 ► ►I ►☶ 🖙 No Filter | Search

97. The "<>" inequality predicate with number data

Find orders for which the shipping cost is not equal to $35

Discussion:

The "<>" inequality predicate means "not equal to". This time, we want to find shipping costs different from the amount of $35 per order. Notice that we do not use quotes or other symbols to enclose numerical data as criteria. In addition, we can use the inequality predicate efficiently with date and text data.

Code:
SELECT OrderID, OrderDate, ShippedDate, ShippingCost
FROM Orders
WHERE ShippingCost <> 35
ORDER BY ShippingCost DESC

Result:

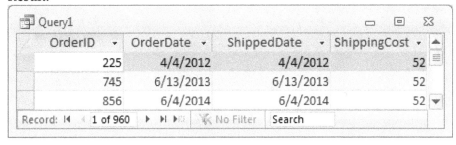

98. The ">" predicate with number and date data concurrently

Find orders placed after a certain date and with shipping cost less than $35

Discussion:

In this example, we are looking for orders placed after June 2012, which also have shipping costs of less than $35.

Code:
SELECT OrderID, OrderDate, ShippedDate, ShippingCost
FROM Orders
WHERE OrderDate > #6/30/2012#
AND ShippingCost < 35
ORDER BY ShippingCost DESC

Result:

CHAPTER 11
THE BETWEEN OPERATOR

The BETWEEN … AND operator is designed to retrieve subsets or ranges from a data set. It works primarily with number and date data. In this sense, it can be used to retrieve records that exist between two values acting as boundaries. Those two boundary values can be numbers or dates. In addition, while we cannot use BETWEEN with wildcard characters or predicates, we can still use functions to augment its range of applicability. It is important to stay aware that BETWEEN is inclusive such that the values acting as boundaries will be included in the recordset. For example, if we use BETWEEN with two date values, the records containing those date values will be included in the result set.

99. The BETWEEN operator with numbers
Find products with prices between $15 and $18
Discussion:
In this example, we are looking for product prices between the $15 and $18 values. The BETWEEN operator is inclusive, so the products with unit prices of 15 and 18 are included in the result set.

Code:
SELECT productname, productunitprice
FROM products
WHERE productunitprice BETWEEN 15 AND 18
ORDER BY productunitprice

Result:

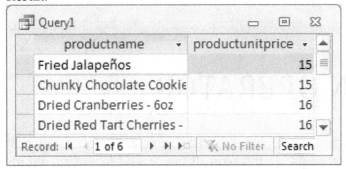

100. The BETWEEN operator with the left function()

Find suppliers with zip codes starting between 12 and 22

Discussion:

In this example, we are looking for a range of zip codes between 12 + any number and 22 + any number. We can use the left() function to extract the two leftmost characters of the zip code and get the result we need.

Of course, one might raise an objection and say: Why do we need to use the left function and not put the lower and upper boundaries in directly as 12189 and 22459? The answer is two-fold: First, the BETWEEN operator does not work with text data and we will get a type mismatch error since the zip code is a text field (and it should be). Second, in working with the supplier table, we deal with only 10 records. If we have hundreds of records to work with, we need to run two SQL statements, one with the min() and max() functions to identify the boundaries, and then a second with BETWEEN.

Code:

```
SELECT companyname, address, city, zip
FROM suppliers
WHERE left(zip, 2) BETWEEN 12 AND 22
ORDER BY zip
```

There is a turnaround to the above code by using a type conversion function (see CHAPTER 25 TYPE CONVERSION FUNCTIONS) to convert the text data in the Zip field into numeric data. Now, if you use the CInt() function you will get a stack overflow error since the CInt() function can convert numbers from -32,768 to 32,767 and with no decimals. Notice in the supplier table, that we have two zip code entries of 52347. Consequently, we can use the CIng() function as it shown below to get the same results!

Code:

SELECT companyname, address, city, zip
FROM suppliers
WHERE clng(zip) BETWEEN 12000 AND 23000
ORDER BY zip

Result:

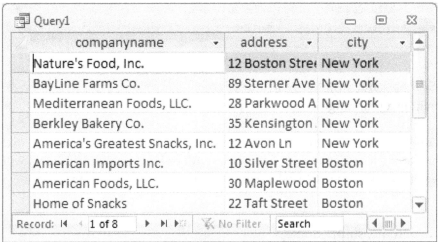

101. The BETWEEN operator with dates

Find orders placed within a date range

Discussion:

In this example, we would like to retrieve order dates that fall between 6/15/2012 and 8/15/2013. The BETWEEN operator is inclusive, and it will include orders placed on 6/15/2012 and 8/15/2013 as it is shown in the result set. In addition, notice the # symbol we use to enclose date values in Access 2010.

Code:

SELECT OrderID, orderdate, shippeddate
FROM orders
WHERE orderdate BETWEEN #6/15/2012# AND #8/15/2013#
ORDER BY orderdate DESC

Result:

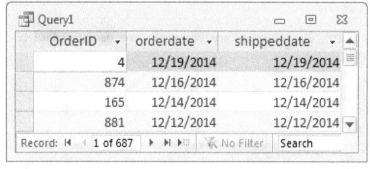

OrderID	orderdate	shippeddate
499	8/15/2013	8/15/2013
278	8/13/2013	8/13/2013
376	8/13/2013	8/13/2013
137	8/12/2013	8/12/2013

Record: ⏮ ◀ 1 of 364 ▶ ▶⏭ ▶✶ No Filter Search

102. The BETWEEN operator with the year() function

Find orders placed within a year range

Discussion:

In this example, we use the year() function to extract the year out of the orderdate field so that we can use year values as the lower and upper boundaries. All orders from 2013 and 2014 will be included in the result set due to the inclusivity characteristic of the BETWEEN operator.

Code:

```
SELECT OrderID, orderdate, shippeddate
FROM orders
WHERE year(orderdate) BETWEEN 2013 AND 2014
ORDER BY orderdate DESC
```

Result:

OrderID	orderdate	shippeddate
4	12/19/2014	12/19/2014
874	12/16/2014	12/16/2014
165	12/14/2014	12/14/2014
881	12/12/2014	12/12/2014

Record: ⏮ ◀ 1 of 687 ▶ ▶⏭ ▶✶ No Filter Search

103. The NOT BETWEEN operator with numbers

Find products with prices outside a price range

Discussion:

In this instance, we are looking for products with prices outside the $10 to $40 range, so we are asking the database to give us all products whose prices do not fall between $10 and $40. In practical terms, when we use the BETWEEN operator with NOT, we are usually looking for extreme values or outliers. The products with prices of exactly $10 or $40 will not be included in the result set.

Code:

```
SELECT productname, productunitprice
FROM products
WHERE productunitprice NOT BETWEEN 10 AND 40
ORDER BY productunitprice ASC
```

Result:

productname	productunitprice
Chocolate Fudge	41
Dried Red Tart Cherries G	43
Oatmeal Raisin Walnut C	43
Fudge Nut Brownie Cook	44

Record: 1 of 15   No Filter   Search

104. Comparison of BETWEEN with "<=" or "=>"

Find products with prices within a price range

Discussion:

In this paradigm, we show that using the BETWEEN operator is the same as using the two inequality predicates "<=" and "=>". Both SQL statements below will produce the same result. However, we should always give preference to equality and inequality predicates since they produce faster results with less overhead for the database engine.

Code:

```
SELECT productname, productunitprice
FROM products
WHERE productunitprice BETWEEN 15 AND 18
ORDER BY productunitprice ASC
```

Or

```
SELECT productname, productunitprice
FROM products
WHERE productunitprice >=15 AND productunitprice <=18
ORDER BY productunitprice ASC
```

Result:

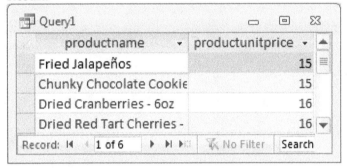

CHAPTER 12
THE IN OPERATOR

The major role of the IN operator is to participate in search conditions for filtering records. It is always used within the WHERE clause of a SQL statement and usually takes the place of multiple OR operators. It is an extremely useful search operator, and it will check the existence of a value against a list of values provided or constructed dynamically. Moreover, the IN operator can be used with text, number, and date data, making it suitable for a wide range of applications. Finally, it is really indispensable when used with subqueries as it will be shown in this chapter and in chapter 31. Using IN with subqueries allows the database professional to obtain results that would have been very difficult or impossible to obtain otherwise. The IN operator should be well understood and at the top of the toolbox of a database user or developer.

105.   The IN operator with text data
Create a report of customers from multiple cities
Discussion:

Our supervisor is requesting a report that lists all customers from the cities of New York, Boston, Chicago, Los Angeles, and Dallas. Of course, we could use the OR operator to produce this report:

```
SELECT LastName, FirstName, city
FROM customers
WHERE (city="New York")
OR (city="Boston")
OR (city="Chicago")
OR (city="Los Angeles")
OR (city="Dallas")
```

Using multiple OR operators to obtain a solution is rather tedious in both time and effort. Then, as soon as we provide the report to the supervisor, she comes back and says: "This is excellent; can I please have another report with our customers in the rest of the cities in the country?" To produce the second report, we will need to create an additional multitude of OR statements with the remaining cities.

The IN operator solves these problems quickly and efficiently. Note that enclosing the names in single or double quotes will produce the same results in Access 2010. In addition, since the ORDER BY clause is not used, the records will appear in the order they are stored in the table.

Code:
SELECT lastname, firstname, city
FROM customers
WHERE city in ('New York', 'Boston', 'Chicago', 'Los Angeles', 'Dallas')

Result:

106. The NOT IN operator with text data
Create a report of customers excluding several cities
Discussion:
This time, our supervisor reverses the request and asks for a report of customers from all cities not included in our previous report—every city except New York, Boston, Chicago, Los Angeles, and Dallas. Since we have the code using the IN operator from the previous example, the only thing we need to do is put the keyword "NOT" in front of the IN operator!

Code:
SELECT lastname, firstname, city
FROM customers
WHERE city NOT IN ('New York', 'Boston', 'Chicago', 'Los Angeles', 'Dallas')

Result:

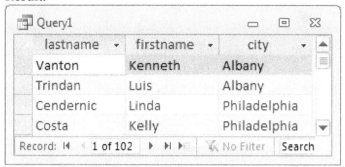

107. The IN operator with numeric data
Create a report of products based on prices
Discussion:

In this scenario, we need to produce a report that lists products from our product catalog with the following prices: 15, 19, 22, 23, and 42. Since the numbers are not sequential, we cannot use the BETWEEN operator to get our results. We can, however, use the IN operator to produce the report almost as fast. In addition, when we employ IN with numbers, we do not use quotes.

Code:
```
SELECT productname, quantityperunit, productunitprice
FROM products
WHERE productunitprice in (15, 19, 22, 23, 42)
```

Result:

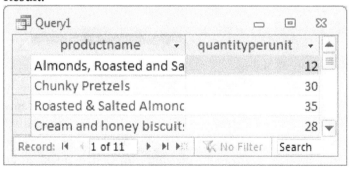

108. The IN operator with date data

Create a report of products based on prices

Discussion:

We have a request from the sales department to have a look at the orders in the first day of the three summer months because they are missing an order. They want to know what happened so that they can communicate it to the customer. We can absolutely use IN with date fields as can be seen in the code below. Notice the special character (#) in which we enclose date criteria in Access 2010. Pay attention that the dates provided are all actual date values and not ranges. We cannot use date ranges with the IN operator. Still, the worth of the IN operator with dates is highly desirable.

Code:
```
SELECT OrderID, OrderDate, ShippedDate, ShippingCost
FROM Orders
WHERE
OrderDate IN (#6/1/2012#, #7/1/2012#, #8/1/2012#)
```

Result:

OrderID	OrderDate	ShippedDate
170	6/1/2012	6/1/2(
201	7/1/2012	7/1/2(
905	7/1/2012	7/1/2(
959	6/1/2012	6/1/2(

Record: ◄ ◄ 1 of 4 ► ►► No Filter Search

109. Search for the same value in multiple fields

Discussion:

Let us suppose we inherited an un-normalized database and we need to search for the same value in multiple fields. For instance, the previous database administrator might have used four "supplier" fields in the products table to keep track of available suppliers for the same product. This is unacceptable under database normalization rules and our first step should be to normalize our database which means creating a separate supplier table. However, if we must do the search now, the IN operator can solve our problem if we use it upside down!

For instance, we usually use the IN operator such as: **Field IN (value1, value2, value3), that is, Supplier IN ("FoodInc1", "FoodInc2", "FoodInc3")**

To search an un-normalized database we do:
Value IN (field1, field2, field3), that is, "Food Inc" in (supplier1, supplier2, supplier3)
Note that we can extend the functionality of this code to search in multiple unrelated fields. For instance, we can search for the value "Mary" in the firstname, lastname, and address fields in the customer table to find a customer whose first name is Mary, or last name is Mary, or we have an address with the name Mary!

Code:
SELECT firstname, lastname, address
FROM customers
WHERE "Mary" IN (firstname, lastname, address)

Result:

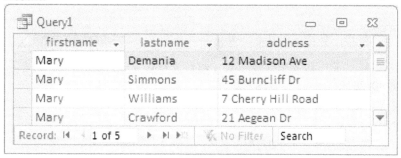

110. Create dynamic lists for the IN operator using subqueries
Generate a report of orders in which there is at least one non-discounted product
Discussion
The IN operator shows its real power when used with lists generated dynamically through SQL code. Instead of typing the values we would like to use with IN in the parenthesis, we can actually use SQL to create value lists automatically. This leads to the concept of subqueries, which we will discuss in detail in chapter 31, but we will go through a few examples here to understand the ultimate use of the IN operator.

In this specific example, management wants to have a report of orders in which no discount was extended for at least one of the products included in the order. Each order might contain multiple products, and for each product, we might or might not have extended a discount. In other words, the database is set up so that discounts are given on a per product basis and not per order. This way, we have the flexibility to extend discounts on a product-by-product basis, which is a much more flexible way of doing business.

To answer this request, we need information from two different tables: the Orders table and the ProductsOrders table. The subquery in this case will generate a list of OrderIDs from the ProductsOrders table for which the discount = 0. Then, this list of OrderIDs will be used as filtering criteria by the IN operator in the main query. Therefore, we have dynamically created a list of values for the IN operator. There are 136 orders with at least one non-discounted product.

Code:
SELECT orderid, orderdate, shippeddate
FROM orders
WHERE orderid
IN (SELECT orderid FROM ProductsOrders WHERE (Discount) =0)

Result:

orderid	orderdate	shippeddate
2	7/30/2013	7/30/2(
5	11/19/2012	11/19/2(
7	12/1/2013	12/1/2(
24	3/12/2012	3/12/2(

Record: 1 of 136   No Filter   Search

111. The IN operator with GROUP BY and HAVING in subqueries

Generate a report of orders for which the total extended discount was 0

Discussion

Continuing from the previous example, we now have a request to produce a report that will list orders in which all of the included products have a discount of zero. So, if four products are included in an order, the discount rate for all four of them will be zero. To reply to this request, we will again use the IN operator to look in the ProductsOrders table for OrderIDs of orders with zero total discounts. The problem here is that we cannot use the WHERE clause since it always runs first and excludes records before the SQL statement is executed. However, our goal is to sum up the discounts for each product in each order first. Our second concern is to somehow make calculations in the ProductsOrders table and find the sum of discount for every order. Third, we need to keep in the result set only the orders with a total discount of zero, and we need to filter out everything else. The final issue is that the filtering needs to happen after the results of the sum() function.

All of the above issues can be solved by using the IN operator, a subquery, the GROUP BY and HAVING clauses, and the sum() function as per the example below. In the example, the GROUP BY clause with the sum() function will run first and produce a list of unique orders and their total discounts. From this list, the HAVING clause will keep only the ones with a zero total discount. Then, the SELECT statement in the subquery will generate a list of OrderIDs as filtered out by the HAVING clause. Finally, the WHERE clause from the main query will use the OrderIDs generated from the subquery to filter orders from the Orders table and produce a result set of orders whose orderID matches the OrderID produced by the subquery.

At this point, we could easily answer the following question as well: Generate a report of orders for which the total extended discount was not 0. We can answer this in no time by replacing the IN operator with NOT IN!

Code:
```
SELECT orderid, orderdate, shippeddate
FROM orders
WHERE orderid
IN (SELECT orderid FROM ProductsOrders GROUP BY orderid HAVING sum(Discount) =0)
```

Result:

112.   The IN operator with subqueries and dates
Find customers who have not placed any orders in the second half of 2012
Discussion
Our task in this scenario is to find customers who have not placed any orders in the second half of the year 2012. Management needs this information for initiating promotions to inactive customers. To achieve this task, we will use the NOT IN and BETWEEN operators and a

subquery. Remember that the purpose of the subquery is always the same—to generate a list of values to be used by the IN operator. Here, the subquery will generate a list of CustomerIDs from the Orders table, which will be used by the main query to filter records from the Customers table. In total, 70 customers have not ordered anything during this six-month period.

Code:
SELECT *
FROM Customers
WHERE CustomerID NOT IN
(Select CustomerID FROM Orders WHERE
OrderDate BETWEEN #6/1/2012# AND #12/1/2012#)

Result:

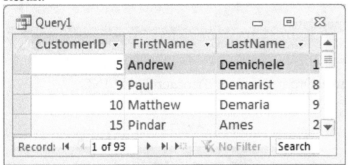

113. The IN operator with subqueries, dates, and date functions
Find customers who have not placed any orders in the year 2012
Discussion
The request in this case is to find customers who have not placed any orders for the year 2012. Of course, we do not track years separately in the orders table, but we can easily extract the year out of the OrderDate filed using the year() function. Then, we can use it in the subquery as shown below. Only 36 customers have not placed any orders in the year 2012. This type of query is excellent to keep track of customer retention rates in a business.

Code:
SELECT *
FROM Customers
WHERE CustomerID NOT IN
(Select CustomerID FROM Orders WHERE
year(orderdate) = 2012)

Result:

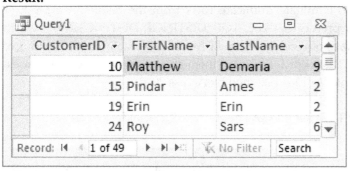

CHAPTER 13
THE DISTINCT PREDICATE

The DISTINCT predicate is used to eliminate duplicate rows from the results of a SELECT statement. It belongs to a set of four predicates (ALL, TOP, DISTINCT, DISTINCTROW) which we can use to manipulate the number of records returned from a SQL statement. All four of them are used right after the SELECT keyword, and all of them are optional. If we do not use a predicate with the SELECT statement, [ALL] is assumed by Access 2010.

SELECT [ALL] [TOP] [DISTINCT] [DISTINCTROW] field1, field2, ... fieldn
FROM table

From the four predicates above, we will focus on DISTINCT in this chapter and TOP in the next one, since they are the two most useful ones. [ALL] is assumed as the default when no predicate is used and the DISTINCTROW has very specific applications. Specifically, the difference between DISTINCT and DISTINCTROW is that DISTINCT is looking for unique values for the field or fields included in the SQL statement. DISTINCTROW will retrieve distinct records overall. We also need to know that the results of a query in which we use DISTINCT are not updatable while the results of a query in which we use DISTINCTROW are updatable. Also, keep in mind that DISTINCTROW might not be supported by other database engines like MSSQL, DB2, Oracle, or MySQL. To conclude, we should focus on understanding the DISTINCT and TOP predicates well because they are essential to retrieving the results we need in various scenarios.

The column on which we use the DISTINCT predicate will return only its unique values. Also, note that if we apply the DISTINCT keyword on a combination of columns—lastname and firstname, for example—the database will return the unique combinations of their values. Let us see how this works through examples in our familiar customers and orders database.

114. Run a SELECT statement without the DISTINCT predicate
Find cities in which we have customers
Discussion:
Using a classic SQL statement to retrieve the column "city" from the customers table will return multiple instances of the same city since it is logical to have multiple customers in the same

150

city. For example, as we can see from the result set, New York appears as many times as the number of customers we have in this city. There are 201 records returned with multiple instances of various cities.

Code:
SELECT city
FROM customers

Result:

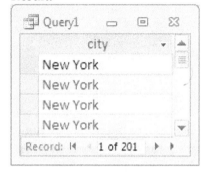

115. Run a SELECT statement with the DISTINCT predicate

Find unique cities in which we have customers

Discussion:

There are cases, however, in which we just want to obtain a report that shows only the unique or distinct names of the cities where we have customers. The business goal is to create a list of cities to know where we do business. Maybe we want to set up shipping centers in several regions. In this scenario, we would like New York to appear only once, Boston only once, and Los Angeles only once. This is a case where we use the DISTINCT predicate. This time, only 15 records returned, and the value for each city is unique. From this recordset, we know that the number of cities where we have customers is 15.

Code:
SELECT DISTINCT city
FROM customers

Result:

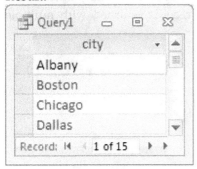

116. Use DISTINCT on one column

Finding unique job titles

Discussion:

Suppose our next business goal is to retrieve the unique job titles of people who replenish our inventory and manage our orders from various corporate suppliers. It is a good thing to know if we deal mostly with managers, directors, or other positions. Maybe we can get better discounts if we talk to people in higher positions with more decision-making flexibility. We can easily achieve this goal using the DISTINCT keyword. The unique corporate titles of people with whom we do business are seven.

Code:

```
SELECT DISTINCT ContactTitle
FROM suppliers
```

Result:

117. Use DISTINCT on multiple columns

Finding unique customer names in various states

Discussion:

Experience indicates that DISTINCT works at its best when applied on a single column. However, if we want to apply DISTINCT on multiple columns, we need to know exactly what to expect. Let's work with our customers table and go through some examples to fully understand this concept.

Code Case 1:

If we run a simple SELECT statement such as:

SELECT firstname, state
FROM customers
WHERE (firstname="John")

We will get four customers with a first name John. Actually, these are all the Johns we have in our customers table.

Result:

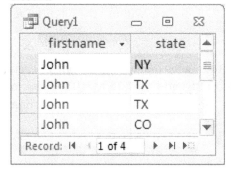

Code Case 1:

If we include the DISTINCT clause such as:
SELECT DISTINCT firstname, state
FROM customers
WHERE (firstname="John")

We will get only three customers with a first name John. This is because we told the database to return unique combinations of first names and states. In the previous result set, we have two Johns in Texas. When we use DISTINCT on both firstname and state, only one of the two appear. This is a problem with DISTINCT on multiple columns. We cannot exactly control

153

which ones will appear in the result set, and we might get results that we haven't intended. So, be very careful when using DISTINCT on multiple columns.

Result:

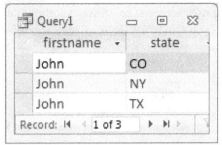

118. Getting more information beyond DISTINCT

Find unique job titles and their Corresponding Numbers

Discussion:

Although it does not thematically belong here, your next logical thought is probably: Okay, I know how to retrieve unique values for names, states, job titles, and other fields. However, what is the total number I have from each? To answer this question, we need to use the GROUP BY clause, which we explore in detail in chapter 17. Here, we will use the job titles as an example to find the number of people holding each title.

As we can see from the result set, we know that we have four sales managers and one of each of the other titles. We simply use one aggregate function count() and the GROUP BY clause to get the result we need. The "CountNumber" is the title we give ourselves to the counting column.

Code:

```
SELECT ContactTitle, Count(ContactTitle) AS CountNumber
FROM suppliers
GROUP BY ContactTitle
```

Result:

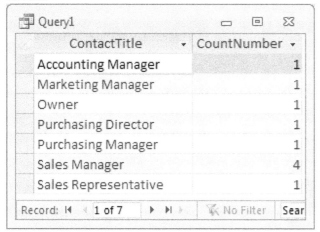

119. The DISTINCTROW predicate

Find customers with at least one order

Discussion:

In this scenario, we are looking for customers who have at least one order in the Orders table. There are three ways to achieve this goal. We can use a subquery (see chapter 31), a join (chapter 30), or DISTINCTROW. I would suggest using a subquery to obtain this result because it is the cleanest way and will provide guaranteed results. We can do it by using joins, but we will create a lot of code, while DISTINCTROW has its own peculiarities. From the result set below, we see that we have 190 unique customers with at least one order. However, we used fields only from the customers table. If we include at least one field from the Orders table, the DISTINCTROW will not work. DISTINCTROW will work with any number of joined tables as soon as we select fields from some of the joined tables but not all of them. Finally, I have included the code using a subquery which will produce the exact same result.

Code:

SELECT DISTINCTROW lastname, firstname, city, zip
FROM Customers
INNER JOIN Orders ON Customers.CustomerID = Orders.CustomerID

Code:

```
SELECT lastname, firstname, city, zip
FROM Customers
WHERE CustomerID
IN (SELECT CustomerID from tbls_Orders)
```

Result:

CHAPTER 14
THE TOP PREDICATE

The TOP predicate is useful for selecting a specified number or a certain percentage of records from a data source like a table or query. It belongs to a set of four predicates (ALL, TOP, DISTINCT, DISTINCTROW) used to manipulate the number of records returned from a SQL statement. All four of them are used right after the SELECT keyword, and all of them are optional. If we do not use a predicate with the SELECT statement, [ALL] is assumed by Access 2010.

SELECT [ALL] [TOP] [DISTINCT] [DISTINCTROW] field1, field2, ... fieldn
FROM table

The TOP predicate used alone is not useful at all since it does not return records in any special order; it simply returns the first n or n% of the records as they are stored in the table. However, when the TOP predicate is used with the ORDER BY, GROUP BY, and WHERE clauses, it shows its real potential and practicality.

120.   The TOP predicate alone with numbers
Retrieve 5 records from the products table
Discussion:
The TOP predicate in this example will return the first five records from the products table in the order these records are stored in the table. This process is practically useless for our business needs since it does not provide any special information at all. This example is given to demonstrate that TOP by itself will not produce any useful results.

Code:
SELECT TOP 5 productname, unitsinstock, unitsonorder
FROM Products

Result:

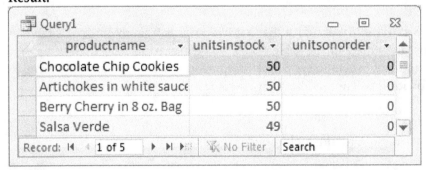

121. The TOP predicate with ORDER BY and numbers

Find the five products with the most units in stock

Discussion:

In this example, the business goal is to find the five products with the highest levels of inventory. The use of the TOP predicate in combination with the ORDER BY clause can show its usefulness and practical application. As you can see from the result set, the five products with the highest inventory levels appear first. We use the DESC keyword with the ORDER BY clause so that highest quantities appear first (see chapter 7 for the ORDER BY clause).

Code:

```
SELECT TOP 5 productname, unitsinstock, unitsonorder
FROM Products
ORDER BY unitsinstock DESC
```

Result:

productname	unitsinstock	unitsonorder
Chocolate Chip Cookies	50	0
Artichokes in white sauce	50	0
Berry Cherry in 8 oz. Bag	50	0
Salsa Verde	49	0

Record: 1 of 5   No Filter   Search

ATTENTION: We need to be very careful when using TOP. In this case we get five records because we have three products with 50 units in stock and two with 49 units in stock. The next biggest quantity is 47 units in stock. If we change this quantity from 47 to 49, then the result set will include six records instead of five. Consequently when in a field we have multiple identical values, we need to use TOP with caution.

122. The TOP predicate with ORDER BY and percentages

Retrieve 10% of the products with the highest prices

Discussion:

This time, management asked for the top 10% of the most expensive products in the inventory. We can easily reply to this request by using the TOP predicate with the ORDER BY clause as shown below. In Access 2010, we use the word "10 PERCENT" and not "10%" with the TOP predicate.

Code:

```
SELECT TOP 10 PERCENT productname, productunitprice
FROM Products
ORDER BY productunitprice DESC
```

Result:

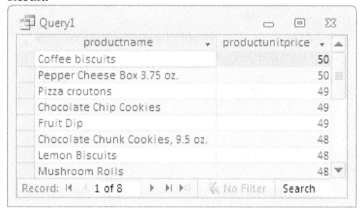

ATTENTION: Again, we need to be very careful when using TOP with percentages. TOP will provide accurate results when the values of the field used in the ORDER BY clause are unique. Any equal values will distort TOP results. For instance, in the products table we have 70 records and in our result set we should have had seven records since we are asking for 10%. However, we have eight. This is because the seventh record has a productunitprice of 48. However, the eighth record has a productunitprice of 48 as well. Since a productunitprice of 48 was included in the result set, all productunitprices of 48 will be included no matter if they are half the table!

123. The TOP predicate with ORDER BY and text data

Select exactly 5 employees sorted by name

Discussion:

In this example, we use TOP in conjunction with ORDER BY to get the first five employees ordered by last name. Of course, the obvious question is: What is the difference with a simple SELECT and ORDER BY without the use of the TOP predicate? The answer is that with TOP we can define the exact number of employees to appear in the result set. The ASC keyword is not used with the ORDER BY clause here because it is assumed by default in Access 2010.

Code:

```
SELECT TOP 5 lastname, firstname, title
FROM SalesReps
ORDER BY lastname
```

Result:

124. The TOP predicate with ORDER BY and dates

Find the 5 most recently hired employees

Discussion:

The TOP predicate is very useful when used with dates. In this example, we are looking for the five most recently hired employees in the corporation. We use the DESC keyword with ORDER BY to obtain this result. We could have used the ASC keyword to retrieve the 5 most senior employees of the corporation.

Code:

```
SELECT TOP 5 lastname, firstname, DateofHire
FROM SalesReps
ORDER BY DateofHire DESC
```

Result:

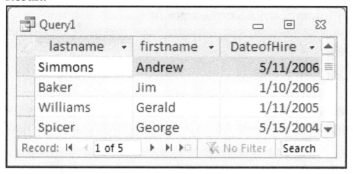

125. The TOP predicate with the GROUP BY clause

Find the 10 largest orders from customers

Discussion:

Let us assume that our manager wants to see the 10 largest orders received from our customers. One somewhat crude way to prepare this report would be to calculate order subtotals (multiply the quantity of each product with its price) for all of the products contained in one order and do a GROUP BY on the orderid, followed by SORT DESC to get on top of the recordset of the largest orders. This way, we get what we need, but the whole affair is a mess. In addition, we get all of the orders we have, which might be a very long list for a printout.

Let us start by assuming that we only have two orders to work with (1 and 2 in the table below). We also notice that order number 1 contains three products, and order number 2 contains two products. We also see the product quantities our customers ordered in the "Quantity" field, as well as the corresponding product prices that we extended to the customers. By the way, the product prices that we finally extended to the customers can be different from the prices in our catalog, which we store in the products table.

ProductsOrders			
OrderID	ProductID	UnitPrice	Quantity
1	1	15	2
1	2	12	3
1	3	18	5
2	1	15	2
2	3	18	8

Code:

SELECT orderid, Sum((([unitprice]*[quantity])) AS orderamount

FROM ProductsOrders

GROUP BY orderid

ORDER BY Sum((([unitprice]*[quantity])) DESC

When using the code above, the database will first multiply the UnitPrice with the Quantity for each product. This temporary calculation is shown in the table below so that you know how the database thinks.

ProductsOrders				
OrderID	ProductID	UnitPrice	Quantity	Temp
1	1	15	2	30
1	2	12	3	36
1	3	18	5	90
2	1	15	2	30
2	3	18	8	144

Then, the database calculates the total (SUM) for each order (this is due to the GROUP BY clause on the ORDERID). Since we have two orders, the grouping looks like the table below. The OrderAmount is an alias or a name that we gave to the calculated field.

OrderID	OrderAmount
1	156
2	174

Still however, we gave another command to the database: to ORDER BY the largest order. The database then shows the following result since 174 is larger than 156.

OrderID	OrderAmount
2	174
1	156

At this point, we are able to get a report of the biggest orders, but we still have a problem with the above code. All of the orders will appear. As you can see from the figure below, 919 orders appear even though we only need to see the 10 largest.

Result:

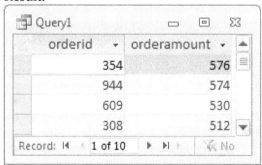

Let us see how we can quickly get the results we need by using the TOP clause.

Code:
```
SELECT TOP 10 orderid, Sum((([unitprice]*[quantity])) AS orderamount
FROM ProductsOrders
GROUP BY orderid
ORDER BY Sum((([unitprice]*[quantity])) DESC;
```

Result:

orderid	orderamount
354	576
944	574
609	530
308	512

Record: |◄ ◄ 1 of 10 ► ►| ► 	No

126. The TOP predicate with calculated fields and WHERE
Get the ten largest orders for a particular product
Discussion:
As in our previous discussion, we can, of course, use ORDER BY, DESC, and WHERE to create result sets that give us powerful information. However, we need to include TOP if we want to get a manageable number of records returned. In this scenario, we have been asked to prepare a report that contains the 15 largest orders for a particular product—for example "Almonds, Roasted and Salted - 18 oz. Bag" (the product with productid = 2).

Code:
```
SELECT TOP 10 orderid, productid, (unitprice*quantity) AS orderamount
FROM ProductsOrders
WHERE (productid=2)
ORDER BY (unitprice*quantity) DESC;
```

Result:

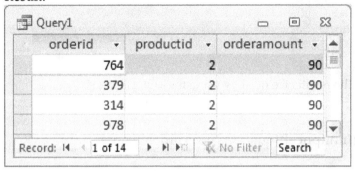

CHAPTER 15
CALCULATED FIELDS

Calculated fields are temporary columns created using arithmetic operators such as (+, *, -, /, ^, Mod). In Access 2010 you can use calculated fields in tables, queries, forms, and reports. However, it is not a good practice to use calculated fields in tables. The third normal form rule of normalization says that all attributes should depend on the key. That is, all table fields need to be related to the entity they describe. That is, all customer fields need to be connected to the CustomerID PK field. A calculation used in a table is an ever changing attribute for the entity and this causes lot of trouble. In addition, a calculated field in a table cannot be indexed which creates additional problems by making the table slower. Finally, you need to pay attention because your Access 2010 database with calculated fields in tables cannot be used by previous versions of Access. The most appropriate place for calculated fields are queries, not even forms or reports.

You can create calculated fields in a variety of ways. For instance, you can multiply a numeric field by a certain number or a certain percentage, and you can multiply two numeric fields themselves. You can multiply two fields and divide the result by another field. You can also create calculated fields conditionally by using the iif() and switch() functions. You can also generate powerful pieces of information by using calculated fields with aggregate functions. Of course, you can use calculated fields in a query with the WHERE clause so that your calculations are applied only to a subset of records. You can also use calculated fields in the HAVING clause in a GROUP BY statement for filtering records after the aggregations from the GROUP BY clause are completed. Finally, you can use calculated fields with UPDATE statements to change hundreds or thousands of records instantly. The applications of calculated fields in databases are essential, and in this chapter, we will present you with multiple examples. However, we will also deal with numeric calculations only. I have devoted two additional chapters on operations with dates and strings so that you can explore each in detail. The arithmetic operators available in Access 2010 appear in the following table:

Operator	Meaning
+	Addition
*	Multiplication
-	Subtraction
/	Division
^	Exponential
mod	Remainder

127. Add a number to a numeric field

Create a product catalog with updated prices on the fly

Discussion:

The business goal here is to create a new product catalog that will appear on the corporate website for a promotional campaign. Management does not want the product prices in the underlying products table to change, however, since this campaign will last only two weeks. We can easily create a query using the SQL code below and use it as the data source for our web catalog. Using these assumptions, management asked to add $2 to the price of each product.

Code:

```
SELECT productname, productunitprice + 2 AS productprice
FROM Products
```

Result:

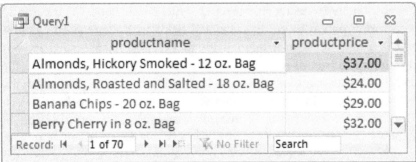

128. Add a percentage to a numeric field

Update product prices on the fly by a certain percentage

Discussion:

This time, due to increased replenishment costs (receiving goods from suppliers), our manager tells us to add a 2% markup for the product catalog we are sending out this month. We multiply by 1.02 and not by 0.02 since the latter will give us only the percentage increase and not the entire new price.

Code:
SELECT productname, productunitprice * (1.02) as productprice
FROM Products

Result:

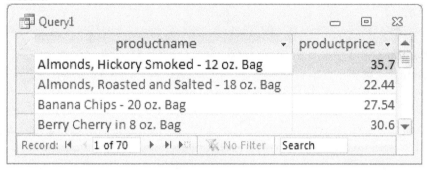

129.   Add two numeric columns
Calculate product inventory quantities
Discussion:
Management asks us for a report about product inventory quantities. Specifically, they want to know not only what units we have in the warehouse but how many are on order as well. To answer this request, we create a new column named TotalUnits, which is simply the sum of the units that we have in stock and the ones we have on order that have not arrived yet.

Code:
SELECT productname, unitsinstock, unitsonorder,
(unitsinstock + unitsonorder)
AS TotalUnits
FROM products

Result:

productname	unitsinstock	unitsonorder	TotalUnits
Almonds, Hickory Smoked	40	5	45
Almonds, Roasted and Salt	32	0	32
Banana Chips - 20 oz. Bag	25	0	25
Berry Cherry in 8 oz. Bag	50	0	50

Record: ◄ ◄ 1 of 70 ► ►I ►☼ No Filter Search

130. Multiply two columns and group their results

Find order totals by order

Discussion:

The request this time is to find order totals for all of the orders that we have had to date. Each order might contain multiple products with multiple quantities for each product. We first need to multiply product prices with quantities for every product in each order and sum the results. Then, we need to group by OrderID so that we can obtain the total for every order. A sample data set on which to make these calculations appears below. The order with OrderID = 1, contains three different products with prices of 15, 12, and 18 and quantities of 2, 3, and 5 respectively. We need to first multiply the product unit price times the quantity for each product, get the subtotals, and sum up the results for each order.

ProductsOrders			
OrderID	ProductID	UnitPrice	Quantity
1	1	15	2
1	2	12	3
1	3	18	5
2	1	15	2
2	3	18	8

Code:

```
SELECT OrderID, Sum([UnitPrice]*[quantity]) AS OrderSubtotal
FROM ProductsOrders
GROUP BY OrderID
```

Result:

OrderID	OrderSubtotal
1	30
2	210
3	231
4	45

Record: I◄ ◄ 1 of 919 ► ►I ► 🦅 No F

131. Subtract a percentage from a numeric column

Provide customers with a 20% discount on every product

Discussion:

Management decided to aggressively sell this month, and they have initiated a promotional campaign with a price discount of 20% for every product in the product catalog. We need to create a new product catalog, which the company wants to send out immediately. We can easily respond to this request using a calculated field as is shown in the code below:

Code:

```
SELECT ProductName, ProductUnitPrice * (1-0.2) as PromotionalPrice
FROM Products
```

Result:

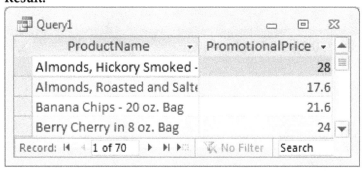

ProductName	PromotionalPrice
Almonds, Hickory Smoked -	28
Almonds, Roasted and Salte	17.6
Banana Chips - 20 oz. Bag	21.6
Berry Cherry in 8 oz. Bag	24

Record: I◄ ◄ 1 of 70 ► ►I ►᠁ 🦅 No Filter Search

132. How to display a currency symbol in calculated fields

Discussion:

Access does not display the currency symbol in calculations even if the field on which calculations are made has a currency format. In this example, we are creating a query in which we increase the value of the productunitprice field by 20%.

Code 1:

SELECT ProductUnitPrice* (1+0.2) AS ProductPrice

FROM products

Although the ProductUnitPrice field is of currency data type in the Products table, the resulting calculation is simply a number.

Result:

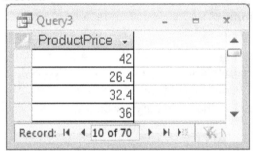

It looks like if we use the cCur() conversion function, we can solve this problem as per the result below. We do, but we need to pay attention not to have any blank entries for the ProductUnitPrice field in the products table. If we do, we will get an error in return.

Code2:

SELECT cCur(ProductUnitPrice* (1+0.2)) AS ProductPrice

FROM products

Result:

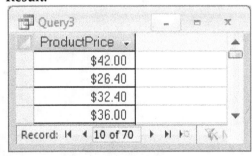

Code3 and 4:
We can also use the iif() function or the nz() function to display the results with a currency symbol and at the same time avoid any errors from the database.

SELECT IIF([ProductUnitPrice] IS NOT Null, CCur(ProductUnitPrice* (1+0.2)), 0) AS Price
FROM products

SELECT CCur(nz(ProductUnitPrice * (1+0.2),0)) AS price from products

Both of the above statements produce the same result: just in case there is a missing value of the ProductUnitPrice field, then they will display a zero.

Result:

Query3		
ProductPrice		
$42.00		
$26.40		
$32.40		
$36.00		
Record: ◄ ◄ 10 of 70 ► ►► ►*		

133.   Use calculated fields with the WHERE clause
Provide customers with a 20% discount on specific products
Discussion:
Since a 20% discount is too much to provide for every product, management has decided to apply it only on products from suppliers with SupplierID 1 and 4. We can quickly change the product catalog to:

Code:
SELECT ProductName, ProductUnitPrice * (1-0.2) as PromotionalPrice
FROM Products
WHERE supplierid = 1 or supplierid = 4

171

Result:

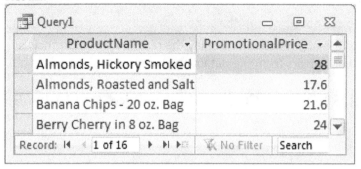

134. Calculated fields with multiple conditions

Provide customers with different discounts based on the product supplier

Discussion:

The previous scenario of providing product discounts by filtering on supplier ids is fine for some cases, but it also has two major drawbacks. First, the same discount rate is applied to every supplier included in the WHERE clause. Second, discount rates can be applied only to suppliers included in the WHERE clause. In some cases, we might want to provide different discount rates for each supplier and include all products from all suppliers in the result set. Suppose we want to provide a 20% discount for products from SupplierID=1, 15% for those from SupplierID=2, 18% for those from SupplierID=3, and 25% for those from SupplierID=4. In addition, we might want to provide a 10% discount for all of the rest of the products regardless of supplier. The switch function comes to the rescue here, providing the flexibility to give us the results we need.

Code:

```
SELECT productname,
SWITCH(
SupplierID = 1,          ProductUnitPrice*(1-0.2),
SupplierID = 2,          ProductUnitPrice*(1-0.15),
SupplierID = 3,          ProductUnitPrice*(1-0.18),
SupplierID = 4,          ProductUnitPrice*(1-0.25),
TRUE,                    ProductUnitPrice*(1-0.1)
)
AS ProductPrice
FROM Products
```

Result:

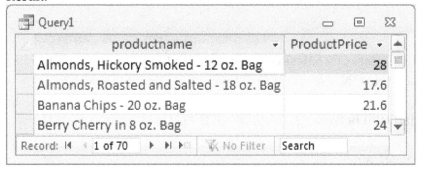

135.   How to use calculated fields with the iif() function

Determine employee bonus eligibility

Discussion:

In this example, we are looking for sales representatives who are eligible for a bonus. To be eligible for a bonus, a sales rep needs to have accumulated sales of $5,000 or more for the year. The SQL code in this example is long but easy.   First, notice that we use three fields only: LastName, Bonus, and OrderDate. We use the OrderDate field to filter orders for 2012 only. Then, we use the lastname field with a GROUP BY clause to display results by employee name. The last field is that of the Bonus. Here, we use the iif() function with the syntax iif (expression, result if expression is true, result if expression is false) to actually make the calculations and determine bonus eligibility:

IIf(Sum([unitprice]*[quantity])>5000,"Bonus","No Bonus") AS Bonus

The iif() function above reads: If the total amount of orders serviced by the sales rep exceeds $5,000, give the sales rep a bonus. Otherwise, no bonus. The AS part means display this field name as "Bonus". Do not pay attention to the joins in this example since we only use them to get fields from three different tables. For a full overview of joins, see chapter 30.

Code:

SELECT SalesReps.LastName, IIf(Sum([unitprice]*[quantity])>5000,"Bonus","No Bonus") AS Bonus

FROM

(SalesReps INNER JOIN Orders ON SalesReps.SalesRepID = Orders.SalesRepID)
INNER JOIN ProductsOrders ON Orders.OrderID = ProductsOrders.OrderID

WHERE (((Orders.OrderDate) Between #1/1/2012# AND #12/31/2012#))

GROUP BY SalesReps.LastName

Result:

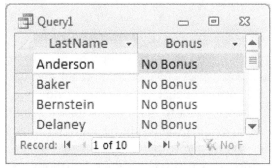

136. Use calculated fields with GROUP BY and aggregate functions

Calculate total discount amounts by order

Discussion:

This time, we have a request to provide a report that will show the total discount amount for each order. Remember that each order might contain multiple products. In addition, for each product in the same order, we might have provided a different discount rate. Our goal is to calculate the discount amount for each product in each order and sum the results. To achieve this task, we will use the ProductsOrders table, which includes the unitprice (the one finally extended to the customer, not the one in the products table used for the product catalog), the quantity of each product, and the discount rate for each product. A sample from the table with two orders appears below:

ProductsOrders				
OrderID	ProductID	UnitPrice	Quantity	Discount
1	1	15	2	20%
1	2	12	3	0

1	3	18	5	15%
2	1	15	2	10%
2	3	18	8	15%

For each product in an order, we need to multiply the unit price by the quantity to get the amount invoiced for that product. Then, we multiply the result by the discount rate to get the total discount for each product in each order. Then, we sum all of the discount amounts in each order. Finally, we group on orderid so that we get the total discount amount by order.

Code:
```
SELECT OrderID, Sum((([UnitPrice]*[Quantity])*[Discount]) AS OrderDiscount
FROM ProductsOrders
GROUP BY OrderID
```

Result:

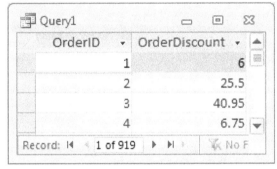

137.   Use a calculated field with an aggregate function

Calculate the average discount amount for all orders

Discussion:

Our business goal is to find the average discount amount we have given away for all of our orders. Discounts are excellent, but we need to keep track of them and evaluate them on a continuous basis. Fortunately, we can do this in no time by simply using the AVG (average) function to get the average amount from all the orders.

Code:
```
SELECT Avg((([UnitPrice]*[Quantity])*[Discount]) AS AverageOrderDiscount
FROM ProductsOrders
```

Result:

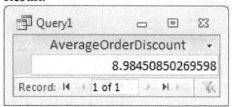

Then, we can compare the above result with the actual average order amount using the code below. Now, we can make the conclusion that an average $9 discount for an average total order of $58 is an acceptable discount rate.

Code:
SELECT Avg([UnitPrice]*[Quantity]) AS AverageOrderAmount
FROM ProductsOrders

Result:

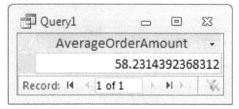

I know you noticed the number of decimals in the results above. We can decrease the number of decimals or eliminate them altogether by using a type conversion function. Actually, calculated fields are extensively used with type conversion functions to format numbers in the most appropriate way. Here, we use the cInt() function to convert the decimal number to an integer. For the full range of type conversion functions, read chapter 25, where they are explained in detail.

Code:
SELECT cInt(Avg([UnitPrice]*[Quantity])) AS AverageOrderAmount
FROM ProductsOrders

Result:

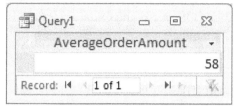

138. Use a calculated field with an aggregate function and WHERE

Calculate the average discount amount for specific orders

Discussion:

Knowing the average discount amount for all of our orders is excellent, but we might want to go a step further and ask: What is the average discount amount provided for customers in the city of Boston? We can easily isolate discount amounts for any city by using multi-table queries like the one below:

Code:

```
SELECT Avg((([UnitPrice]*[Quantity])*[Discount]) AS AverageOrderDiscount
FROM Customers
INNER JOIN (Orders INNER JOIN ProductsOrders ON Orders.OrderID =
ProductsOrders.OrderID) ON Customers.CustomerID = Orders.CustomerID
WHERE (((Customers.City)="Boston"));
```

Result:

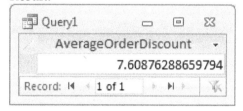

139. Storing the results of calculated fields with SELECT INTO

Storing total order amounts in a separate table

Discussion:

Sometimes, we might want to store the results of our calculations in a backup, archive, or temporary table. This is very easy to achieve using SELECT INTO statements that were covered in the SELECT chapter. Storing results of calculated fields in production tables is not a good idea because these fields will interfere with normalization rules. However, for archiving purposes, we can go ahead.

In this example, we take the OrderID and OrderTotal fields from the ProductsOrders table and transfer their records in a new table named ArchivedOrders. Of course, the OrderTotal field is calculated from three different fields in the ProductsOrders table.

Code:
```
SELECT OrderID, SUM((unitprice*Quantity)*(1-Discount)) AS OrderTotal
INTO ArchivedOrders
FROM ProductsOrders
GROUP BY OrderID
```

Result:
The database will first ask you if you want to go ahead.

Then, in the objects pane, we can see the new table with a name exactly as we defined it in the SQL code.

CHAPTER 16
CONCATENATED FIELDS

Concatenating columns means nothing more than displaying the contents of two or more columns in one. The operation of concatenation happens through a query on the fly, and the resulting column and its contents are not saved in the underlying table. There are no special arithmetical or logical calculations involved. Simply put, if we want a query or report to display the contents of the first and last name fields as one, we just concatenate the two fields. Though the concept sounds simple, its applicability in every day work tasks is indispensable.

Concatenation in databases can achieve much more than simply displaying the contents of two or more columns together, however. We can create mailing labels, write letters with the correct punctuation, combine field data with plain text, perform conditional concatenation based on the values of any field, and use string and other functions for truly powerful results.

To concatenate fields in MS Access 2010, we can use the "&" character or the "+" character. Since the "+" character is the one used with most databases, we will be using this one for our examples.

140. Column concatenation without spaces
Put all customer address information in one field
Discussion:
Suppose we have a job to create mailing labels for letters to our suppliers. My experience indicates that most people will go to Word, connect to Access, and go through multiple steps and a painful process to achieve this task. There is no need to go to this trouble since we can easily achieve this task using Access 2010 alone. There are two steps we need to follow: First, we create a query, namely qry_suppliers_labels, with a field that concatenates values from the address, city, state, and zip fields from the suppliers table. Second, we create a report that formats our data to the label size we want, and we set the query with the concatenated field as its data source. This is it—we are done forever.

Why? Because let's say in the future, we need to create mailing labels only for a subset of our suppliers in the city of Boston or in the state of California. We can just modify our qry_suppliers_labels, add the city field or the state field, and enter any criteria expressions we need. Then, we can just run our report again. We might also face another scenario in which we need to create labels of different sizes. It will take a few seconds to modify our report and get the label sizes we need.

I will show you how to use punctuation and spaces for formatting your concatenated columns so that you can do everything in Access. In this example, we create a simple concatenation of four fields. Using this code, there will be no spaces between the field values in the result set.

Code:

```
SELECT  (address+city+state+zip) AS FullAddress
FROM Customers
```

which is the same as

```
SELECT  (address&city&state&zip) AS FullAddress
FROM Customers
```

Result:

As you can see, the four fields are concatenated into one. However, the data is cramped in a continuous string of characters. We need to add spaces between the fields so that we can easily read them and print the results in a way that will make sense to USPS.

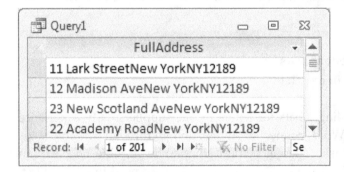

141.   Column concatenation with spaces

Put all customer address information in one field with spaces between values

Discussion:

In this example, we just add spaces between the concatenated columns. We use single quotes with a space between them to achieve this output.

Code:

```
SELECT  (address +' '+ city +' '+ state +' '+ zip)  AS FullAddress
FROM Customers
```

Result:

142.   Concatenation of columns and text

Writing customer letters in Access 2010

Discussion:

What if we would like to write a letter using a database? We can indeed combine plain text with field data with enough flexibility to write automatic letters! There is a sample letter below. Notice how punctuation marks are enclosed in double quotes. In addition, the SELECT statement is practically one field named ""CustomerLetter".

Code:

```
SELECT "Dear" + ' '+ (lastname + ' ' + firstname) +"." + ' '+ "It is our pleasure to
announce that we reviewed your resume, and we have set up an interview time for
you.  Can you please verify that your address is" + ' ' + (address +' '+ City +' '+ State +'
'+ Zip) + ' ' + "to send you corporate policy details and directions?"  AS CustomerLetter
FROM Customers
```

Result:

143.   Use the left() string function with concatenated fields

Displaying only the first letter from the customers' first names.

Discussion:

Let's say we want to write a letter, but instead of using the complete first name of the customer, we only want the first letter to appear. We can achieve this result and more by using string (text) functions. In this example, we use the left() function, but we can use anyone that suits our needs. (I have devoted a whole chapter on string functions to which you can refer for details). The left function in this example will extract the first character from the first name field.

Code:

SELECT "Dear" + ' '+ (lastname + ' ' + left(firstname, 1)) +"." + ' '+ "Please complete the enclosed forms so that we can ship your order to your country." AS CustomerLetter
FROM Customers

Result:

144. Use the ucase() string function with concatenated fields

Uppercasing customer last names

Discussion:

This is an additional example of using a string function in conjunction with concatenated columns. Consult chapter 26 regarding text and string operations for a full understanding of the role of string functions, as well as some cool examples. Our goal here is to have the last and first names of our customers capitalized.

Code:

```
SELECT "Dear" + ' '+ (ucase(lastname)) + ' ' + (ucase(firstname)) +"." + ' ' + "Please
complete the enclosed forms so that we can ship your order to your country." AS
CustomerLetter
FROM Customers
```

Result:

145. Use concatenated fields with criteria

Send letters to a select group of customers

Discussion:

The goal behind this example is to show that we can use additional fields in a query with concatenated fields to sort and filter data. This way, we have total control to retrieve exactly the records we want for concatenation. In this particular example, we restrict the output to customers from the city of Boston.

Code:

SELECT "Dear" + ' '+ (ucase(lastname)) + ' ' + (ucase(firstname)) +"." + ' ' + "Please complete the enclosed forms so that we can ship your order to your state." AS CustomerLetter, city
FROM customers
WHERE city = "Boston"

Result:

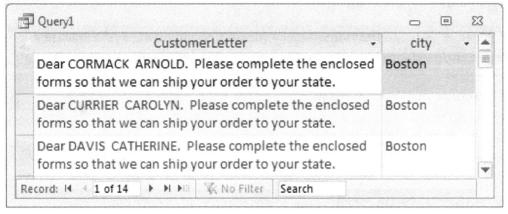

146. Using commas, periods, and other characters

Use correct punctuation with concatenated columns

Discussion:

Commas, periods, question marks, and other punctuation characters can become a pain when constructing concatenated fields. The answer is to enclose them in double quotes. In addition, if they come right after or before the concatenated field, we need to use the + character as well. For example, notice the period, in both statements below at the end of the parenthesis of the first name.

This will work: SELECT (lastname) + ' '+ (firstname) + "." FROM Customers

This will not work: SELECT (lastname) + ' '+ (firstname) "." FROM Customers

Code:

SELECT (lastname) + ' '+ (firstname) + "." AS CustomerName
FROM Customers

184

Result:

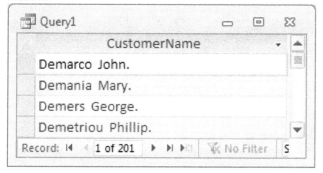

147. Conditional concatenation with the iif() function

Concatenating supplier fields using state as a condition

Discussion:

Sometimes, we might not want to apply the same concatenation rules for all of the records in the query. For example, we might want to create a certain label or letter for suppliers in NY and a different label or letter for everyone else, all in the same query. We can absolutely do this by using conditional statements and the iif() function in particular. However, someone might ask why we need to do this and not use simple criteria to do the same thing. First, in databases, we can achieve the same task in twenty different ways. There is always another less time-consuming and more effective way. Second, in this case, if we use a simple criterion such as (state = 'NY'), we only get the suppliers in NY. What we want is to send two different letters—one formatted for the state of NY and one for everyone else!

Using the iif(condition, true, false) function below, we tell the database to concatenate the companyname, contacttitle, and contactname fields if the state is NY. If it is not, we tell the database to concatenate only the contacttitle and contactname fields. This way, we can create two different sets of labels in the same query. Of course, we can use our imagination and modify the SQL statement below to use it for letters with plain text or any other concatenation task we need.

Code:

```
SELECT IIf((([State]='NY'),[Companyname]+' '+[ContactTitle]+' '+[Contactname],
[ContactTitle]+' '+[Contactname]) AS MailTo
FROM Suppliers
```

Result:

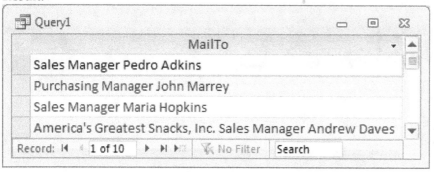

148. More powerful conditional concatenation with the switch() function

Concatenating supplier columns different for each city

Discussion:

Now that we know conditional concatenation is possible, what if we want to create different letters for suppliers based on the city where they reside? Notice in the suppliers table that there are three cities: Boston, New York, and Dallas. Our task is to create a different letter for suppliers in each city using the same query. We cannot use the iif() function to achieve this task since it takes only two parameters, and we need three. We can, however, use the switch() function as shown below:

Code:

```
SELECT
SWITCH(
[city]= 'Boston',      "Dear" +' '+ [contactname]+"," +' '+ "for our current sale we offer a
25% discount in" +' '+ [city] ,
[city] ='Dallas',      "Dear" +' '+ [contactname]+"," +' '+ "for our current sale we offer a
10% discount in" +' '+ [city] ,
[city] ='New York',    "Dear" +' '+ [contactname]+"," +' '+ "for our current sale we offer a
25% discount in" +' '+ [city] ,
)
AS SupplierLetter
FROM suppliers
```

Result:

149. Conditional concatenation with the switch(), left(), and instr() functions

Concatenate supplier fields conditionally for each city

Discussion:

In the previous example, we saw how to use the switch() function to create a different letter for suppliers based on the city where they reside. However, we used the full name of the supplier since the contactname field in the suppliers table contains both the first and last names of the supplier. This time, we would like to send a more personal letter to them by using only the first name. This means that we need to isolate the first name from the contactname field and use it in the query. We can achieve this task by using the instr() function to find the space between the first and last name strings in the contacttitle field. Then, we can use the left function to isolate whatever characters are left from the space we found with instr(). The whole SQL statement is shown below. As you can see in the result set, only the first names of the suppliers appear now.

Code:
```
SELECT
SWITCH(
[city]= 'Boston',        "Dear" +' '+ left(contactname, InStr(1,contactname," ")-1)
 +"," +' '+ "for our current sale we offer a 25% discount in" +' '+ [city] ,
[city] ='Dallas',        "Dear" +' '+ left(contactname, InStr(1,contactname," ")-1) +"," +' '+
"for our current sale we offer a 10% discount in" +' '+ [city] ,
[city] ='New York',    "Dear" +' '+ left(contactname, InStr(1,contactname," ")-1) +"," +' '+
"for our current sale we offer a 25% discount in" +' '+ [city] ,
)
AS SupplierLetter
FROM suppliers
```

Result:

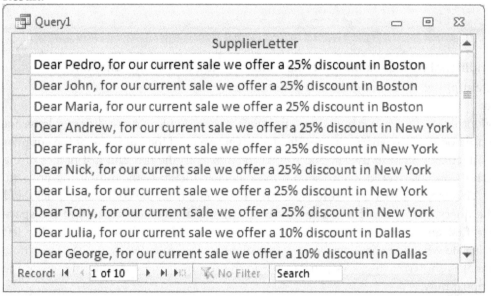

CHAPTER 17
THE GROUP BY CLAUSE

The GROUP BY clause is one of the foggiest keywords for both beginners and intermediate database professionals. Because of its intricacies, users and developers do not have a clear understanding of the circumstances when the GROUP BY clause is used. In this chapter, we have two goals: First, to understand in detail how and when the GROUP BY clause should be used, and second, to understand exactly what results to expect from it. The fundamental goal of the GROUP BY clause is to summarize data. The general syntax of the GROUP BY clause appears below but you do not need to memorize it since we will explore the role of each option in detail in the subsequent examples. Notice that in the statement below the WHERE, HAVING, and ORDER BY clauses are optional. However, we always need to use an aggregate function (sum, avg, min, max, etc.) in conjunction with the GROUP BY clause.

SELECT fields, aggregate function (field or calculated field)
FROM table
WHERE criteria (optional)
GROUP BY field(s)
HAVING criteria (optional)
ORDER BY field – (optional)

Before we do anything else, let's have a look at the table I prepared especially for this chapter. It is a simple table with only twelve records about customers and their orders. The goal is to run the GROUP BY examples on this table and give you the ability to do the calculations manually so that you know exactly how every result is obtained. The name of the table is tbls_customersgr.

LastName ▾	OrderID ▾	OrderDate ▾	ProductName ▾	UnitPrice ▾	Quantity ▾
Mahoney	57	5/29/2012	Chocolate Chip Brow	15	1
Mahoney	57	5/29/2012	Mushrooms Sauce	5	2
Mahoney	57	5/29/2012	Dark Chocolate Apric	28	5
Spicer	509	9/17/2013	All-Purpose Marinad	15	2
Spicer	509	9/17/2013	Oatmeal Raisin Wal	8	3
Spicer	509	9/17/2013	Corn Chips Bag	15	2
Spicer	509	9/17/2013	Dark Chocolate Apric	28	3
Martin	494	9/30/2013	Cream and honey bis	32	3
Martin	494	9/30/2013	Traditional Swedish	5	5
Riegert	1	11/6/2013	Dried Red Tart Cherri	15	2
Mahoney	502	8/3/2014	Roasted No-Salt Alm	15	1
Mahoney	502	8/3/2014	Sesame Crackers in :	15	3

tbls_customersGR

Record: 1 of 12 — No Filter — Search

First, notice that there are four customers in total. Second, the customer, Mr. Mahoney, ordered twice: orders 57 and 502. Third, the rest of the three customers have one order only. Fourth, Mr. Riegert has one order with one product only, but he ordered two units of it. Fifth, orders 57, 494, 502, and 509 contain multiple products. Sixth, dark chocolate is a product included in two orders (in 57 and 509). At this point, we are ready to go through our first example.

150. The GROUP BY clause on one column and one aggregated field
Retrieve the total product units ordered by customer
Discussion:
In this scenario, the objective is to calculate the total product units ordered by each customer. There are only two fields used in the SQL code below. LastName is the field on which we apply the GROUP BY clause, and TotalUnits is the aggregated field that results from applying the sum() function on the Quantity column.

Code:
```
SELECT LastName, SUM(quantity) AS TotalUnits
FROM tbls_customersgr
GROUP BY LastName
```

Result:

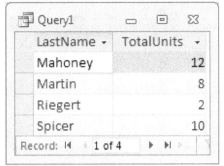

151. The GROUP BY clause on one column and one aggregated-calculated field

Retrieve the total order amount by customer

Discussion:

In this scenario, we have a request from management to calculate the total order amounts by customer to create a list with our best customers. There are two fields used in the SQL code. LastName is the field on which we apply the GROUP BY clause. TotalUnits is the aggregated field. However, this time, the aggregation occurs on the result of the multiplication of two columns. It is necessary to multiply the unitprice with the quantity columns to retrieve the total for each product in each order and then, sum the results by customer lastname.

Code:

SELECT LastName, SUM(unitprice*quantity) AS OrderTotal
FROM tbls_customersgr
GROUP BY LastName

Result:

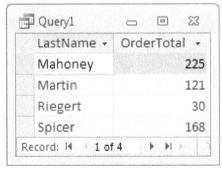

We see some interesting results here. First, since we grouped by customer last name, the result set produced four records, which is the exact number of unique customers we have in the tbls_customersgr table. We need to check the results to verify the database made the calculations correctly. We use Mahoney as an example.

LastName	Unit Price	Quantity	UnitPrice* Quantity
Mahoney	15	1	15
Mahoney	15	3	45
Mahoney	15	1	15
Mahoney	5	2	10
Mahoney	28	5	140
		SUM()	225

First, the database will do the multiplication of (unitprice * quantity) as we defined it in the calculated field named OrderTotal. This means that the database will multiply the price of each product ordered * its quantity ordered for all products in all orders for the particular customer. Then, it will simply SUM()results since we used the sum() function. Doing the calculations manually, we arrived at 225 for Mr. Mahoney, which is the same number the database produced for this customer.

152.   The GROUP BY clause on one column and two aggregated fields

Find total and average order amounts by customer

Discussion:

In this scenario, the goal is to produce a report that will show the total and average order amounts grouped by customer. There are three fields used in the SQL code: LastName, OrderTotal, and AvgOrder. The lastname is the field used with the GROUP BY clause. The fields OrderTotal and AvgOrder are the two aggregated fields.

Code:

SELECT lastname, SUM(unitprice*quantity) AS OrderTotal, AVG(unitprice*quantity) AS AvgOrder
FROM tbls_customersgr
GROUP BY lastname

Result:

lastname	OrderTotal	AvgOrder
Mahoney	225	45
Martin	121	60.5
Riegert	30	30
Spicer	168	42

Record: I◄ ◄ 1 of 4 ► ►I ⊳ 🔾 No Filter | Search

153. The GROUP BY clause on one column, one aggregated field, and WHERE
Find total order amounts for a subset of customers
Discussion:
Sometimes, we want to exclude certain records from our aggregate calculations. In these cases, we can use the WHERE clause to exclude records we are not interested in working with. Using WHERE, we exclude records before the GROUP BY clause takes effect. Therefore, if we have a source dataset with 3,000 records and use WHERE, the GROUP BY clause takes effect on the remaining records only. Later, you will learn the use of HAVING, which is a filtering statement like WHERE that takes effect after the GROUP BY calculates the summarized field values. Consequently, you need to know exactly what you want to do and use the appropriate filtering statement with GROUP BY.

In this example, we look for order totals by customer, but we want to exclude the orders from our customer Spicer. Mr. Spicer has only one order with orderid = 509. We use three fields in this SQL statement: Lastname, OrderTotal, and OrderID. LastName is the GROUP BY field, OrderTotal the aggregated field, and OrderID the filtering field.

Code:
```
SELECT LastName, SUM(unitprice*quantity) AS OrderTotal
FROM tbls_customersgr
WHERE orderid <> 509
GROUP BY LastName
```

Result:

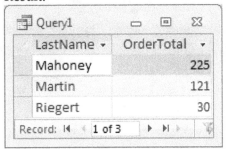

154. The GROUP BY clause on one column, one aggregated field, and HAVING

Find customer orders with total order amount exceeding $100

Discussion:

In this example, we want to exclude from the result set all customers whose order totals are less than $100. However, we do not know beforehand who these customers are. We need to run the GROUP BY clause, find the totals, and exclude those below $100. This is exactly the case in which HAVING is used. Using HAVING with GROUP BY is a powerful and flexible way to filter records. By the way, we use the HAVING clause only in conjunction with the GROUP BY clause. Looking at the result set, we can see that only three customers appear. The customer named Riegert does not appear because his order total is only 30.

Code:

```
SELECT LastName, SUM(unitprice*quantity) AS OrderTotal
FROM tbls_customersgr
GROUP BY LastName
HAVING SUM(unitprice*quantity)>100
```

Result:

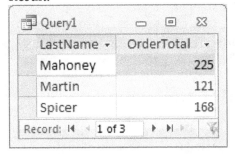

155. The GROUP BY clause on one column, one aggregated field, WHERE and HAVING

Calculate order totals above $100 excluding a subset of products

Discussion:

In this example, pay attention to the combined use of WHERE and HAVING. We want to calculate customer order totals, but we want to exclude from the result set customers whose order totals are less than $100. In addition, we want to exclude the calculation amounts related to the product "Chocolate Chip Brownie". Perhaps management wants to see how customer order amounts differ if this product is excluded from their orders. Maybe they are thinking of discontinuing this particular product.

In general, when it comes to filtering records in GROUP BY statements, we need to make some quick decisions: Do we need to use WHERE, HAVING, or a combination of the two? Your way of thinking should always be the same: Use the WHERE clause to exclude records that you do not want to be included in the aggregate calculations, and use HAVING to exclude values after the aggregations by GROUP BY are made. In this case, we use WHERE to exclude the product "Chocolate Chip Brownie" from the recordset, and we use GROUP BY to create the aggregations on whatever records remain. After the aggregations are made, the HAVING clause takes effect to exclude order totals less than $100. The bottom line is that in the SQL statement below, the WHERE clause will run first, then the GROUP BY, and finally the HAVING clause.

Code:

```
SELECT LastName, SUM(unitprice*quantity) AS OrderTotal
FROM tbls_customersgr
WHERE productname <> "Chocolate Chip Brownie"
GROUP BY LastName
HAVING SUM(unitprice*quantity)>100
```

Result:

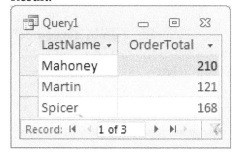

156. The GROUP BY clause with WHERE, HAVING, and ORDER BY

Sorting customer order totals

Discussion:

In this example, we put together all of the statements we learned about GROUP BY up to this point and introduce the ORDER BY clause. When the ORDER BY clause is used with GROUP BY, it takes effect after the database makes the calculations resulting from the GROUP BY clause. Furthermore, in this example, we exclude from the calculations a particular order with orderid=509.

Code:

```
SELECT LastName, SUM(unitprice*quantity) AS OrderTotal
FROM tbls_customersgr
WHERE orderid <> 509
GROUP BY LastName
HAVING SUM(unitprice*quantity)>100
ORDER BY Lastname DESC
```

Result:

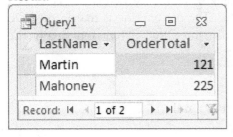

157. The GROUP BY clause with NULLS

Calculate average customer order amounts with and without nulls

Discussion:

For the purposes of this example, delete from the tbls_customersgr table the unit price for one of the products in Mahoney's order. Specifically, delete the unit price for Dark Chocolate Appricots. The idea is to demonstrate exactly what happens when nulls exist in data needed for calculations in GROUP BY clauses. Using 5 records in this table, you can check the results manually and learn so that when you deal with 5,000 records, you know exactly what to do.

tbls_customersgr					
LastName	OrderID	OrderDate	ProductName	UnitPrice	Quantity
Mahoney	57	5/29/2012	Dark Chocolate Apricots in 20 oz. Bag		5
Mahoney	57	5/29/2012	Mushrooms Sauce	5	2
Mahoney	57	5/29/2012	Chocolate Chip Brownie	15	1

Let us run two pieces of code:

Code:

SELECT OrderID, Avg(([unitprice]*[quantity])) AS AverageOrderAmount
FROM tbls_customersgr
GROUP BY OrderID

Result with null values:

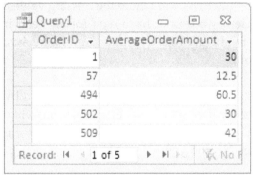

Now replace the deleted unit price for Dark Chocolate Appricots at $28 and run the SQL statement again:

Code:

SELECT OrderID, Avg(([unitprice]*[quantity])) AS AverageOrderAmount
FROM tbls_customersgr
GROUP BY OrderID

Result without null values:

OrderID	AverageOrderAmount
1	30
57	55
494	60.5
502	30
509	42

Record: ◄ ◄ 1 of 5 ► ►► No

As you can see from the first result set, all of the calculations look right except for orderid = 57. In this case, the database is giving us an average of 12.5. In other words, it takes into consideration only the two products in that order and leaves out the third—the one with the missing quantity. I will not express an opinion whether this is correct or not. I simply want you to know that when missing data exists, aggregate functions will ignore the missing values. Some people might argue that this is correct because if we do not have data for an item, it should not be included in the calculations. Others might say that when missing data exists, aggregate functions should take this into consideration.

We will not miss the forest for the trees in this case. Instead of becoming bogged down by database peculiarities, the most effective action when you make calculations like multiplications or when you use the GROUP BY clause is to first check your fields for missing data. It takes a few seconds to check for nulls (chapter 24), and you will not have to worry how aggregate functions will handle your data.

158. The GROUP BY clause on multiple columns

Find order totals grouped by customer and order number at the same time
Discussion:
Sometimes, you want to have a more detailed view of your data. For example, you might want to find order totals by customer and OrderID at the same time. You can easily achieve this with GROUP BY in Access 2010. Since you grouped first by last name and then by OrderID, orders will be totaled by lastname first, followed by OrderID. You can reverse the order of grouping or add more grouping fields according to the level of the detail you would like to see.

Code:

SELECT lastname, OrderID, SUM([unitprice]*[quantity]) AS OrderTotal
FROM tbls_customersgr
GROUP BY lastname, OrderID

Result:

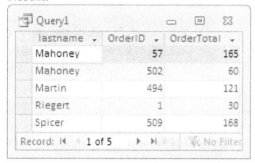

lastname	OrderID	OrderTotal
Mahoney	57	165
Mahoney	502	60
Martin	494	121
Riegert	1	30
Spicer	509	168

Record: 1 of 5   No Filter

CHAPTER 18
AGGREGATE FUNCTIONS

Aggregate functions like sum(), avg(), count(), count(*), max(), and min() have the main goal of summarizing data and converting this data into useful pieces of information. Aggregate functions process values from a table column to produce a summary value, whether a summation, an average, or a maximum value.

Aggregate functions can and are often used on calculated fields as well (chapter 15) which fields are themselves the result of the multiplication, summation, or division of two or more fields.

With aggregate functions, you need to pay attention to any null values in your data. In this chapter, you will understand well the effect of null values on aggregate calculations. However, no matter how much knowledge you have regarding the behavior of aggregate functions with null values, you should have one goal in mind: To eliminate null values from the columns on which you conduct aggregations. In other words, you need to develop a habit to examine your data for nulls before you even use aggregate functions. Of course, advanced developers by design do not allow null values in their tables. They will use default values, constraints, or validation rules to avoid nulls altogether.

Finally, aggregate functions are extremely useful when combined with the GROUP BY clause. We examined GROUP BY in the previous chapter and are now ready to go a step further, using it with aggregate functions to observe the power of the results obtained.

In this chapter, we will use aggregate functions with calculated fields, the GROUP BY clause, the WHERE clause, the HAVING clause, and a few operators so that you learn the combined use of aggregate functions—and not in isolation. For the purposes of this chapter, we have created a special table called tbls_customersag with only 20 records so that you can check the results against the dataset, make calculations manually, and fully understand the effects of aggregate functions. Before you start the examples in this chapter, open this table to understand its structure and have a look at its 20 records.

159.   The count() function

Count the number of orders

Discussion:

The count() function, used alone, will calculate the number of records in a dataset as soon as it is used on a field that contains no null values. In practice, the count() function is usually applied on the primary key of the table since it is the one field that is certain not to contain nulls. In this example, we use it on the OrderID field, which is not the primary key, but I use it to show you the different results produced by count() in the subsequent examples. In this case, the count() function returned the number of records in the table, i.e. 20. We can be certain of one thing from this result: The OrderID field does not contain any null values since the number returned from the count() function is equal to the number of records in the table.

Code:

SELECT count(orderid) as NumberofOrders

FROM tbls_customersag

Result:

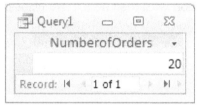

160.   The count() function with DISTINCT

Count the number of unique orders from customers

Discussion:

The previous example is fine, but we need to find a way to count the number of unique orders in this table. The proper way to accomplish this task in SQL is to use the COUNT and DISTINCT statements together as:

SELECT Count (Distinct orderid) as NumberofOrders FROM tbls_cusotmersag

This is excellent, but our problem is that it does not work in Access 2010. We need to deviate thematically for a second and use a subquery with DISTINCT to achieve the result we want (See chapter 31 on subqueries). From the result set below, notice that the number of orders produced by the count() function is now 15. This is actually the number of unique orders in the table, which is exactly what we need.

201

Code:

SELECT Count(*) AS NumberofOrders
FROM
(SELECT DISTINCT orderid FROM tbls_customersag)

Result:

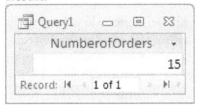

161. The count() function with the GROUP BY clause

Count the number of orders by customer

Discussion:

The objective in this scenario is to calculate how many orders we received from each customer. We can provide an answer quickly by using the count() function with the GROUP BY clause. From the result set, you obtain two pieces of information. First, you know that you have 9 unique customers in the dataset of 20 records. Second, you have a count of the number of orders by each customer.

Code:

SELECT lastname, count(orderid) as NumberofOrders
FROM tbls_customersag
GROUP BY lastname

Result:

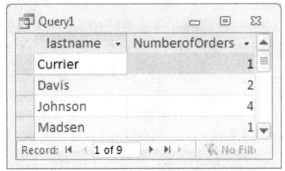

162. The count() and count(*) functions in comparison

Count the number of records in a table using count(*)

Discussion:

In this scenario, the objective is to clearly understand the differences between Count(), Count(*), and count() DISTINCT so that you can take full advantage of them in your data tasks. For this purpose, I have temporarily deleted the name of customer Davis from the table tbls_customersag. Now, we have 20 records in the table with the last name of a customer missing.

			tbls_customersag		
PK	LastName	OrderID	ProductID	UnitPrice	Quantity
1		4	55	15	3
2	Sterling	60	56	12	5
3	Sterling	60	21	15	4

Let's use the count() function first. As you can see from the result set, the number returned is 19. This is because we used count() on the lastname field in which a value is missing. Consequently, while the table contains 20 records, we received only 19. You do not need to worry about these intricacies if you follow a simple piece of advice: Any time you work with aggregate functions, calculated fields, or GROUP BY, check your records for null values, and make the necessary edits and replacements (see chapter 23 for details on null values). Then, you do not need to worry about the intricacies of how aggregate functions or calculated fields behave with missing data.

Code:

SELECT count(lastname) as NumberofCustomers
FROM tbls_customersag

Result:

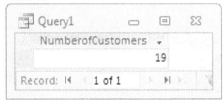

Now, let's use the count(*) function. As you can see from the result set, the count(*) function returned the correct result of 20 records in the table.

Code:

SELECT count(*) as NumberofCustomers
FROM tbls_customersag

Result:

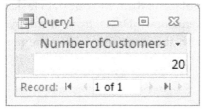

Now, let's use count(*) with a subquery and DISTINCT. As you can see from the result set, the number of unique customers returned is 10. We know already, however, that we have 9 unique customers in the table. This time, the count(*) function returned 10 because it counted the "blank" customer as an additional unique customer.

Code:

SELECT Count(*) AS NumberofCustomers
FROM
(SELECT DISTINCT lastname FROM tbls_customersag)

Result:

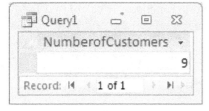

163.   The AVG() function

Calculate the average order amount by customer

In this example we calculate the number of orders and the average order amount by customer. In a previous example, we learned how to calculate the number of orders by customer. This is good information but not enough for our business. For example, some customers might have many orders but with minimal order amounts. If we depend on the number of orders only, we might miss some good customers with big orders, and our marketing promotions and resources might be off target. Calculating the average order amount solves this problem.

Code:
```
SELECT lastname, count(orderid) as NumberofOrders, AVG(unitprice*quantity)
AS AvgOrderAmount
FROM tbls_customersag
GROUP BY lastname
```

Result:

lastname	NumberofOrders	AvgOrderAmount
Currier	1	30
Davis	2	60
Johnson	4	18.75
Madsen	1	30
McGrath	1	10
Miller	2	25
Ming	2	60
Powers	4	31
Sterling	3	50

Record: 1 of 9   No Filter   Search

164. The avg() function with the WHERE clause

Calculate the number of orders and average order amounts for specific customers

Discussion:

We have the flexibility to use the WHERE clause with aggregate functions to manipulate the result set and retrieve the exact pieces of information we need. Using WHERE will cause the database engine to first eliminate records per the WHERE clause and perform any calculations on the remaining ones. In this particular example, we exclude two customers using the NOT IN operator.

Code:
```
SELECT lastname, count(orderid) as NumberofOrders, AVG(unitprice*quantity)
AS AvgOrderAmount
FROM tbls_customersag
WHERE lastname NOT IN ("Johnson", "Madsen")
GROUP BY lastname
```

Result:

lastname	NumberofOrders	AvgOrderAmount
Currier	1	30
Davis	2	60
McGrath	1	10
Miller	2	25
Ming	2	60
Powers	4	31
Sterling	3	50

Record: 1 of 7   No Filter   Search

165. The sum() function

Calculate the number of orders, average, and total order amounts by customer

Discussion:

Here, we use everything we have written in the previous example and add the sum() function to calculate the total order amount by customer. We are still excluding two customers from the calculations using the NOT IN operator in the WHERE clause.

Code:

```
SELECT lastname, count(orderid) as Num, avg(unitprice*quantity)
AS Avg, sum(unitprice*quantity) AS Total
FROM tbls_customersag
WHERE lastname NOT IN ("Johnson", "Madsen")
GROUP BY lastname
```

Result:

lastname	Num	Avg	Total
Currier	1	30	30
Davis	2	60	120
McGrath	1	10	10
Miller	2	25	50
Ming	2	60	120
Powers	4	31	124
Sterling	3	50	150

Record: ◀ ◀ 1 of 7 ▶ ▶▶ ▷ ⫬ No Filter | Search

166. The min() function

Calculate the minimum (lowest value) of customer orders

Discussion:

Let's assume we now have an additional request to find the minimum order amount for each customer. We can achieve this using the code below:

Code:

```
SELECT lastname, count(orderid) as Num, min(unitprice*quantity) AS Min,
avg(unitprice*quantity) AS Avg, sum(unitprice*quantity) AS Total
FROM tbls_customersag
WHERE lastname NOT IN ("Johnson", "Madsen")
GROUP BY lastname
```

Result:

lastname	Num	Min	Avg	Total
Currier	1	30	30	30
Davis	2	45	60	120
McGrath	1	10	10	10
Miller	2	20	25	50
Ming	2	60	60	120
Powers	4	15	31	124
Sterling	3	30	50	150

Record: 1 of 7 | No Filter | Search

167. The max() function

Calculate the maximum value of customer orders

Discussion:

The max() function will calculate the value of the biggest order for each customer, and it will report just that in the result set.

Code:

```
SELECT lastname, count(orderid) as Num, min(unitprice*quantity) AS Min,
avg(unitprice*quantity) AS Avg, max(unitprice*quantity) AS Max,
sum(unitprice*quantity) AS Total
FROM tbls_customersag
WHERE lastname NOT IN ("Johnson", "Madsen")
GROUP BY lastname
```

Result:

lastname	Num	Min	Avg	Max	Total
Currier	1	30	30	30	30
Davis	2	45	60	75	120
McGrath	1	10	10	10	10
Miller	2	20	25	30	50
Ming	2	60	60	60	120
Powers	4	15	31	45	124
Sterling	3	30	50	60	150

Record: I◄ ◄ 1 of 7 ► ►I ► 🔍 No Filter | Search

168. The Standard Deviation and Variance functions

Calculate the standard deviation and variance of customer order amounts

Discussion:

Using SQL, we can do much more than the usual arithmetic calculations. Actually, we can even perform some statistical analysis. In this example, we are looking for the standard deviation and variance of order amounts from each customer. In the SQL code, we used the cint() conversion function to avoid multiple decimals for the standard deviation column (chapter 25). In the result set, Currier and McGrath have only one order and, as it is logical, no variance and standard deviation can be calculated. From a business point of view, customers Davis, Sterling, and Powers are prone to making orders that vary a lot in size.

Code:

```
SELECT lastname, count(orderid) as Num, min(unitprice*quantity) AS Min,
avg(unitprice*quantity) AS Avg, max(unitprice*quantity) AS Max,
sum(unitprice*quantity) AS Total, cint(stdev(unitprice*quantity)) As stdev,
var(unitprice*quantity) as var
 FROM tbls_customersag
WHERE lastname NOT IN ("Johnson", "Madsen")
GROUP BY lastname
```

Result:

lastname	Num	Min	Avg	Max	Total	stdev	var
Currier	1	30	30	30	30	#Error	
Davis	2	45	60	75	120	21	450
McGrath	1	10	10	10	10	#Error	
Miller	2	20	25	30	50	7	50
Ming	2	60	60	60	120	0	0
Powers	4	15	31	45	124	15	218
Sterling	3	30	50	60	150	17	300

Record: I◄ ◄ 1 of 7 ► ►I ►   ☒ No Filter   Search

169. Aggregate functions with GROUP BY and HAVING

Calculate order amounts and filter records based on results of aggregate functions

Discussion:

This time, our manager wants a report that shows the number of orders, minimum, average, maximum, and total order amounts calculated by customer. In addition, he wants products with productID 13, 56, and 30 to not participate in the calculations. He wants us to exclude from the result set any customers with total order amounts of less than $100. He also wants us to exclude from the calculations any customers with average order amounts of less than $40. Finally, he wants us to exclude from the calculations any customers with a standard deviation in their order amounts of 20 and above, but the standard deviation calculation should not appear in the result set.

The above sounds complicated, and it is complicated to a degree. Still, it is not difficult to achieve. I would like you to learn to follow a process when it comes to complicated SQL statements. This process involves the incremental building of the SQL statement instead of trying to think about everything at once. Essentially, we will build the solution one step at a time.

Our first step in any complicated problem involving SQL is to try to identify the fields. In this example, we need seven fields to do our job, and this step is straightforward. The SELECT statement with the seven fields appears below. We include the type conversion function cint() so that we restrict the number of decimals for the standard deviation field.

SELECT lastname, count(orderid) as Num, min(unitprice*quantity) AS Min,
avg(unitprice*quantity) AS Avg, max(unitprice*quantity) AS Max,
sum(unitprice*quantity) AS Total, cint(stdev(unitprice*quantity)) As stdev
FROM tbls_customersag

Since our manager wants results produced by customer, we add the GROUP BY clause on lastname.

SELECT lastname, count(orderid) as Num, min(unitprice*quantity) AS Min,
avg(unitprice*quantity) AS Avg, max(unitprice*quantity) AS Max,
sum(unitprice*quantity) AS Total, cint(stdev(unitprice*quantity)) As stdev
FROM tbls_customersag
GROUP BY lastname

Our next step is to exclude products with productID 13, 56, and 30. For this task, we make use of the WHERE clause with the NOT IN operator (chapter 12) as it appears below:

SELECT lastname, count(orderid) as Num, min(unitprice*quantity) AS Min,
avg(unitprice*quantity) AS Avg, max(unitprice*quantity) AS Max,
sum(unitprice*quantity) AS Total, cint(stdev(unitprice*quantity)) As stdev
FROM tbls_customersag
WHERE productID NOT IN (13,56,30)
GROUP BY lastname

The next step is to exclude from the result set any customers with total order amounts of less than $100 or any customers with average order amounts of less than $40. Here, we have a problem since we must first perform the aggregate calculations and run the GROUP BY clause to find out who those customers are. How can we do this in one SQL statement? For cases like this one, we make use of the HAVING clause, which is the filtering clause you can use to filter records after aggregate calculations have been performed. The code will now look like this:

SELECT lastname, count(orderid) as Num, min(unitprice*quantity) AS Min,
avg(unitprice*quantity) AS Avg, max(unitprice*quantity) AS Max,
sum(unitprice*quantity) AS Total, cint(stdev(unitprice*quantity)) As stdev
FROM tbls_customersag
WHERE productID NOT IN (13,56,30)
GROUP BY lastname
HAVING sum(unitprice*quantity) > 100 AND avg(unitprice*quantity) > 40

The final step in building the SQL statement is to exclude from the calculations any customers with a standard deviation in their order amounts of 20 and above but without including the standard deviation calculation in the result set. In the SQL code below, we took out the expression cint(stdev(unitprice*quantity)) from the SELECT statement and put it in the HAVING clause. This way, the filtering happens, but the standard deviation calculations do not appear in the result set.

Code:
SELECT lastname, count(orderid) as Num, min(unitprice*quantity) AS Min,
avg(unitprice*quantity) AS Avg, max(unitprice*quantity) AS Max,
sum(unitprice*quantity) AS Total FROM tbls_customersag
WHERE productID NOT IN (13,56,30)
GROUP BY lastname
HAVING sum(unitprice*quantity) > 100 AND avg(unitprice*quantity) > 40 AND
cint(stdev(unitprice*quantity)) < 20

After all of the filtering, only one customer out of nine satisfied all of the criteria.

Result:

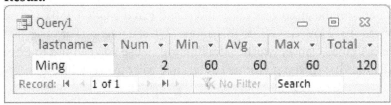

lastname	Num	Min	Avg	Max	Total
Ming	2	60	60	60	120

Record: I◄ 1 of 1 ► ►I   No Filter   Search

CHAPTER 19
CROSSTAB QUERIES

Crosstab queries have a reputation of being complicated and intricate objects. This should not be the case. You can really work efficiently with crosstab queries once you recognize their basic structure. In essence, to create a crosstab query, you use three fields only. One field will function as the column heading, the second as the row heading, and the third as the value field. The value field is the actual field on which calculations occur using aggregate functions like sum(), avg(), count(), count(*), max(), and min(). From the previous chapter, you know very well how to work with aggregate functions. Let us apply this knowledge in crosstab queries.

Suppose you want to calculate order totals by state and year. In other words, you would like to know how much you sold in every state in every year. Since you know already that to create a crosstab query, you need to have a field as a column heading, a field as a row heading, and a value field, your query will look like this in its basic design:

	Year
State	Value

When you run the query, since you have multiple states and years in your data, your result set will look like this:

	Year1	Year2	Year3
State1	Value	Value	Value
State2	Value	Value	Value
State3	Value	Value	Value

The state row field will expand automatically to include data for as many states as you have in your database. The year field will expand to include as many columns as the number of years you have in your data. The value field will present the sum of order amounts for all of the combinations of year and state.

The above diagram represents the basic structure of a crosstab query in Access 2010. However, you have a couple of bonuses at this point. Once you understand how crosstab queries work in Access 2010, you also understand how pivot tables work in Excel, how pivot charts summarize their data, and you definitely have an advantage over someone who creates pivot tables and charts without full knowledge of data summaries under the hood. In the following examples, we start with basic crosstab queries and incrementally add techniques that will make your crosstab queries powerful tools for your work. I also provide the design code for all the crosstab queries so that they are easier to understand.

Working with crosstab queries usually involves the joining of multiple tables. We might need a field from the customers table, a field from the orders table, and a field from the products table. Since joins are not the focus of this chapter, I would like to spare you the intricacies of joining tables and focus on the actual crosstab queries themselves. That is why the examples in this chapter are based on a query purposely made for this chapter. Its name is "Qry_Crosstab_Base" from which we will take all of the fields we need to work with. Of course, I also provide chapter 30 toward the end of the book to explain joins inside out so that you can professionally and easily work with joined tables.

170.   A crosstab query with three fields - example 1
Find total sales by state and year
Discussion:
As you can see from the design view and the SQL code, we use three fields to create this very informative crosstab query. The first is the state field, which we use as the row heading. The second is the OrderDate field, which we use for column headings. For the OrderDate field there is a catch: We use the year() function to extract only the year out of the multitude of order dates we have in the database. The third field is the value field, which we call OrderTotal. This is a calculated field that sums the unitprice * the quantity of each product for each of our customer orders.

When you look at the SQL code, you will notice the use of a new statement called TRANSFORM. The TRANSFORM statement relates to the value field in a crosstab query, and it always precedes the SQL statement. Additionally, it is always followed by the aggregate function used for the value field, which in this case is sum(Quantity * UnitPrice). Below is the SQL code for the crosstab query explaining it step by step:

TRANSFORM Sum([unitprice]*[quantity]) AS Ordertotal
The TRANSFORM statement is used for the value field in a crosstab query.

SELECT State FROM Qry_Crosstab_Base

The SELECT statement is used only for the row-heading field of the crosstab query, which in this case is the State field.

GROUP BY State

The GROUP BY clause follows next, and it is applied on the same field used in the SELECT statement. Since we used State for the SELECT statement, we use State for the GROUP BY clause as well.

PIVOT Year([OrderDate])

The PIVOT statement is the last one used in a crosstab query, and it is applied on the column-heading field.

Below is the general structure of a crosstab query in SQL code.

```
TRANSFORM ValueField
SELECT ColumnField
FROM DataSource
GROUP BY ColumnField
PIVOT RowField
```

Design Code:

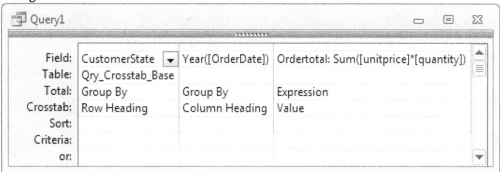

Code:

```
TRANSFORM sum([unitprice]*[quantity]) AS Ordertotal
SELECT CustomerState
FROM Qry_Crosstab_Base
GROUP BY CustomerState
PIVOT Year([OrderDate])
```

Looking at the results below, we can quickly understand and compare sales volumes by each state and each year. For example, the biggest sales revenues come from California, and they grow year by year. In Florida, we need to have a look at what is happening because sales dropped a lot for 2014. This is the power of crosstab queries. We get summarized results in seconds.

Result:

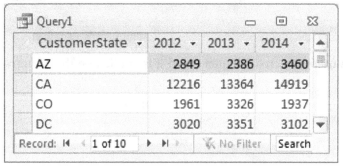

171.   A crosstab query with three fields—example 2

Find total sales by city and year

Discussion:

Our business manager is very happy with the comprehensive sales report we provided by state and year. Now that she knows what our database can do, she asks for an additional report that will show sales volumes by city and year. In about three seconds we replace the state field with the city field in our query, and our new crosstab query is ready!

Design Code:

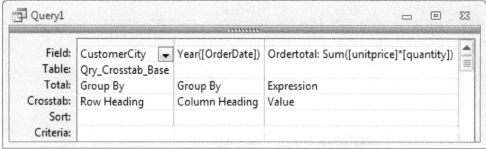

Code:

```
TRANSFORM Sum([unitprice]*[quantity]) AS Ordertotal
SELECT CustomerCity
FROM Qry_Crosstab_Base
GROUP BY CustomerCity
PIVOT Year([OrderDate])
```

Result:

CustomerCity	2012	2013	2014
Albany	1199	1214	1356
Boston	1999	2020	859
Chicago	2353	4924	3076
Dallas	2691	4174	3292

Record: 1 of 15   No Filter   Search

172. The issue of uniqueness of values in crosstab queries

Find total sales by customer and year

Discussion:

Now, our supervisor asks for additional detail. Specifically, he wants a sales report by customer and year. Again, in a few seconds, we replace the city field from the previous example with lastname and presumably, we are done!

Unfortunately, that isn't the case this time! Our problem is that multiple customers might have the same last names. Since we are grouping on the last name field, all of the customers with the same lastname will be grouped together! This is a very common problem in crosstab queries and when using the GROUP BY clause. Consequently, I would like you to develop a process to think thoroughly about the uniqueness of values when using the GROUP BY clause. For instance, you should think about the possibility of having the same last name in your data for multiple customers. The same is true for city fields since the same city name might refer to multiple distinct cities, as is the case with Portland, Oregon and Portland, Maine. We will see how we can solve this problem in the next example with concatenated fields.

In addition, notice from the result set that there are some blank values. For example, there are blank values for Ames in 2012 and 2013. These blanks mean that Ames has not placed any orders in 2012 and 2013 respectively.

Design Code:

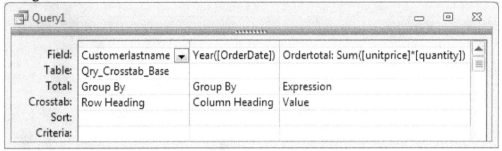

Code:

TRANSFORM sum([unitprice]*[quantity]) AS Ordertotal
SELECT Customerlastname
FROM Qry_Crosstab_Base
GROUP BY Customerlastname
PIVOT year([OrderDate])

Result:

Customerlastname	2012	2013	2014
Ackerman	120	32	207
Ames			871
Andersen	350		393
Anderson	965	924	1434

Record: 1 of 171   No Filter   Search

173. Crosstab queries with concatenated fields

Find total sales by customer and year displaying full customer names

Discussion:

In the previous example, we discussed that the results of the crosstab query were incorrect because multiple distinct customers might have the same last name. In this example, we need to make sure that we summarize sales volumes by unique customers. The knowledge acquired from the concatenated fields chapter (chapter 16) comes in handy here. In this example, we will GROUP BY the field resulting from the concatenation of the last and first name fields of the customers to obtain accurate results.

I know what you are thinking: What if there are customers with the same last and first names? This is a possibility, after all. We have three ways to solve this problem depending on its nature. First, if two customer entries pertain to the same customer, (there are duplicated records in the data set), read chapter 23 on duplicate and orphaned records to explore a range of solutions.

Second, if the two customer entries pertain to two different customers, we can add middle names, zip codes, and even part of the address information to the concatenated expression to obtain unique results.

Third, to avoid this problem in its conception, we can add to the customer table a unique multiple-field index on the last and first name fields so that values of customers with the same last and first names are not accepted at all in the table. See chapter 3 for the exact syntax of multiple-field indexes.

I have created an additional problem on purpose: When you look at the result set in this example, you will notice that the first record is blank! If this is the case, go immediately to your record set, and check the values of the fields you use in the concatenated expression for blanks. You will notice that customer "Corelli" does not have a first name entry! Add a first name for this customer, and your blank record will disappear when you run your crosstab again.

Design Code:

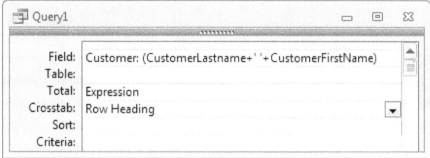

Code:
```
TRANSFORM Sum([unitprice]*[quantity]) AS Ordertotal
SELECT (CustomerLastname+' '+CustomerFirstName) AS Customer
FROM Qry_Crosstab_Base
GROUP BY (CustomerLastname+' '+CustomerFirstName)
PIVOT Year([OrderDate]);
```

Result:

Customer	2012	2013	2014
Ackerman Nicholas	120	32	207
Ames Pindar			871
Andersen Thomas	350		393
Anderson Joseph	110	575	477
Anderson Paul	371	72	513

Record: ◄ ◄ 2 of 190 ► ►► No Filter | Search

174. Display row totals in crosstab queries

Find customer sales by state and year and calculate grand totals

Discussion:

There are two ways to calculate grand totals in crosstab queries. The first is to calculate grand totals for column fields. For example, the grand totals of orders in all states for 2012, 2013, and 2014. Grand totals of columns will appear at the bottom of the crosstab grid. To accomplish this task, we can use the $\sum$ command on the ribbon. We can find it at the "Home" tab in the "Records" group. By clicking on $\sum$, an additional row will become available at the bottom of the crosstab query grid where we can select any grand total calculations we want as the following figure shows:

Code:

```
TRANSFORM sum([unitprice]*[quantity]) AS Ordertotal
SELECT CustomerState
FROM Qry_Crosstab_Base
GROUP BY CustomerState
PIVOT Year([OrderDate])
```

Result:

CustomerState ▾	2012 ▾	2013 ▾	2014 ▾
AZ	2849	2386	3460
CA	12216	13364	14919
CO	1961	3326	1937
DC	3020	3351	3102
Total	44230	51164	45002

Record: I◀ ◀ 1 of 10 ▶ ▶I ▶ ⎚ No Filter Search

The other way is to calculate grand totals for row fields when we might want to see grand totals from all years for the states of AZ, CA, CO, etc., for example. To accomplish this task, we need to perform a little trick in the design of the crosstab query grid: We take the value field, in this case OrderTotal, and we create an additional column in the design grid that we name Grand Total. We leave the calculated field the same (Sum(Unitprice*quantity)) and assign this new column to be an additional row heading in the query. Check the design of the Grand Total field in the figure below:

Design Code:

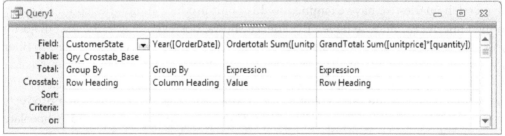

Field:	CustomerState ▾	Year([OrderDate])	Ordertotal: Sum([unitp	GrandTotal: Sum([unitprice]*[quantity])
Table:	Qry_Crosstab_Base			
Total:	Group By	Group By	Expression	Expression
Crosstab:	Row Heading	Column Heading	Value	Row Heading
Sort:				
Criteria:				
or:				

If we want to accomplish this task in SQL, the only thing we need to do is to add the value field expression Sum([unitprice]*[quantity]) AS GrandTotal in the SELECT line of the SQL statement as it appears below:

Code:

```
TRANSFORM Sum([unitprice]*[quantity]) AS Ordertotal
SELECT CustomerState, Sum([unitprice]*[quantity]) AS GrandTotal
FROM Qry_Crosstab_Base
GROUP BY CustomerState
PIVOT Year([OrderDate]);
```

Result:

CustomerState	GrandTotal	2012	2013	2014
AZ	8695	2849	2386	3460
CA	40499	12216	13364	14919
CO	7224	1961	3326	1937
DC	9473	3020	3351	3102

Record: ◄ ◄ 1 of 10 ► ►► No Filter | Search

175. Limit the number of rows in crosstab queries using WHERE

Find total sales by product and year for certain products only

Discussion:

All of the crosstab queries we have examined to this point produce summaries counting every record in the underlying database table. Experience shows, however, that in the vast majority of cases, we will make calculations on a subset of data. We can use the WHERE clause to filter the data we want to cross tabulate. The WHERE clause always affects the number of records returned from a query whether this query is a simple SELECT or a crosstab one. In this specific example, the goal is to provide sales volumes by product and year, excluding some products from the calculations. Specifically, the products 'Chocolate Chip Cookies' and 'Chocolate Fudge' should be excluded from the calculations. We can use the WHERE clause in conjunction with the NOT IN operator to get exactly the results we need. The design view of the crosstab query appears below, as well as in the SQL code. When it comes to the result set, the two products we excluded will not appear in the cross-tabulated calculations.

Design Code:

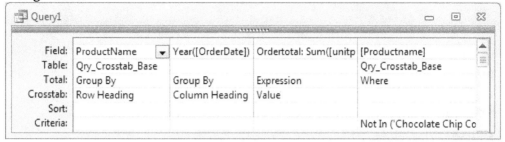

Code:

```
TRANSFORM Sum([unitprice]*[quantity]) AS Ordertotal
SELECT ProductName
FROM Qry_Crosstab_Base
WHERE ((Productname) NOT IN ('Chocolate Chip Cookies','Chocolate Fudge '))
GROUP BY ProductName
PIVOT Year([OrderDate])
```

Result:

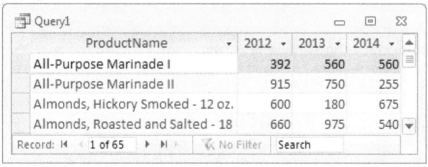

176.   Limit the number of columns in crosstab queries using PIVOT IN

Find total sales by product and year for specific years

Discussion:

In the previous example, we discussed how we can use the WHERE clause to filter the number of products included in the crosstab results. We learned how to limit the number of rows in a crosstab query, but there is a way to limit the number of columns as well.

For instance, what if our dataset contains sales data for the last ten years, and we do not want to include all of them in our crosstab results? We might want to see only the last two or three years. In this scenario, we are looking to control the number of columns appearing in the crosstab results. To achieve this task, we can use the PIVOT IN statement. In this particular example, we only want to see sales volumes for the years 2012 and 2013.

Code:
```
TRANSFORM Sum([unitprice]*[quantity]) AS Ordertotal
SELECT productname
FROM Qry_Crosstab_Base
GROUP BY productname
PIVOT Year([OrderDate]) IN (2012,2013)
```

Result:

productname	2012	2013
All-Purpose Marinade I	392	560
All-Purpose Marinade II	915	750
Almonds, Hickory Smoked - 12 oz.	600	180
Almonds, Roasted and Salted - 18	660	975

Record: 1 of 67   No Filter   Search

177.   Filter crosstab queries using any field for criteria

Find total sales by product and year in AZ, CA, and OH

Discussion:

In the previous two examples of filtering crosstab queries, we used the WHERE clause on the productname field and the PIVOT IN on the Orderdate field. Both of these fields are part of the crosstab query. The productname field is used for rows, and the orderdate field for columns. I would like you to know, however, that you can use any field in your dataset to filter records in a crosstab query without this field being an integral part of the crosstab query. You simply designate it as a "WHERE" field as it appears in the design grid below, or you use it in a WHERE clause as it appears in the SQL code. In addition, the state field, used as a "WHERE" field in this example, will not appear in the result set.

Design Code:

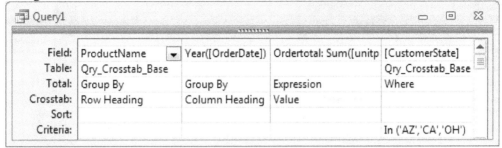

Code:

```
TRANSFORM Sum([unitprice]*[quantity]) AS Ordertotal
SELECT ProductName
FROM Qry_Crosstab_Base
WHERE ((CustomerState) IN ('AZ','CA','OH'))
GROUP BY ProductName
PIVOT Year([OrderDate])
```

Result:

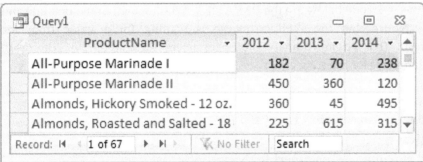

178.   Using parameters with crosstab queries

Find sales by customer and year using state as a parameter

Discussion:

Now, we have a new situation. Corporate managers are ecstatic about our ability to produce such useful results with crosstab queries. However, they call on us constantly to design the queries they need, and we spend a lot of time defining simple criteria. To solve this problem, we can use parameters with crosstab queries. Parameters in crosstab queries need a little attention. We need to enter the parameter twice: First in the query design grid as seen in the figure below:

Design:

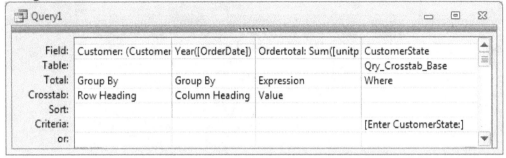

Second, we need to enter it in the parameters dialog box that we can find in the "Show/Hide" group of the "Query Design" tab as in the figure below:

Make sure the parameter data type is the same as the one in the field where you are using it. The items to notice in the SQL code below are the PARAMETERS statement in the first line and the WHERE clause. Notice that the WHERE clause is waiting for a value from the PARAMETERS statement. (For a detailed analysis on parameters, see chapter 20). The result set produced in this example is for the state of NY.

Code:
```
PARAMETERS [Enter CustomerState:] Text ( 255 );
TRANSFORM Sum([unitprice]*[quantity]) AS Ordertotal
SELECT (CustomerLastname+' '+CustomerFirstName) AS Customer
FROM Qry_Crosstab_Base
WHERE (((Qry_Crosstab_Base.CustomerState)=[Enter CustomerState:]))
GROUP BY (CustomerLastname+' '+CustomerFirstName)
PIVOT Year([OrderDate])
```

Result:

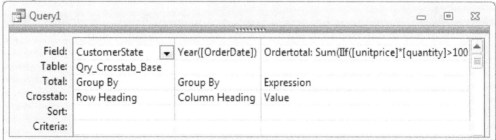

179. Conditional processing of crosstab queries using the iif() function

Calculate discounted sales volumes depending on revenue volumes

Discussion:

Our business assignment in the first example of this chapter was to give our manager a print out of total of sales by state and year. We were able to do that successfully and in no time. Now, however, our task is a little bit more complicated. Management wants to know the sales volumes if they gave a 10% discount to customers in states with total sales of more than $10,000. In addition, they want to know the sales volumes if they gave a discount of 5% to customers in states with total sales of less than $10,000. And they want to see all results in one report.

This is not a problem at all. The key here is to use the iif() function with the crosstab query. The expression for the value field in the crosstab query is the expression shown below. We ask the database to apply a 10% discount if total sales are bigger than $10,000 or to apply a 5% discount if total sales are less than $10,000.

Sum(iif([unitprice]*[quantity]>10000, ([unitprice]*[quantity])*(0.9), ([unitprice]*[quantity])*(0.95))) AS Ordertotal

Design Code:

Code:

```
TRANSFORM Sum(iif([unitprice]*[quantity]>10000, ([unitprice]*[quantity])*(0.9),
([unitprice]*[quantity])*(0.95))) AS Ordertotal
SELECT CustomerState
FROM Qry_Crosstab_Base
GROUP BY CustomerState
PIVOT Year([OrderDate])
```

Result:

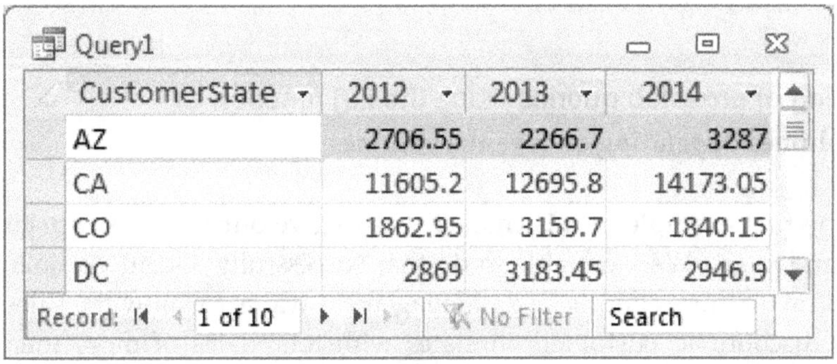

CustomerState	2012	2013	2014
AZ	2706.55	2266.7	3287
CA	11605.2	12695.8	14173.05
CO	1862.95	3159.7	1840.15
DC	2869	3183.45	2946.9

Record: 1 of 10   No Filter   Search

180.   Format output in crosstab queries

Find total sales by product and year and show results as currency

Discussion:

There might be some instances in which we would like to format the results of the value field of a crosstab query as currency so that the dollar sign appears in front of the numbers. This can be accomplished by using the format() or Ccur() functions right in the TRANSFORM statement as it appears below. Both will produce the same output.

Code:

```
TRANSFORM Format(Sum([unitprice]*[quantity]), "Currency") AS Ordertotal
SELECT ProductName
FROM Qry_Crosstab_Base
GROUP BY ProductName
PIVOT Year([OrderDate]);


TRANSFORM Ccur(Sum([unitprice]*[quantity])) AS Ordertotal
SELECT ProductName
FROM Qry_Crosstab_Base
GROUP BY ProductName
PIVOT Year([OrderDate]);
```

Result:

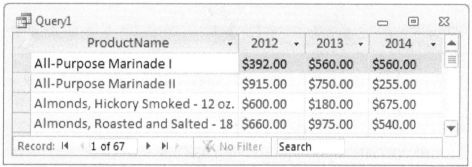

181.   Using the nz() function in crosstab queries

Find total customer orders by customer and year

Discussion:

In the cross-tabbed results below, the many blanks in the grid are immediately noticeable and do not appear very professional.

Code:

```
TRANSFORM Sum([unitprice]*[quantity]) AS Ordertotal
SELECT (CustomerLastname + ' ' + CustomerFirstName) AS customer
FROM Qry_Crosstab_Base
WHERE ((CustomerState) In ('AZ','CO','MD'))
GROUP BY (CustomerLastname + ' ' + CustomerFirstName)
PIVOT Year([OrderDate])
```

Result:

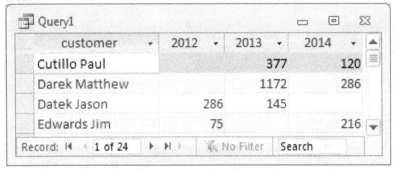

There is a way to replace these blank values with zeros using the nz() function. Notice how we use three functions in the TRANSFORM line to obtain the results we need.

Code:

```
TRANSFORM Ccur(Nz(Sum([unitprice]*[quantity]))) AS Ordertotal
SELECT (CustomerLastname + ' ' + CustomerFirstName) AS customer
FROM Qry_Crosstab_Base
WHERE ((CustomerState) In ('AZ','CO','MD'))
GROUP BY (CustomerLastname + ' ' + CustomerFirstName)
PIVOT Year([OrderDate])
```

Result:

customer	2012	2013	2014
Cutillo Paul	$0.00	$377.00	$120.00
Darek Matthew	$0.00	$1,172.00	$286.00
Datek Jason	$286.00	$145.00	$0.00
Edwards Jim	$75.00	$0.00	$216.00

Record: ◄ ◄ 1 of 24 ► ►► ❑ No Filter | Search

182. Conditional crosstab queries

Calculate order totals for "expensive" and "inexpensive" products

Discussion:

This time, management wants to know the contribution to the total sales volume of products selling above $25 per unit and the contribution of products selling below $25 per unit. Depending on the results we give them, they will change their sales priorities to focus more on products that will generate the most sales for the company. In addition, they would like to have the results by year so that they can also distinguish any trends in sales volumes. We can use the switch function right in the PIVOT statement to create product categories exactly the way management has asked.

Code:

```
TRANSFORM Sum([unitprice]*[quantity]) AS Ordertotal
SELECT Year([OrderDate]) As Year
FROM Qry_Crosstab_Base
GROUP BY Year([OrderDate])
PIVOT
SWITCH(
unitprice >= 25 ,      "ExpensiveProducts",
unitprice < 25,        "InexpensiveProducts"
)
```

Result:

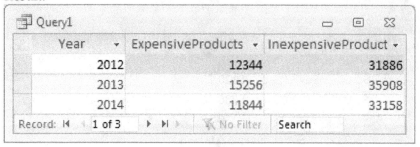

Year	ExpensiveProducts	InexpensiveProduct
2012	12344	31886
2013	15256	35908
2014	11844	33158

CHAPTER 20
PARAMETER QUERIES

The primary goal of a parameter query is to provide flexibility in criteria expressions. Instead of hard coding criteria values in the query code, it provides users the capability to supply the values they want to work with. For example, instead of hard coding the value "NY" for the state field, a parameter query allows users to supply any state they want and get the corresponding results.

Parameter queries in their simplest form will include one or two parameterized fields. However, you should know that parameter queries can be used with multiple parameters of any data type, wildcard characters, operators, equality and inequality predicates, and even functions. We will go through examples of all the above in this chapter so that you can make full use of the power and flexibility of parameter queries.

183. Creating a query with one parameter field
Retrieve order information using state as a parameter
Discussion:
The simplest form of a parameter query is one with a single parameter field. The parameter field always appears in the WHERE clause of the query and its parameter prompt is enclosed in brackets. In this example, the parameter field is "state", and its prompt will appear as [Enter State:]. The colon at the end of the prompt is optional, and you can omit it if you want. In this specific example, we used the equality predicate "=" in the expression ((State)=[Enter State:]). This is because the parameter in this query is waiting for complete state values like "NY", "AZ", "FL", or "CA". However, you are not restricted to equality or inequality predicates such as (=, <>, <, <=, >, =>). Later, you will learn how you can enter only part of the value you are looking for, in which case you can use an operator such as LIKE. You could also use the BETWEEN operator or even wildcard characters and functions as you will see in this chapter.

Code:
```
SELECT OrderID, OrderDate, City, State
FROM Qry_Parameters_Base
WHERE ((State)=[Enter State:])
```

Parameter Prompt:

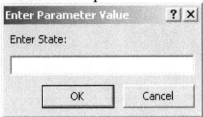

Result:

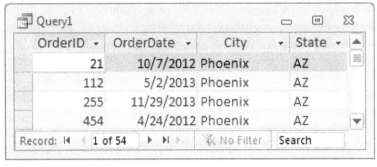

184. Creating a query with two parameter fields

Retrieve order information using state and city as parameters

Discussion:

Creating multi-field parameter queries is a possibility in Access 2010. In this example, we use the state and city as parameter fields using the AND operator. This means that we force our users to select a state first and then, a city within that state like NY and New York. We can just as easily use the OR operator so that our users can select any state and any city they want.

Code:

```
SELECT OrderID, OrderDate, City, State
FROM Qry_Parameters_Base
WHERE ((((State)=[Enter State:]) AND (City)=[Enter City:]))
```

Result:

OrderID ▾	OrderDate ▾	City ▾	State ▾
43	5/6/2013	New York	NY
115	1/27/2012	New York	NY
264	2/9/2012	New York	NY
642	3/16/2013	New York	NY

Record: 1 of 118   No Filter   Search

185. Creating a query with three parameter fields, one of them an expression
Retrieve order information using state, city, and ordertotal as parameters
Discussion:
In this example, we use three parameters for the State, City, and TotalOrder fields. Notice the third parameter ">[Enter Amount Bigger Than:]" for the TotalOrder field. Here, we use the ">" greater than inequality predicate to retrieve orders from "NY" state and "New York" city, which are bigger than $200 in this example. Of course, we could have used any amount for order totals to retrieve the orders we want. Equality and inequality predicates allow amazing flexibility in parameter queries. For a review of equality and inequality predicates, review chapter 10.

Code:
```
SELECT OrderID, OrderDate, City, State
FROM Qry_Parameters_Base
WHERE ((((State)=[Enter State:]) AND (City)=[Enter City:]) AND (totalorder)>[Enter Amount Bigger Than:])
```

Result:

OrderID ▾	OrderDate ▾	City ▾	State ▾
341	4/24/2012	New York	NY
411	8/29/2014	New York	NY
429	3/28/2014	New York	NY
447	4/21/2012	New York	NY

Record: 1 of 30   No Filter   Search

186. Define the order of the parameter prompts

Retrieve order information using orderdate, state, and ordertotal as parameters

Discussion:

Using multiple parameters might present a problem if we enter them directly in the query design grid in Access 2010. In this case, Access will present the parameters from left to right according to the lineup of the columns in the grid. Some sources suggest entering parameters in the "Parameters" sheet in the "Show/Hide" group of the "design" tab to force order. It is really not necessary to type our parameters a second time. In our SQL statement, we just type our parameters in the order we would like them to appear. However, always think about the logic behind the parameter lineup. In this example with the AND operator, the order will not make a difference in the result set since all three parameter values will apply concurrently on the fields for which they are specified. However, there might be cases in which we want a certain date range to be specified first and then, use operators to search for data within that range using operators different from AND.

In this example, the parameters are: NY, 1/1/2012, and $200.

Code:

SELECT OrderID, OrderDate, City, State

FROM Qry_Parameters_Base

WHERE ((((State)=[Enter State:]) AND (orderdate)>[Enter Date Later Than:]) AND (totalorder)>[Enter Amount Bigger Than:])

Result:

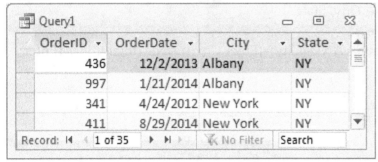

187. How to retrieve records by providing only part of the parameter value

Find customers by supplying only part of the name

Discussion:

We want to give our users the ability to search orders by customer name without remembering the exact last name of the customer. In this example, we use the * wildcard character and lastname as the parameter field. Of course, we can use our creativity and employ any wildcard character we want (see chapter 8) with any kind of equality or inequality predicates to achieve amazing results. In this example, we will look for all customer names starting with "Ba". As you might expect, the same customer will come up multiple times since each customer might have multiple orders. That is why the name Balfur appears multiple times.

Code:
SELECT lastname, firstname, city, state
FROM Qry_Parameters_Base
WHERE ((lastname) LIKE [Enter last name:] + "*")

Result:

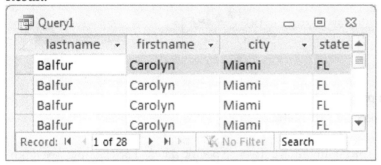

188. Using numeric ranges in parameter queries

Find sales volume ranges from customer orders

Discussion:

Suppose we have a request to provide managers the ability to retrieve sales volumes. This is easy with a parameter query. As you can see from the result set, there are 159 orders between $200 and $300. In this example, we used the "<" and ">" inequality predicates instead of the BETWEEN operator. The lower and upper limits of our boundaries ($200, $300) will not appear in the result set. However, if we used BETWEEN (chapter 11), which is inclusive, the boundaries would have been included in the result set. The same would happen if we used the "<=" and "=>" inequality predicates.

Code:
SELECT OrderID, OrderDate, City, State, TotalOrder
FROM Qry_Parameters_Base
WHERE (((TotalOrder)>[Enter Min Order Amount:]) AND (totalorder)<[Enter Maximum Order Amount:])

Result:

OrderID ▾	OrderDate ▾	City	▾	State ▾
507	5/2/2013	Houston		TX
517	7/5/2014	Houston		TX
508	10/21/2014	Orlando		FL
96	3/6/2013	Washington		DC

Record: 1 of 159   No Filter   Search

189. Using date ranges in parameter queries
Find total order amounts between specific dates
Discussion:
This time, our goal is to retrieve order amounts between specific dates. For example, we might want to retrieve sales volumes only for a period of five days, ten days, a few months, or years. In this example, we are looking for orders between 1/1/2014 and 1/7/2014.

Code:
SELECT OrderID, OrderDate, City, State, TotalOrder
FROM Qry_Parameters_Base
WHERE (((OrderDate)>[Enter Min Date:]) AND (OrderDate)<[Enter Max Date:])

Result:

OrderID ▾	OrderDate ▾	City	▾	State ▾	TotalOrder ▾
146	1/4/2014	New York		NY	120
473	1/4/2014	Los Angeles		CA	415
331	1/5/2014	Philadelphia		PA	255
402	1/5/2014	New York		NY	75

Record: 1 of 6   No Filter   Search

190. Using functions in parameter queries

Find orders for a specific month for any range of years

Discussion:

Now, we have a very peculiar request from our company. Management wants to do some decision-making, and they have asked us for a way to run multiple scenarios such as: What were the sales volumes in the months of May for the last two years? Or for the month of June in the last three years? Or for any month for any range of years? They want to be able to perform these scenarios at will. To achieve this goal, we use the month() function to extract the month out of the OrderDate field, the year() function to extract years out of the OrderDate field, and the BETWEEN operator!

In this example, we used May (5) for the month and 2012 to 2013 for the year range. As you can see from the result set, we only retrieved orders for May of 2012 and May 2013.

Code:

```
SELECT OrderID, OrderDate, City, State, TotalOrder
FROM Qry_Parameters_Base
WHERE (((Month([OrderDate])=[Enter Month Number:]) AND ((Year([OrderDate]))
BETWEEN [ Enter Min Year:] And [Enter Max Year:])));
```

Result:

191. Calculations and functions in parameter queries

Find fulfillment cycle times for customer orders for specific periods

Discussion:

Management now wants to find fulfillment cycle times for customer orders for internal efficiency indicators. They would like us to retrieve the amount of time it took the company to ship an order from the time it received the order and for any range of dates. This is not as bad as it sounds. In this example, we measure the lag time in days for the period of 1/1/2012 to 1/30/2012. We use twice the day() function to construct a calculated field (lagTimesInDays) and then, two parameters for the OrderDate field.

Code:
SELECT OrderID, (day(ShippedDate) - day(OrderDate)) AS LagTimeInDays,
TotalOrder
FROM Qry_Parameters_Base
WHERE (((OrderDate)>[Enter Min Date:]) AND (OrderDate)<[Enter Max Date:])

Result:

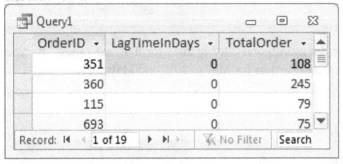

CHAPTER 21
CONDITIONAL DATA MANIPULATION

The iif(), switch(), and partition() functions are the most useful and practical functions for conditional data manipulation in Access 2010. Keep in mind that CASE does not work in Access 2010, so do not bother wasting your time looking for it.

What exactly do we mean by conditional data processing? Let's assume we have a customer database we use for promotional campaigns. We might decide we want to provide different discount levels for customers in the Northeast, Midwest, West, Southeast, and Southwest states. Since we do not have region information in our database, we need to create multiple SELECT queries for these categories and apply the appropriate discount for each region. Using conditional data processing, on the other hand, will enable us to do our job in just one query.

You might be thinking at this point that it does not bother you to create four queries to do your job. What matters in the end is getting the job done. I totally agree. However, what will happen after a couple of years at work is that you will end up with several hundred queries. In the end, you will not remember what was what, and you will be afraid to delete even one of them since you no longer know what it was used for. During the last 15 years, I have seen this happen countless times with departmental databases.

To encourage you to use conditional processing, let me give you another example. Let's say we have a database in which we store our products, along with the corresponding suppliers. Every now and then, our suppliers send us updated prices, and we need to update our own product catalog as well. We have only 20 suppliers and 200 products in our database, and we need to update our prices every few weeks.

Of course, thinking logically, suppliers will provide us with different price updates. Some of them will increase their prices by 3%, some by 5%, some by 3.5%, some by 4%, ending up with four clusters in this example. Still, we will have to create four update queries and include the specific calculated fields for the updates and specific criteria so that the appropriate supplier products are updated and with the correct percentages.

Furthermore, every time we have price updates, we will need to modify our current update queries, create new ones, modify their criteria, and calculate new prices for the updates. We will end up with an unmanageable number of queries even for this simple scenario. Using conditions, on the other hand, we can do the job very effectively using just one single query!

A final point on conditional statements: Those who understand conditional statements will produce much better database designs and entity relationship diagrams since they know in advance what needs to be stored and what can be produced automatically by the database.

192. Display yes/no instead of checked/unchecked boxes
Discussion:
We start with a simple example to see how we can use the iif() function to display actual text values instead of checkboxes. By default, a yes/no field in Access will display its contents in a query as checkboxes even if you set its format property in the underlying table to yes/no.

Code:
SELECT Productname, ProductUnitPrice, Active
FROM products

Result:

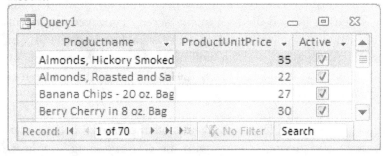

What if we want to see a "yes", "no" value instead? We can achieve this by using the iif() logical function as in the code below. The iif() logical function takes three arguments with the syntax iif (expression, result if expression is true, result if expression is false). The iif() function below reads: If the active field value is -1 then display the text "yes", otherwise display the text "no".

Code:

SELECT Productname, ProductUnitPrice, iif([Active] = -1, "yes", "no") As YN_Active
FROM products

Result:

Productname	ProductUnitPrice	YN_Active
Almonds, Hickory Smoked	35	yes
Almonds, Roasted and Sal	22	yes
Banana Chips - 20 oz. Bag	27	yes
Berry Cherry in 8 oz. Bag	30	yes

Record: 1 of 70 — No Filter — Search

193. Using the iif() and switch() functions with two simple conditions

Produce a product catalog with special discounts for one product only

Discussion:

We received an urgent message from the inventory department saying we have a large quantity of Chocolate Fudge which needs to go out into the market fast. We only have a few hours to produce a new product catalog for this week and send it to our customers. All of the product prices in the catalog should remain the same except for Chocolate Fudge, which will be reduced by 50%. We must not make this percentage change right in the table because this price will be valid only for a week.

Solution 1: using the iif() function

We can solve this problem using an iif() function. The translation of the iif() function in this example says: For the product with productid = 14, change the value of the field ProductUnitPrice by 50%, and for the rest of the products in the catalog, leave the price as is in the table. In addition, notice that a second function is used, cCur(), to display numbers with the dollar sign in front of them. Notice also that we changed the title of the ProductUnitPrice field to appear as "ProductPrice" in this week's catalog. Finally, notice in the result set that the price of Chocolate Fudge is now $20.50 in the query, while it remains $41 in the products table.

Code:

SELECT ProductID, ProductName, QuantityPerUnit,
cCur(iif([productid]=14,[productunitprice]*0.5,[productunitprice])) AS ProductPrice
FROM Products

Result:

ProductID	ProductName	QuantityPerUnit	ProductPrice
14	Chocolate Fudge	28	$20.50
15	Chocolate Blueberries in 10 oz. Bag	28	$24.00
16	Chocolate Almonds in 8 oz. Bag	25	$25.00
17	Dark Chocolate Apricots in 20 oz. Bag	35	$46.00

Record: 1 of 70 No Filter Search

Solution 2: using the switch() function

There is no need to use the switch function in this case since the conditions are very simple. However, I would like to show you its syntax and how it works with respect to an iif() function. In this example, we again used the Ccur() function in front of the switch function to obtain the dollar sign in front of the product prices. There is no doubt that the switch() function is much cleaner and comprehensible than the iif() function. This becomes more evident as the number of conditions goes up.

Code:

SELECT ProductID, ProductName, QuantityPerUnit,
SWITCH(
productid = 14,   productunitprice*0.5,
productid <>14,   productunitprice
)
AS ProductPrice
FROM Products

Result:

ProductID ▾	ProductName ▾	QuantityPerUnit ▾	ProductPrice ▾
1	Almonds, Hickory Smok	12	35
2	Almonds, Roasted and S	12	22
3	Banana Chips - 20 oz. Ba	12	27
4	Berry Cherry in 8 oz. Bag	15	30

Record: ◄ ◄ 1 of 70 ► ►I ►❋ 🔽 No Filter | Search

194. Using the iif() and switch() functions with two conditions but multiple criteria
Provide discounts for customers in NY, TX, and CA only
Discussion:

This time, management initiates a new promotional campaign. They want to offer a 20% discount to customers in large states such as NY, TX, and CA and 10% to everyone else around the country. They want a list of customers and their corresponding discount rates for review.

Solution 1: using the iif() function
Using the iif() function becomes a bit more complicated this time and requires two OR operators. The iif() function translates to: If the customer is in NY, CA, or TX, provide him or her with a discount of 20%. Otherwise, provide the customer with a discount of 10%.

Code:
```
SELECT State, lastname, firstname,  OrderTotal,
IIf([state]= 'NY' Or [state]= 'CA' Or [state]= 'TX',"20%","10%")
AS Discount
FROM Qry_Conditions
```

Result:

State ▾	lastname ▾	firstname ▾	OrderTotal ▾	Discount ▾
NY	Riegert	Joanne	30	20%
DC	Read	Lisa	210	10%
AZ	Moore	Gerald	231	10%
MA	Davis	Catherine	45	10%

Record: ◄ ◄ 1 of 919 ► ►I ► 🔽 No Filter | Search

Solution 2: using the switch() function

The use of the switch function with two conditions and multiple criteria is again more legible than using the iif() function and, therefore, easily editable if we need to update our criteria later on.

Code:

```
SELECT State, lastname, firstname, OrderTotal,
SWITCH(
[state]= 'NY' Or [state]= 'CA' Or [state] = 'TX',       "20%",
[state] <> 'NY' Or 'CA' Or 'TX',                  "10%"
)
AS Discount
FROM Qry_Conditions
```

Result:

State	lastname	firstname	OrderTotal	Discount
NY	Riegert	Joanne	30	20%
DC	Read	Lisa	210	10%
AZ	Moore	Gerald	231	10%
MA	Davis	Catherine	45	10%

Record: 1 of 919   No Filter   Search

195. Working with multiple conditions and criteria

Determine discount amounts based on customer sales volumes

Discussion:

Our sales manager wants to provide order discounts to customers based on their historical sales volume with the company. Thus, if a customer has a certain recorded sales volume, the next time she orders, she will get a predetermined discount rate regardless of her new order amount.

If the total order amount for a customer is less than $200, that customer will receive no discounts. If it is between $200 and $300, the customer will get a 5% discount. If it is between $300 and $500, the customer will get a 10% discount. For anything above that, our manager will offer a generous 25% discount to the customer. Our job is to create a datasheet that will list customers and show the corresponding discount rate for each customer.

Solution 1: using nested iif() functions

Our first option is to use a series of nested iif() functions as shown below—four iif() functions, one inside the other to accomplish our goal. However, the use of nested iif() functions is a convoluted process. In addition, if we need to change the business logic behind our statement by adding additional categories, the task is not a clear and clean preposition. The problem originates from the fact that the iif() function takes only two arguments. For more outcomes or categories, we need to nest, which, in turn, results in complicated statements.

Code:

```
SELECT lastname, firstname, OrderTotal, IIf([ordertotal]<200,0,IIf([ordertotal]>=200
And [Ordertotal]<300,'5%',IIf([ordertotal]>=300 And
[ordertotal]<500,'10%',IIf([ordertotal]>500,'25%')))) AS Discount
FROM Qry_Conditions;
```

Result:

lastname	firstname	OrderTotal	Discount
Riegert	Joanne	30	0
Read	Lisa	210	5%
Moore	Gerald	231	5%
Davis	Catherine	45	0

Record: 1 of 919   No Filter   Search

Solution 2: using the switch() function

In this example, the first observation is that the switch() function does not limit the number of expressions we can use, so we need no nesting. In addition, our logic becomes immediately apparent to us and anyone else who will need to edit the SQL statement later on. The cleanliness of the SQL statement is obvious:

Code:

```
SELECT lastname, firstname, ordertotal,
SWITCH(
ordertotal < 200,                            "0" ,
ordertotal >= 200 and ordertotal < 300,      "5%" ,
ordertotal > 300 and ordertotal <= 500,      "10%" ,
ordertotal > 500 ,                           "25%"
)
AS Discount
FROM qry_conditions
```

Result:

lastname	firstname	OrderTotal	Discount
Riegert	Joanne	30	0
Read	Lisa	210	5%
Moore	Gerald	231	5%
Davis	Catherine	45	0

Query1

Record: 1 of 919 — No Filter — Search

196. An effective trick with the switch() function

Calculate customer discounts based on location

Discussion:

This time, the task is to provide customer discounts in specific states. At the same time, a general discount percentage should be extended to all customers in states not included in the specific state list. We can achieve this task by using the TRUE keyword as part of the last expression in a switch() function. This last expression will evaluate true for every state not included in the specific state list, and we will extend the 10% discount to all of the customers in states different from NY, AZ, CO, FL, and MA.

Code:

```
SELECT State, lastname, firstname,  OrderTotal,
SWITCH(
[state]= 'NY',    "20%",
[state] ='AZ',    "15%",
[state] ='CO',    "12%",
[state] ='FL',    "18%",
[state] ='MA',    "18%",
TRUE,             "10%",
)
AS Discount FROM Qry_Conditions
```

Result:

State	lastname	firstname	OrderTotal	Discount
NY	Riegert	Joanne	30	20%
DC	Read	Lisa	210	10%
AZ	Moore	Gerald	231	15%
MA	Davis	Catherine	45	18%

Record: 1 of 919   No Filter   Search

197. Using switch() with WHERE, IN, and ORDER BY

Calculate discounted order totals based on customer sales volume

Discussion:

Our goal now is to calculate sales totals for specific customer categories. These categories are obtained by calculating customer total order amounts. We only offer discounts to customers with order totals between $200 and $500. No one else receives discounts. In addition, we want to extend these discounts only to customers in AZ, CO, TX, and FL. After the switch function ends, we can absolutely use the WHERE clause with the IN operator to define the exact records for which our calculations will apply.

249

Code:

```
SELECT OrderID, lastname, firstname, State,
SWITCH(
ordertotal>= 200 and ordertotal < 300,    Ordertotal*(1-0.1) ,
ordertotal> 300 and ordertotal <= 500,    OrderTotal*(1-0.15) ,
ordertotal> 500 ,                          OrderTotal*(1-0.2),
TRUE,                                      OrderTotal
)
as DiscountedOrders
FROM qry_conditions
WHERE state in ('AZ', 'CO', 'TX', 'FL')
ORDER BY ordertotal DESC
```

Result:

OrderID	lastname	firstname	State	DiscountedOrders
944	Corelli		TX	459.2
308	Darek	Matthew	CO	409.6
404	Crandil	Joseph	TX	408
932	Weinberger	Fred	FL	386.75

Query1

Record: 1 of 301   No Filter   Search

198. Using switch() with calculated fields

Produce product categories based on product prices

Discussion:

This time, the request we have from management is to provide a product list categorized arbitrarily by price. They want to see a product list that specifies each product as "economical", "moderate", and "expensive" based on its price. Although we carry no such field in the database, we can absolutely create the list in seconds by using a switch() function combined with calculated fields. In essence, we calculate the unit price times its quantity per unit to get the total price we pay, and we then assign categories based on price. For instance, if the price falls between $500 and $1000, we designate these products as "moderately" priced. We can save this query and update it at will if management wants more, less, or otherwise defined categories.

Code:

```
SELECT ProductName, UnitsInStock, UnitsOnOrder,
SWITCH(
ProductUnitPrice*QuantityPerUnit < 500,    "Economical",
ProductUnitPrice*QuantityPerUnit >= 500 AND
ProductUnitPrice*QuantityPerUnit<1000,     "Moderate",
ProductUnitPrice*QuantityPerUnit >= 1000,  "Expensive",
)
as PricingCategory
FROM Products
ORDER BY  ProductUnitPrice*QuantityPerUnit DESC
```

Result:

ProductName	UnitsInStock	UnitsOnOrder	PricingCategory
Chocolate Chunk C	15	20	Expensive
Dark Chocolate Ap	38	0	Expensive
Buttermilk Muffins	31	0	Expensive
Coffee biscuits	24	0	Expensive

Record: 1 of 70   No Filter   Search

199. Using switch() with aggregate functions

Calculate employee commissions and bonuses based on their sales volume

Discussion:

There are multiple tasks in this example. First, we need to calculate employee commissions as a percentage of their sales. Second, we need to calculate employee bonuses based again on sales volumes. Third, we need to add commission and bonus amounts. Fourth, we need to make these calculations only for 2012. Fifth, we need to present the results as currency.

Do not be intimidated by the long SQL statement. It is long but not as tough as it looks. In two minutes, you will have a total grasp of it. First, notice we use only three fields in this SQL statement: lastname, orderdate, and CommissionAndBonus. We use the lastname field as is. For the orderdate field, we use the function year() to extract the year part of the date. The CommissionAndBonus field will be the result of the switch function calculations.

Next, notice that we use three functions, sum(), Ccur(), and switch(), one after the other. We use the sum() function to obtain the total order amounts sold by our salesperson. Since we do not have a field for order totals in the database (correctly, since we can calculate them), we need to multiply the quantity of each product sold by its price in every order and sum() the results. Then, we use the Ccur() function to convert the data type of the CommissionAndBonus field to appear as currency. Finally, we use the switch function to assign commissions and bonuses according to sales volumes.

Next, we have a FROM statement but do not pay attention to the joins since Access will create the joins automatically when we paste this code in a query and look at its design. We devote a whole chapter on joins (chapter 30).

In the final part of the SQL statement, we group by employee and year since we need to have commissions and bonuses shown by employee. We filter the year by using the HAVING clause as we examined in our "GROUP BY" chapter.

In the end, the whole query is reduced to three fields: lastname and year by which we group by and the commissionandbonus field on which we apply the sum() aggregate function.

Code:
SELECT LastName, Year([OrderDate]) AS [Year],

```
SUM(CCur(SWITCH(
([UnitPrice]*[quantity]) < 5000,        ([UnitPrice]*[quantity])*(0.1) + 500 ,
([UnitPrice]*[quantity]) >= 5000 and  ([UnitPrice]*[quantity]) <10000,
([UnitPrice]*[quantity])*(0.15) + 1000,
([UnitPrice]*[quantity]) >= 10000 and  ([UnitPrice]*[quantity]) <15000,
([UnitPrice]*[quantity])*(0.2) + 3000,
([UnitPrice]*[quantity]) >= 15000 ,     ([UnitPrice]*[quantity])*(0.25) + 5000,
)))
as CommissionAndBonus
```

FROM SalesReps INNER JOIN (Orders INNER JOIN ProductsOrders ON Orders.OrderID = ProductsOrders.OrderID) ON SalesReps.SalesRepID = Orders.SalesRepID

```
GROUP BY LastName, Year([OrderDate])
HAVING (((Year([OrderDate]))=2012))
ORDER BY Sum([UnitPrice]*[quantity]) DESC
```

Result:

LastName	Year	CommissionAndBonus
Zensons	2012	$47,092.40
Spicer	2012	$46,563.40
Anderson	2012	$39,988.80
Baker	2012	$44,976.60

Record: I◄ ◄ 1 of 10 ► ►I ► | No Filter | Search

200. Using partition() for data visualization
Calculate sales volume intervals and count orders included
Discussion:
What if we encounter a request for a visualization of the distribution of our orders? For example, we would want to know how many orders fall between 0 and $50, how many

between $50 and $100, how many between $100 and $150, etc. We can provide an answer using the partition() function.

The partition() function has the syntax:

$$\text{Partition(field, beginning number, ending number, interval)}$$

For instance, if we want to categorize orders in $50 increments starting at $0 and ending at $500, we can write: Partition(ordertotal, 0, 500, 50).

In this example, we use two fields: "Range" and "Count". Both of these fields are calculated fields. The contents of the Range field are produced by the partition function, and the contents of the Count field are produced by counting the number of orders in each partition according to their order total amount. We can change the parameters of the partition function at will to produce any intervals we want.

A fact to keep in mind about the partition function is that in this example, we defined the boundaries between $0 and $500 with intervals of $50. This does not mean that the partition function will stop at $500. It will stop producing intervals at $500, and from $501 and above, it will put all remaining orders in the same category. We will still know how many orders we have above $501.

Code:
```
SELECT DISTINCTROW Partition([ordertotal],0, 500, 50) AS Range,
Count(ordertotal) AS Count
FROM Qry_Conditions
GROUP BY Partition([ordertotal],0, 500, 50)
```

Result:

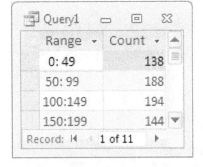

201. Using switch() with update queries

Update multiple product prices from multiple suppliers conditionally

Discussion:

Now, this is an occasion where a switch() function will show its true and unique power. When we combine it with update statements, we can produce highly effective updates that otherwise would have required multiple update queries to obtain.

In this example, we want to update 70 products from ten suppliers, and for each supplier, we apply different update percentages. Those percentages start from 2% all the way up to 11%, as you can see from the SQL code below. By combining the switch() function with the UPDATE statement, we can do everything in one single query. We can save this query and use it every time we need to update our prices. Even if we do not receive price updates for one or some of the suppliers, we can leave the query as is and simply do not use any percentage updates for that supplier. We can just write: ProductUnitPrice = ProductUnitPrice.

Code:

```
UPDATE tbls_Products_Upd
SET ProductUnitPrice =
SWITCH (
supplierid=1,     ProductUnitPrice*(1.1) ,
supplierid=2,     ProductUnitPrice*(1.08),
supplierid=3,     ProductUnitPrice*(1.07) ,
supplierid=4,     ProductUnitPrice*(1.05) ,
supplierid=5,     ProductUnitPrice*(1.03) ,
supplierid=6,     ProductUnitPrice*(1.02) ,
supplierid=7,     ProductUnitPrice*(1.03) ,
supplierid=8,     ProductUnitPrice*(1.07) ,
supplierid=9,     ProductUnitPrice*(1.11) ,
supplierid=10,    ProductUnitPrice*(1.08) ,
)
```

Result:

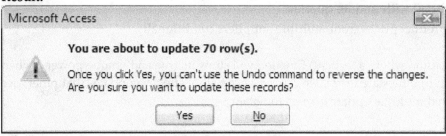

202.   Using switch() with crosstab queries

Create a crosstab query that calculates order totals for "big" and "small" cities

Discussion:

This time, we have a request from management to calculate sales volumes by year and, at the same time, categorize results by small and big cities in the country. They told us specifically that they want to see combined sales volumes for big cities like New York and Los Angeles and combined sales volumes for every other city in which we do business. This is an excellent occasion to combine the power of the switch function with the flexibility of crosstab queries. Instead of pivoting by the city field as we did in the crosstab queries chapter, we use the switch function right in the PIVOT statement to create city categories of our own imagination and creativity.

Code:

```
TRANSFORM Sum([unitprice]*[quantity]) AS Ordertotal
SELECT Year([OrderDate]) As Year
FROM Qry_Crosstab_Base
GROUP BY Year([OrderDate])
PIVOT
SWITCH(
[CustomerCity]= 'New York' Or [CustomerCity]= 'Los Angeles' ,        "BigCities",
[CustomerCity] <> 'New York' Or 'Los Angeles',              "SmallCities"
)
```

Result:

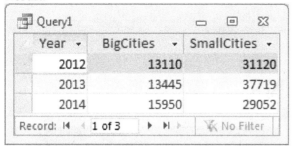

CHAPTER 22
UNION OPERATIONS

The primary goal of the UNION statement is to combine records from multiple data sets. In this respect, you can merge records from two or more SQL statements, from a SQL statement and a table, or from two or more tables. In contrast to popular belief, you can combine records with fields of different data types and sizes in Access 2010. In addition, the fields do not have to be similar in content or name! The number of fields, however, does need to be the same. The UNION operator will return no duplicate records, while the UNION ALL operator will return all records from the combined data sets.

The UNION operator is not just a dull SQL statement that we use to combine records from multiple tables. You will see throughout this chapter that you can combine it with clauses like WHERE, ORDER BY, and GROUP BY, operators like IN, NOT IN, and BETWEEN, and even subqueries for powerful results. Understanding the UNION operator will enable you to perform operations and achieve results that other database users could not even imagine possible.

In this chapter, we will work with two customer tables under the assumption that we have two distribution centers with one as our main center and the other as a regional center. For the most part, customers order from one of the two distribution centers. However, just to complicate our scenario a bit, we do have customers who will order from both. Consequently, we need to pay attention to how customer records are merged in order to exclude duplicate ones.

We will use two tables: The customers table with 201 records and the tbls_customers_un table with 20 records. Fifteen of the customers in the tbls_customers_un table are identical to the customers table, while five are different. The similarities or dissimilarities of data among tables are important for UNION statements, as we shall see in a second.

203. The UNION operator with similar fields

Combine unique customer records from two datasets

Discussion:

In this example, we use a simple UNION statement to combine customer records from the two distribution centers. Notice that the number of customers returned is 206. This is because we combined 201 customers from the first table and 20 from the second. Since 15 customers are identical in both tables, and we use the UNION operator, we will only get 206 unique customers. If we used the UNION ALL operator, we would get 221 records.

Code:

```
SELECT lastname, firstname, city, state, zip
FROM customers
UNION
SELECT lastname, firstname, city, state, zip
FROM tbls_customers_un
```

Result:

204. The UNION operator with dissimilar fields

Combine customer and supplier records from two different tables

Discussion:

Here, we demonstrate the ability of the UNION statement to combine data from two dissimilar tables. Notice the different field names from the customer and supplier tables. In addition, check the numbers. We get all of the customers from the customers table (201) and all of the suppliers (10) from the suppliers table.

Code:

SELECT lastname, firstname, city, state, zip

FROM customers

UNION

SELECT companyname, contactname, city, state, zip

FROM suppliers

Result:

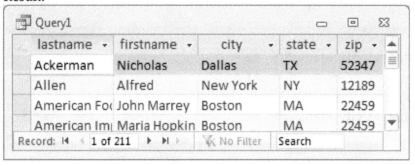

205. The UNION operator with tables and SQL statements

Combine all customer records from a table and some from a SQL statement

Discussion:

In this example, we will combine all of the records from the customers table with some of the records from the tbls_customers_un table. Essentially, we merge a table and a SQL statement. Notice the absence of a SELECT statement for the customers table and the use of the WHERE clause in the code below:

Code:

TABLE [customers]

UNION

SELECT *

FROM tbls_customers_un

WHERE state='TX'

Result:

CustomerID ▾	FirstName ▾	LastName ▾	Address ▾
1	John	Demarco	11 Lark Street
2	Mary	Demania	12 Madison Av
3	George	Demers	23 New Scotlan
4	Phillip	Demetriou	22 Academy Rc

Record: 1 of 208 · No Filter · Search

206. Using multiple UNION operators

Combine records from two customer tables and a supplier table

Discussion:

We can use UNION to merge records from multiple data sources. In this example, we employ two UNION statements to merge data from three data sources. Notice that while the first two SELECT statements contain identical fields, the third one uses different ones. Also, we must pay attention to our numbers. The first table (customers) contains 201 records, the second (tbls_customers_un) 20, and the third (suppliers) 10. We have a total of 231 records, but our result set contains only 216. This is correct since we have 15 identical customers. Consequently, the final result is 231-15 = 216 records.

Code:
```
SELECT lastname, firstname, city, state, zip
FROM customers
UNION
SELECT lastname, firstname, city, state, zip
FROM tbls_customers_un
UNION
SELECT companyname, contactname, city, state, zip
FROM suppliers
```

Result:

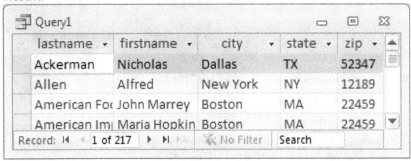

207.   The UNION ALL operator

Combine customer records from two data sources and allow duplicates to appear

Discussion:

The UNION operator will exclude duplicate records. Suppose we want to combine two lists, but we also want to include duplicates. For this purpose, we need to use the UNION ALL operator. Have a look at the number of records returned. In this case, it should be 201 + 20 for a total of 221, and this is exactly what we get. (Remember we have 201 records in the customer table and 20 in the tbls_customers_un).

Code:

```
SELECT lastname, firstname, city, state, zip
FROM customers
UNION ALL
SELECT lastname, firstname, city, state, zip
FROM tbls_customers_un
```

Result:

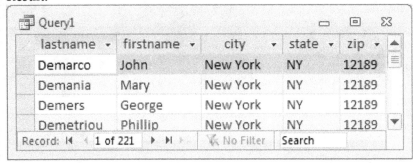

208. Using UNION with ORDER BY

Sort customer records correctly when using UNION

Discussion:

The ORDER BY clause should be used at the end of the whole SQL statement when using UNION operators, not after the individual SQL statements.

Code:

```
SELECT lastname, firstname, city, state, zip
FROM customers
UNION
SELECT lastname, firstname, city, state, zip
FROM tbls_customers_un
ORDER BY lastname
```

Result:

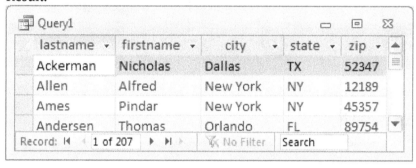

209. Using UNION with WHERE

Create customer lists with filtering criteria using WHERE

Discussion:

In this example, notice the use of the WHERE clause in each individual SELECT statement. We can absolutely use multiple WHERE clauses to get exactly what we need from the individual data sets. In this example, we wanted to get only customers from New York from the first and customers from Texas from the second.

Code:

SELECT lastname, firstname, city, state, zip
FROM customers
WHERE state = 'NY'
UNION
SELECT lastname, firstname, city, state, zip
FROM tbls_customers_un
WHERE state ='TX'
ORDER BY state

Result:

lastname	firstname	city	state	zip
Allen	Alfred	New York	NY	12189
Ames	Pindar	New York	NY	45357
Anderson	Peter	New York	NY	12189
Anthopolis	Ricky	New York	NY	12189

Record: 1 of 38   No Filter   Search

210. Using UNION with IN and NOT IN

Create customer lists with filtering criteria using IN and NOT IN

Discussion:

We can perform detailed filtering using the WHERE clause and the IN or NOT IN operators within each individual SELECT statement in this UNION operation. Notice we can apply criteria with different operators on different fields. We might have used the WHERE clause with the AND operator in the first SELECT and the IN operator in the second. In addition, we could have applied some criteria on the city field in the first SELECT and some criteria on the state field in the second.

Code:

SELECT lastname, firstname, city, state, zip

FROM customers

WHERE city IN('New York', 'Los Angeles')

UNION

SELECT lastname, firstname, city, state, zip

FROM tbls_customers_un

WHERE city IN('Dallas', 'Miami', 'Orlando', 'Ontario')

ORDER BY lastname

Result:

lastname	firstname	city	state	zip
Ackerman	Nicholas	Dallas	TX	52347
Allen	Alfred	New York	NY	12189
Ames	Pindar	New York	NY	45357
Andersen	Thomas	Orlando	FL	89754

Record: 1 of 68   No Filter   Search

211. Using UNION with BETWEEN

Find customers in a certain zip code range who ordered from multiple distribution centers

Discussion:

We can use the BETWEEN clause to filter results in UNION statements. As soon as we satisfy the basic requirements of a UNION statement, we can filter records as we please using any filtering clauses such as LIKE, "=", or BETWEEN. Notice in this example that we must use the cLng() number conversion function (chapter 25) to convert zip codes to numbers since in the original table, they are stored as text. Otherwise, the BETWEEN operator will not work since it cannot find text ranges. We can use any conversion functions we want with no problems in UNION statements.

265

Code:

```
SELECT lastname, firstname, city, state, zip
FROM customers
WHERE cLng(zip) BETWEEN 12000 AND 12999
UNION
SELECT lastname, firstname, city, state, zip
FROM tbls_customers_un
WHERE cLng(zip) BETWEEN 12000 AND 12999
ORDER BY lastname
```

Result:

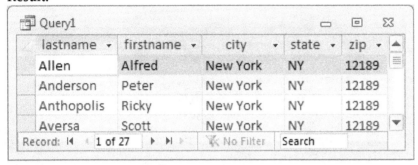

212. A trick with UNION and the aggregate function count()

Display total customer numbers dynamically

Discussion:

Here, we use a trick to display all of the customer records from the customers table and a total row at the end of the recordset. We can do this by using a single SQL statement and UNION. Notice in the second SQL statement we use quotes instead of fields to satisfy the UNION requirement of same field numbers in both statements. In addition, notice that we start the name of the first field of the second SQL statement with a "z", which has no other meaning but to force the total row to appear last in the recordset. Finally, for our trick to succeed, we need to use the ORDER BY clause on the first field of the first SQL statement.

Code:
```
SELECT lastname, firstname, city, state, zip, CustomerID
FROM customers
UNION
SELECT
'zTotal customer count', '', '', '', '', Count(CustomerID)
FROM customers
ORDER BY lastname ASC
```

Result:

lastname ▾	firstname ▾	city ▾	state ▾	zip ▾
Ackerman	Nicholas	Dallas	TX	52347
Allen	Alfred	New York	NY	12189
Ames	Pindar	New York	NY	45357
Andersen	Thomas	Orlando	FL	89754

Record: I◄ ◄ 1 of 202 ► ►I ▸   No Filter   Search

213. Using UNION with SELECT INTO

Combine customer data from multiple tables and save the combined dataset dynamically in a different table

Discussion:

This is a useful trick to get data from multiple data sources and save it in a different table. We can use SELECT INTO to pull this off, but we must pay attention! The first SQL statement may naturally come to mind, but it will not work. We need to use a subquery (chapter 31) as can be seen in the second SQL statement. Pay attention to the number of records. It has to be 206 (201 from the first table and 5 from the second) since we are asking for unique records to be moved. If we want to move everything, we can use UNION ALL.

Code: (Will not work)
```
SELECT lastname, firstname, city, state, zip INTO UnionTable
FROM customers
UNION
SELECT lastname, firstname, city, state, zip
FROM tbls_customers_un
```

Code: (Will work)

SELECT lastname, firstname, city, state, zip INTO tempTable

FROM

(SELECT lastname, firstname, city, state, zip

FROM customers

UNION

SELECT lastname, firstname, city, state, zip

FROM tbls_customers_un

)

Result:

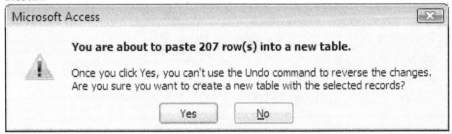

214.   Using UNION with INSERT INTO

Combine records from multiple data sources, filter them, and append them into an existing table

Discussion:

There are occasions in which we need to combine data from multiple tables and append it in an existing table. We can use INSERT INTO and UNION to accomplish these tasks. The table "tempTable_un" used in this example needs to exist before we run the SQL statement. Also, notice the use of the WHERE clause through which we can transfer the records we want.

Code:
INSERT INTO tempTable_un (lastname, firstname, city, state, zip)
SELECT lastname, firstname, city, state, zip
FROM
(SELECT lastname, firstname, city, state, zip
FROM customers
WHERE state = 'NY'
UNION
SELECT lastname, firstname, city, state, zip
FROM tbls_customers_un
WHERE state = 'NY'
)

Result:

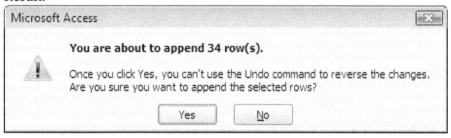

215. Using UNION with GROUP BY within each SELECT statement

Combine customer data from all distribution centers, count the totals, and show in the query the center they came from

Discussion:

Here, we use a number of tricks and functions to arrive at the result we need. First, notice we use a GROUP BY clause in both SQL statements in the query. Second, we use the count() function to get the number of customers by state. Third, we create a field of our own ("Main" and "Regional) in the beginning of each of the two SQL statements to display customer numbers according to distribution center. Finally, we use the ORDER BY clause to present results by state for easy comparison of numbers.

Code:
SELECT "Main" As DisCenter, state, count(CustomerID) AS Customers
FROM customers
GROUP BY state
UNION
SELECT "Regional" As Center, state, Count(CustomerID) AS Customers
FROM tbls_customers_un
GROUP BY state
ORDER BY STATE

Result:

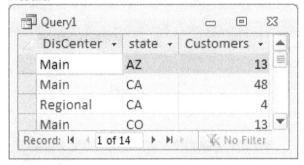

DisCenter	state	Customers
Main	AZ	13
Main	CA	48
Regional	CA	4
Main	CO	13

Record: ◄ ◄ 1 of 14 ► ►► ◌ No Filter

216. Using UNION with GROUP BY outside each SELECT statement

Combine customer data from all distribution centers, count the totals, and group results by state

Discussion:

In this example, the GROUP BY clause produces combined results from each state regardless of distribution center. Unlike what we did in the previous example, we first combine the data and then, use the GROUP BY clause. Notice the use of the subquery with the UNION operator that enables us to GROUP results from the two data sets.

Code:
SELECT state, count(customerid) as Customers
FROM

(SELECT state, CustomerID
FROM customers
UNION
SELECT state, CustomerID
FROM tbls_customers_un
)

GROUP BY state
ORDER BY STATE

Result:

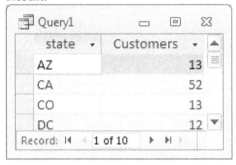

217. Using UNION with two subqueries to filter records for aggregations

Compare customer data from two tables only for states existing in both tables

Discussion:

Our goal this time is to compare customer numbers from both distribution centers, but we only want to see states from the "Main" center for which a corresponding state exists in the "regional" center. We need a subquery in the first SELECT statement to achieve the desired output. The subquery in the first SELECT statement will search for matching records in the table in the second SELECT statement.

Code:

```
SELECT "Main" As DisCenter, state, count(CustomerID) AS Customers
FROM customers
WHERE State in (SELECT state from tbls_customers_un)
GROUP BY state
UNION
SELECT "Regional" As Center, state, Count(CustomerID) AS Customers
FROM tbls_customers_un
GROUP BY state
ORDER BY STATE
```

Result:

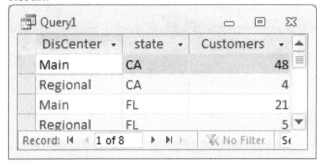

218. Trick for knowing which table the row came from when using UNION

Discussion:

In certain occasions with UNION operators it is useful to know the source table for each record in the result set. In this example, we combine data from the suppliers and customers table but we want to know who is a customer and who is a supplier. To achieve this we simply add a text entry in each of the SQL statements used with the UNION operator.

Code:

```
SELECT lastname, firstname, city, state, zip, "customer" AS TypeOfContact
FROM customers
UNION
SELECT companyname, contactname, city, state, zip, "supplier"
FROM suppliers
```

Result:

CHAPTER 23
DUPLICATE, ORPHANED, and UNRELATED RECORDS

This chapter focuses on four specific learning goals: The identification of duplicate, orphaned, related, and unrelated records. Orphaned and duplicate records will affect your database integrity, while related and unrelated records will affect your business decisions.

Orphaned records occur when there are no primary key values for corresponding foreign key values in a one-to-many relationship. For example, in a relationship between customers and orders, you might have orders without corresponding customers. This scenario can occur if referential integrity for this relationship is off (chapter 4). This will allow a user to delete a customer without any warning that there are existing orders for this customer. Alternatively, it might allow a user to enter an order without first entering a customer.

We need to have referential integrity on in order to avoid the occurrence of orphaned records. Yet, what happens when we already have orphaned records in the database? There are two solutions with orphaned records. The first is to delete orphaned records from the database. However, to eliminate orphaned records, we first need to find them. In this chapter, there will be plenty of examples to locate orphaned records.

The second solution is to keep orphaned records such as orders in the database, but in this case, we need to enter their corresponding customer information. In any case, we must be able to retrieve orphaned records.

A second common occurrence in business databases is duplicate records. In this chapter, you will learn several techniques to isolate and deal with duplicate records, which are not, by the way, synonymous with identical records. Two customer records might be duplicates even if they have the same name but different address information. So, you will learn how to find duplicate records based on the values of one, two, or multiple fields.

A third case involves unrelated records. For example, we might have customers in the database who have not placed an order for quite some time. These customers have no relations in the orders table. This is a business and not a database problem. However, we need to act, and we have two choices for inactive customers. The first is to use a marketing campaign to entice them to start buying again. If this is not feasible, we might want to delete them from the database or move them to a historical customer table. To delete or move these records, we need to be able to find them first.

The fourth scenario is related records. We might want to know how many customers placed orders over a period of a year, month, or quarter. In other words, we want to know how many customers have related order entries in the orders table. In this chapter, you will learn how to quickly identify these customers to increase the effectiveness of your business operations.

Finally, so that you can check your numbers, you will use the table named tbls_orders, which contains a number of orphaned and duplicate records. Specifically, the records with OrderID = 8, 45, 254, 820, 993 are duplicate records. In addition, there are two records with null OrderIDs, which I put in to make our work a bit more complicated.

SECTION 1 – DUPLICATE RECORDS

219. Find duplicate records in a table based on the values of one field
Find duplicate customer orders based on the value of the orderID
Discussion:
In this example, we are looking for records in the tbls_Orders table that have the same value for the OrderID field. In addition, we use the count(*) function to calculate the number of instances of duplicate records. We can use the code below to look for duplicate values for any field. We will just replace the OrderID field with the field on which we want to search for duplicate values. Remember that this example will give us duplicate field values and not necessarily duplicate records. Though the OrderID values are the same, the rest of the fields in the returned records might have different values. Still, it is very useful to know how to search for duplicate values on one field. As you can see from the result set, two records have null values for the blank OrderID. In addition, there are two instances of duplicate records for OrderIDs with values 8, 45, 254, and 820. Finally, the OrderId with value 993 appears in three records in the table.

Code:
SELECT OrderID, Count(*) AS NumberofDuplicates
FROM tbls_Orders
GROUP BY OrderID
HAVING count(*)>1

Result:

OrderID	NumberofDuplicate
	2
8	2
45	2
254	2
820	2
993	3

Record: I◄ ◄ 1 of 6 ► ►I No Fil

220. Find duplicate records in a table based on the values of two fields

Find duplicate customer orders based on the values of OrderID and CustomerID

Discussion:

In this example, we are looking for duplicate records based on the values of OrderID and CustomerID. If the values of the OrderID and CustomerID are the same for at least two records, they will appear in the result set as duplicates. In addition, the count(*) function is used to calculate the number of records with identical OrderID and CustomerID values. We can replace the two fields used in this example with any fields on which we would like to look for duplicate values. Keep in mind that while two records might have matching values for two fields, this does not necessarily mean that they have identical values for the rest of their fields. This code will allow us to locate potential duplicate records based on the values of two fields. We need to examine the individual records to verify that they are indeed duplicates.

Code:

```
SELECT OrderID, CustomerID, Count(*) AS NumberofDuplicates
FROM tbls_Orders
GROUP BY OrderID, CustomerID
HAVING count(*)>1
```

Result:

OrderID	CustomerID	NumberofDuplicates
8	71	2
45	93	2
254	198	2
820	46	2

Record: 1 of 5 — No Filter — Search

221. Find duplicate records in a table based on the values of multiple fields

Find duplicate customer orders based on the values of multiple fields

Discussion:

In this example, we are looking for duplicate records based on the values of eight fields. In other words, if the values of eight fields of at least two records are identical, those records will appear as duplicates. Of course, with eight identical values, two records will most probably be duplicate entries. Notice that there are two identical records for each OrderID with values 8, 45, 254, and 820, while there are three identical records with OrderID = 993.

Code:

```
SELECT Count(*) AS NumberofDuplicates, OrderID, CustomerID, SalesRepID,
ShipperID, OrderDate, RequiredDate, ShippedDate, ShippingCost

FROM tbls_Orders

GROUP BY OrderID, CustomerID, SalesRepID, ShipperID, OrderDate, RequiredDate,
ShippedDate, ShippingCost
HAVING count(*)>1
```

Result:

NumberofDuplicates	OrderID	CustomerID	SalesRepID	ShipperID
2	8	71	3	1
2	45	93	1	3
2	254	198	3	2
2	820	46	8	1

Record: 1 of 5 — No Filter — Search

222.   Find and display all duplicate records in a table

Find and display all duplicate records in the Orders table

Discussion:

In the previous examples, we were able to find duplicate records in the table but display only one instance from each in the result set. There are cases, however, in which we will want to display all instances from all duplicate records. We can achieve this goal by using a subquery. In this example, we will display all instances of all duplicate records based on the values of the OrderID field, or put another way, based on the values of one field.

Code:

```
SELECT *
FROM tbls_Orders WHERE OrderID IN(
SELECT OrderID
FROM tbls_Orders
GROUP BY OrderID
HAVING count(*)>1)
ORDER BY OrderID
```

Result:

OrderID	CustomerID	SalesRepID	ShipperID	OrderDate
8	71	3	1	4/1/2014
8	71	3	1	4/1/2014
45	93	1	3	10/23/2012
45	93	1	3	10/23/2012
254	198	3	2	7/15/2012
254	198	3	2	7/15/2012
820	46	8	1	9/4/2014
820	46	8	1	9/4/2014
993	99	10	2	10/14/2012
993	99	10	2	10/14/2012
993	99	10	2	10/14/2012

Query1

Record: 1 of 11   No Filter   Search

SECTION 2 – ORPHANED RECORDS

223.   What are orphaned records and how to deal with them

In the figure below, there are five orders in the Orders table with OrderIDs from 1 to 5. For the first four orders, there are corresponding customers in the Customers table. For orders with OrderID=5, there does not exist a corresponding customer in the database. This is an order that belongs to no one. The record in the Orders table with OrderID=5 is called an orphaned record.

CUSTOMERS		ORDERS		
CustID	Name	OrderID	CustID	OrderDate
1	John	1	2	9/10/2009
2	Mary	2	2	10/10/2010
3	George	3	1	11/10/2010
4	Stacy	4	3	11/11/2010
		5	7	11/15/2010

A reason for this might be that when the database was created and relationships established, referential integrity was not turned on. The immediate consequence is that a user of the database deleted the customer with CustomerID=7 either by mistake or on purpose. Although the customer record is gone, his or her orders are still in the database, useless and compromising data integrity. Another reason might be that a user received an order from a new customer. The correct process would have been to check if the customer existed and then enter the order. If referential integrity is off a representative can enter an order without an existing customer. To avoid orphaned records, referential integrity should be turned on for a relationship between two tables.

224.   Find orphaned records using a subquery

Find orders for which there are no customers using a subquery
Discussion:

Let us assume that we want to turn on referential integrity for the relationship between the Customers and Orders tables (chapter 4). If Access 2010 does not allow us to do this, our first action should be to look for orphaned records in the Orders table or in the table in general in the many side of the relationship. We can use the code below to do just that. In this example, we use the tbls_Orders table since in the original Orders table, there are no orphaned records. As you can see in the result set, there are three orders (OrderID= 1500, 1501, and 1502) that came up as orphaned records. This in turn means that the customers with CustomerID values of 250, 251, and 252 do not exist in the Customers table. If we open the customers table, we will not find any customers with these CustomerID values.

Code:
SELECT *
FROM tbls_Orders
WHERE CustomerID
NOT IN (SELECT CustomerID from Customers)

Result:

OrderID	CustomerID	SalesRepID	ShipperID	OrderDate
1500	250	11	2	1/20/2012
1501	251	12	2	11/18/2012
1502	252	14	3	2/5/2013

Record: 1 of 3 — No Filter — Search

225. Find orphaned records using a join

Find orders for which there are no customers using a join

Discussion:

There is a second and faster way to locate orphaned records in a table. Specifically, we can use a LEFT join (chapter 30) between Customers and tbls_Orders to locate any orphaned records in the tbls_Orders table. As you can see, the result set is identical to the one using a subquery in the previous example.

Code:
SELECT *
FROM tbls_Orders
LEFT JOIN Customers ON tbls_Orders.[CustomerID] = Customers.[CustomerID]
WHERE ((((Customers.CustomerID) Is Null));

Result:

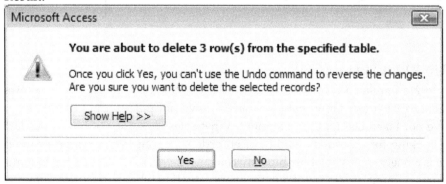

226. Delete orphaned records using a subquery

Delete orders for which there are no customers using a subquery

Discussion:

We can use a subquery to find and delete orphaned records in one step. In the code below, we use the DELETE statement to delete orders in the tbls_Orders table for which there are no customers in the customers table. The subquery will isolate CustomerID values in the tbls_Orders table for which there are no corresponding CustomerID values in the Customers table. Notice that the CustomerID is the primary key in the Customers table and the foreign key in the tbls_Orders table.

Code:

```
DELETE
FROM tbls_Orders
WHERE CustomerID
NOT IN (SELECT CustomerID FROM Customers)
```

Result:

Microsoft Access

You are about to delete 3 row(s) from the specified table.

Once you click Yes, you can't use the Undo command to reverse the changes. Are you sure you want to delete the selected records?

Show Help >>

Yes   No

227.   Delete orphaned records using a join

Delete orders for which there are no customers using a join

Discussion:

We can also use a LEFT join to isolate and delete orphaned records in the tbls_Orders table. Notice the WHERE clause in the code below which looks for CustomerID values in the LEFT JOIN with a null value, i.e. CustomerID or foreign key values in the tbls_Orders table for which no primary key values exist in the customers table. Joins work faster than subqueries especially on indexed fields, and while they are more complicated, their use might well be justified in cases with many records. However, this does not mean that a join will always be faster than a subquery. The bottom line is that we have the option to isolate and delete orphaned records using joins.

Code:

```
DELETE  tbls_Orders.*
FROM tbls_Orders
LEFT JOIN Customers ON tbls_Orders.[CustomerID] = Customers.[CustomerID]
WHERE ((((Customers.CustomerID) Is Null))
```

Result:

SECTION 3 – UNRELATED RECORDS

The knowledge to locate unrelated records is fundamental in database applications. It allows us to reply to questions such as: How many customers have not placed any orders? How many students have not taken classes this semester? What sales reps did not have sales last week? So, we are looking for customers who have no orders (maybe over a period of time) knowing that there is a one-to-many relationship between customers and orders. Keep in mind that finding customers without orders is not a problematic situation when it comes to database integrity; it is simply a business fact. However, finding orders without customers represents a database integrity problem, and we call these orphaned records.

228. Find unrelated records using a subquery

Find customers for whom there are no orders using a subquery

Discussion:

In this example, we use a subquery with the NOT IN operator to find customers who do not have any orders. We are looking for records in the customers table that have no related records in the Orders table. In other words, we are looking for CustomerID values (1, 2, 3 etc.) in the Customers table, which do not exist in the Orders table. Put it yet in another way, we are looking for primary key values (CustomerID) in the customers table with no corresponding foreign key values (CustomerIDs) in the Orders table. The code appears below:

Code:

```
SELECT *
FROM Customers
WHERE CustomerID
NOT IN (SELECT CustomerID from tbls_Orders)
```

Result:

229. Find unrelated records using a subquery and criteria

Find customers for whom there are no orders using date criteria

Discussion:

In the previous example, you learned how to identify customers without orders for all sales years in the database. This is excellent knowledge, but in actual business practice, you will need some additional criteria to derive insightful pieces of information. For example, we might want to know what customers have not placed any orders in the last year, quarter, month, or even week. Alternatively, we might want to know what customers from NY have not placed any orders in the last two months. It is possible to use criteria to extract these amazing pieces of information fast and efficiently. In this example, we are looking for customers who have not placed any orders in 2012. As you can see from the result set, we have 49 such customers. Of course, we can use the vast arsenal of date functions in the upcoming chapter 27 to extract any period we feel we need to look into.

Code:
```
SELECT *
FROM Customers
WHERE CustomerID NOT IN
(SELECT CustomerID
FROM tbls_Orders
WHERE OrderDate BETWEEN #1/1/2012# AND #12/31/2012#)
```

Result:

CustomerID	FirstName	LastName	Address
10	Matthew	Demaria	90 Park Ave
15	Pindar	Ames	23 Cornell Dr
19	Erin	Erin	28 Karrie Terrace
24	Roy	Sars	65 Sunset Terrace

Record: 1 of 49   No Filter   Search

SECTION 4 – RELATED RECORDS

230. Find related records using a subquery
Find customers who placed orders
Discussion:
There will be occasions in your work in which you will need to find related records. In other words, you might want to find customers who placed orders, suppliers who sent raw materials, or products that sold some units. We can achieve this task by using a subquery. In this example, we are looking for customers who placed orders, such as which of the 201 customers in the customers table actually placed orders. Since we know from previous examples that out of the 201 customers, 11 never placed any orders, we would expect to retrieve 190 records. This is exactly the result from the following code. Remember that we can add additional criteria to identify customers who placed orders in certain periods such as years, quarters, or months, as we will see in the next example.

Code:
```
SELECT *
FROM Customers
WHERE CustomerID
IN (SELECT CustomerID from tbls_Orders)
```

Result:

231.   Find related records using a subquery and criteria

Find customers who placed orders during the 4th quarter of 2012

Discussion:

In this scenario, we are looking for customers who placed orders in the 4th quarter of 2012. Notice that we use two date functions, datepart() and year(), to extract the quarter and year out of the OrderDate field respectively. Using the subquery and the two date functions, we are able to extract exactly the information we need about our customers. This list of customers can definitely help in our marketing and promotional campaigns, and we can retrieve it in seconds.

Code:
```
SELECT *
FROM Customers
WHERE CustomerID
IN (SELECT CustomerID from tbls_Orders WHERE
DatePart("q",[OrderDate]) = 4 AND  year(OrderDate) = 2012)
```

Result:

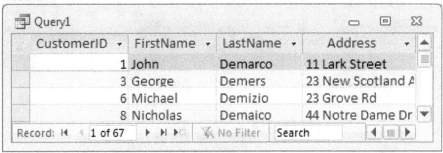

CHAPTER 24
WORKING WITH NULLS

There are three concepts you need in order to understand null values in full: First, a zero (0) value is not a null value. It means that there is a value, and it is zero. Second, a zero-length string, also called an empty string, is not a null value. It means that there should be a value, but there is none. In Access 2010 we can designate an empty string value by typing two double quotation marks with no space between them (""). Third, a null value means that we do not know whether there should be a value or not.

Zero-length strings and null values appear as empty cells in Access 2010. We have no way of distinguishing which cell actually has a null value and which one has an empty string in it; they both appear empty. Do not be concerned about this because in our examples, we will see how to take care of this situation. The best way to avoid tricky and problematical situations with nulls and zero-length values is to avoid them altogether. When designing a new database, we can assign default values to fields that users might leave blank. For example, for a customer middle name, we can set a default value of "NA" when none is entered. For existing databases, we can run effective update statements (chapter 28 in this book) to replace null and empty string values with default values.

Null values will affect your calculations in aggregate functions, searching expressions, union operations, and will leave doubts about the validity of your results. Let us explore in detail all of the scenarios around nulls and the ways to eliminate them. For this chapter, so that you can verify the effects of null values and zero-length strings, I have created a table called "ProductsN" which contains only ten records. Using these ten records, you will be able to verify your calculations and learn to work with nulls effectively. Then, you will be able to apply the same techniques for thousands of records.

232. Looking for nulls using criteria
Find products whose stock keeping unit codes (SKUs) are null
Discussion:
Our task is to find all products for which the SKU code is missing. Of course, with only ten products, we can just eye the table and tell right away that there are four SKU codes missing. Let us try to write the code to retrieve them and see if the database agrees. In this example, we

are looking for null values using the criterion "is null" in the WHERE clause, and as you can see, the SQL statement returned four records.

Code:
SELECT productID, productname, productunitprice, SKU
FROM tbls_ProductsN
WHERE SKU IS NULL

Result:

productID ▾	productname ▾	productunitprice ▾	SKU ▾
3	Banana Chips (Zero-Length)	30	
4	Berry Cherry (Zero-Length)	30	
71	Almonds (Null)		
72	Almonds Roasted (Null)		

Record: ◄ ◄ 1 of 4 ► ►I ►⊞ ☒ No Filter   Search

233.   Looking for nulls using the IsNull() function

Display all products to find the ones whose SKU is null

Discussion:

The isnull() function provides us with additional functionality in looking for nulls. Specifically, it will produce a true or false value for all of the entries in the field we are inspecting. In this example, we use isnull() to check the SKU field for nulls. For every value in the SKU field, we will get a true or false response from the database. In Access 2010, the value 0 means false, and the value -1 means true. In the following datasheet, we will get -1 for the four records with null values.

Code:
SELECT ProductID, productname, productunitprice, IsNull(SKU) AS SKUCheck
FROM tbls_ProductsN

Result:

ProductID ▾	productname ▾	productunitprice ▾	SKUCheck ▾
3	Banana Chips (Zero-Length)	30	-1
4	Berry Cherry (Zero-Length)	30	-1
5	California Original Pistachios	29	0
6	Choice Apricots - 16 oz. Bag	32	0
7	Cran Raisin Mix in 17 oz. Bag	31	0
8	Dried Blueberries - 1 lb. Bag	28	0
9	Dried Cranberries - 34 oz.	35	0
10	Raw Sunflower Seeds in 19 o	25	0
71	Almonds (Null)		-1
72	Almonds Roasted (Null)		-1

Record: I◄ ◄ 1 of 10 ► ►I ►▒ ✕ No Filter   Search

234. Looking for nulls using the iif() function

Display the word "null" for products with null SKUs

Discussion:

You can use the iif() function to find nulls in a field and obtain more readable results. The iif() function in this example will display the word "null" for every null value it finds in the SKU field. In this particular example, we indicate null values by the word "null", but we could have used "unknown", "empty", or anything else we would have liked.

Code:

```
SELECT ProductID, productname, productunitprice, IIf(IsNull([SKU]),"NULL", [SKU])
AS SKUCheck
FROM tbls_ProductsN
ORDER BY SKU
```

Result:

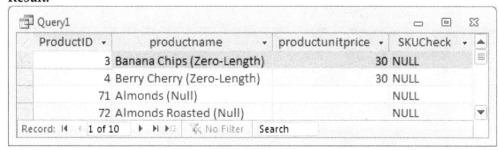

ProductID ▾	productname ▾	productunitprice ▾	SKUCheck ▾
3	Banana Chips (Zero-Length)	30	NULL
4	Berry Cherry (Zero-Length)	30	NULL
71	Almonds (Null)		NULL
72	Almonds Roasted (Null)		NULL

Record: I◄ ◄ 1 of 10 ► ►I ►▒ ✕ No Filter   Search

235.   Calculations with nulls

Calculate product inventory subtotals where some values are nulls

Discussion:

In this example, we want to multiply the ProductUnitPrice with the QuantityPerUnit to calculate the value of our inventory by product. In the ProductsN table, there are blank values for both the ProductUnitPrice and the QuantityPerUnit fields. Let's see how our result set will come up.

Code:

```
SELECT productID, productname, (productunitprice*quantityperunit) As Subtotal
FROM tbls_ProductsN
ORDER BY (productunitprice*quantityperunit) DESC
```

Result:

As you can see, for the records with null values for either one of the two multiplied fields, there will be no result. This will have consequences in our inventory results since at least for productid=72, we know that we do have 25 units on hand. Since their price is missing, the inventory report will be erroneous. To avoid this situation, we need to make it a habit to look for nulls before we do any calculations.

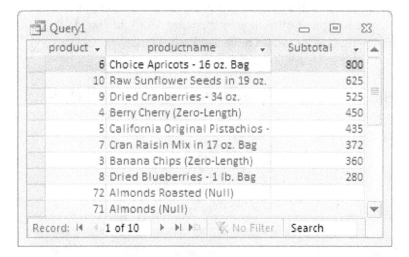

product	productname	Subtotal
6	Choice Apricots - 16 oz. Bag	800
10	Raw Sunflower Seeds in 19 oz.	625
9	Dried Cranberries - 34 oz.	525
4	Berry Cherry (Zero-Length)	450
5	California Original Pistachios -	435
7	Cran Raisin Mix in 17 oz. Bag	372
3	Banana Chips (Zero-Length)	360
8	Dried Blueberries - 1 lb. Bag	280
72	Almonds Roasted (Null)	
71	Almonds (Null)	

Record: I◄ ◄ 1 of 10 ► ►I ►▤ ⟨ No Filter   Search

236. Using sum() with null values

Calculate the total inventory value

Discussion:

The situation becomes even worse when we use aggregate functions since we cannot see the empty field values to realize we have missing data. When aggregate functions encounter null values, they will leave them out of the calculations altogether and report only on known values.

In this case, products with productID 71 and 72 will be missing from the calculations. For productid=72, we have no quantity or price data, and we do not know if this is correct or not. For productid=71, we know that we have a quantity on hand = 25 but no price, and our results are definitely wrong. The best way to avoid the above situations is to check the data for nulls and make every effort to fill in the missing values.

Code:

```
SELECT SUM(productunitprice*quantityperunit) As Total
FROM tbls_ProductsN
```

Result:

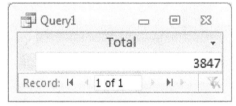

237. Using count() with nulls

Count the number of products in the inventory correctly

Discussion:

As I have mentioned countless times in this book, our primary goal is to rid the database of nulls by replacing them with concrete values in our tables such as "NA" for text fields or zeros for numeric ones. Now, our goal is to calculate the number of products in our inventory table. If we apply the count() function on the SKU field, we will get six records. This is because the four null values in the SKU field have not been counted!

Code:

```
SELECT Count(SKU) As CountSKUs
FROM tbls_ProductsN
```

Result:

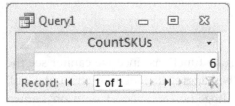

Discussion:

My recommendation to this problem is to use count() or other arithmetic functions on fields that, by default, do not allow nulls in their values. For example, we could use count() on the ProductID field which is the primary key of the table.

Code:

```
SELECT Count(ProductID) As CountSKUs
FROM tbls_ProductsN
```

Result:

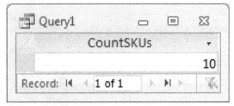

Discussion:

Another solution for correct counts is to use the count(*) function, which will return the actual number of records in the table independently of any null values in any field.

Code:

```
SELECT Count(*) As CountRecords
FROM tbls_ProductsN
```

Result:

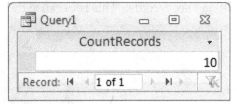

238. Leaving nulls out of the result set

Find products for which the SKU code is not null

Discussion:

We can obtain a list of products that do not contain null values in the SKU field by using the IS NOT NULL clause. The IS NOT NULL clause is not a panacea to null values problems. The real solution would be to use UPDATE statements to replace null values with concrete values such as "NA" for text or zeros for numeric fields. As we expected, the SQL statement returned six records with non-null values for the SKU field.

Code:

```
SELECT productID, productname, productunitprice, SKU
FROM tbls_ProductsN
WHERE SKU IS NOT NULL
```

Result:

productID	productname	productunitprice	SKU
5	California Original Pistachios	29	PDK-2347
6	Choice Apricots - 16 oz. Bag	32	PDK-2347
7	Cran Raisin Mix in 17 oz. Bag	31	PDKLS-1889
8	Dried Blueberries - 1 lb. Bag	28	PDKLS-1889

Record: 1 of 6 — No Filter — Search

239. Using the NZ() function to deal with null values

Calculate inventory replenishment amounts

Discussion:

Our task this time is to replenish our inventory. We need to know how many units of a product we need to have so that we will have enough to operate. We must take into consideration the units we have on hand, how many we have already ordered, and the reorder level that will trigger more orders. All of this information is available in the "tbls_ProductsN" table.

We need to add the units in stock to the units we have already ordered and subtract the result from the reorder level amount which is preset. This is easier said than done because the awful null values will get in the way again. Of course, with ten records in the table, we can easily check for null values, but with 10,000 product records, we will not be able to tell. If we try to

293

do the calculations while ignoring the presence of nulls, we will end up with the database unable to produce results for 40% of our products—four out of ten!

Code:

SELECT ProductID, (ReorderLevel-(UnitsInstock+UnitsOnOrder)) AS UnitsToOrder
FROM tbls_ProductsN

Result:

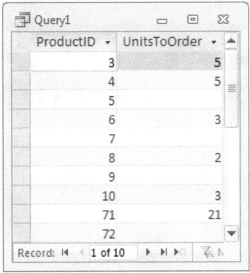

Some people resort to sorting as a way of dealing with null values. This is impractical and amateurish for solid business databases, as well as an obstacle to automation. Even if you find them, what are you going to do with them? Thankfully, in Access 2010, there is a function for situations like this one, and it is called the nz() function. The nz() function has two arguments as shown below:

Nz(field, value of field if it is null)

For the "value of field if it is null" argument, we can put any value we want to like 0, 1, 2, etc. for numeric fields or "hi my name is John" for text fields. In this particular example, the nz() function will replace the null values of the fields unitsinstock and unitsonorder with zeros so that the calculations can go ahead. Please notice from the result set that the database was now able to produce results for 100% of our records.

Code:

SELECT ProductID, (ReorderLevel-(nz(UnitsInstock,0)+nz(UnitsOnOrder,0))) AS
UnitsToOrder
FROM tbls_ProductsN

Result:

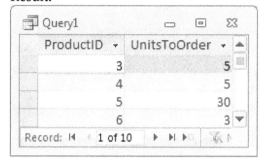

240.   Permanently replace nulls using an update statement

Use UPDATE to replace null values in the SKU field

Discussion:

We can replace the null values in the SKU field by using the UPDATE statement with the
WHERE clause and the IS NULL expression. As you can see from the result set, the database is
asking to replace the four existing null values in the SKU field. (Check chapter 28 for an in
depth look at the update statement).

Code:

```
UPDATE tbls_ProductsN
SET SKU = "NA"
WHERE SKU IS NULL
```

Result:

CHAPTER 25
TYPE CONVERSION FUNCTIONS

Type conversion functions are an excellent tool in the arsenal of the database power user and developer. Unfortunately, they usually go underneath the radar screen of even advanced users because their functionality is not apparent or because they use other methods to accomplish the same result. For instance, to convert a column from a text data type to number data type, some users go to the table design view and force a change there.

There are three problems with this approach: First, by changing the field data type forcefully, data might be lost. Second, if something goes wrong, there is no turning back to the original data. Third, Access might function as the front-end to enterprise databases like MSSQL, Oracle, or IBM DB2, in which case the administrators will not allow a change to the design of the back-end database. The solution is to use type conversion functions to change data types on the fly without affecting table design. In Access 2010, the range of type conversion functions at our disposal are:

FUNCTION	RETURN TYPE	RANGE FOR *EXPRESSION* ARGUMENT
CBool	Boolean	Any valid **string** or numeric expression.
CByte	Byte	0 to 255.
CCur	Currency	-922,337,203,685,477.5808 to 922,337,203,685,477.5807.
CDate	Date	Any valid date expression.
CDbl	Double	-1.79769313486231E308 to -4.94065645841247E-324 for negative values; 4.94065645841247E-324 to 1.79769313486232E308 for positive values.
CDec	Decimal	+/-79,228,162,514,264,337,593,543,950,335 for zero-scaled numbers, that is, numbers with no decimal places. For numbers with 28 decimal places, the range is +/-7.9228162514264337593543950335. The smallest possible non-zero number is 0.0000000000000000000000000001.

CInt	Integer	-32,768 to 32,767; fractions are rounded.
CLng	Long	-2,147,483,648 to 2,147,483,647; fractions are rounded.
CSng	Single	-3.402823E38 to -1.401298E-45 for negative values; 1.401298E-45 to 3.402823E38 for positive values.
CStr	String	Returns for CStr depend on the *expression* argument.
CVar	Variant	Same range as **Double** for numerics. Same range as **String** for non-numerics.

Source: office.microsoft.com

http://office.microsoft.com/en-us/access-help/type-conversion-functions-HA001229018.aspx

We will start by examining the conversion functions CByte(), CInt(), CLng(), CSng(), and CDbl(). All of these functions relate to the number data type in Access 2010, and we use them for two purposes: First, to change numeric data from one format to another such as to change a numeric field from an integer to a double size. Second, to convert text data to numeric data. For instance, suppose a developer created a table and assigned the "Quantity" as a text field. If we later need to make calculations on this field, we first need to convert it to a numeric data type.

Let's say we have a table field called "PartWeight": Although the data type is number, you can see from the figure below that you have various choices for its size. Shifting dynamically between these choices of Byte, Integer, Single, Double, or Decimal is exactly the job of conversion functions like CByte(), CInt(), CLng(), CSng(), and CDbl().

Field Size	Long Integer ▼	▲
Format	Byte	
Decimal Places	Integer	
Input Mask	**Long Integer**	
Caption	Single	
Default Value	Double	
Validation Rule	Replication ID	
Validation Text	Decimal	▼

241. The CByte() function

Convert numbers to byte size

Discussion:

The CByte() function will convert any numbers with decimals such as doubles to a number between 0 and 255, which is one byte according to extended ASCII. There are few occasions when we need this transformation. Suppose, however, that we have a column or a number that we want to convert to a byte.

Code:

SELECT cbyte(245.2346) as Number_Byte

Result:

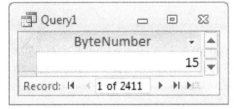

If we try to use cbyte() on a number bigger than 255, we get an overflow error, and the conversion is not possible. In addition, we can dynamically use the cbyte() function on a column without affecting the table design as the code indicates below:

Code:

SELECT cbyte(unitprice) as ByteNumber
FROM ProductsOrders

Result:

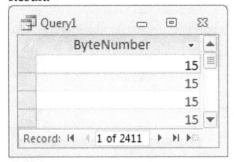

242.   The CInt() function

Convert numbers to integer size

Discussion:

An integer number size will hold numbers between -32,768 to 32,767 and with no decimals. Consequently, if we want to convert the number 234.2345 to an integer value, we can write:

Code:

SELECT cint(234.2345) as Number_Integer

Result:

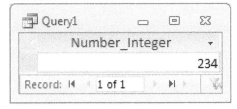

243.   The CLng() function

Convert expressions to long integer numbers

Discussion:

A long integer number size will hold numbers between -2,147,483,648 to 2,147,483,647 with no decimals. If we want to convert the number 50,234.2345 to a long integer value, we will write clng(50234.2345). Notice that we cannot convert to an integer in this case since this number exceeds the integer's capabilities.

Code:

SELECT clng(50234.2345) as Number_Long

Result:

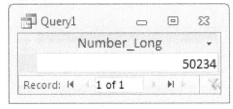

244. The CSng() and CDbl() functions

Convert numbers to Single or Double sizes

Discussion:

We can use the Single and Double number sizes when working with high precision floating numbers. Both single and double sizes are high precision field sizes, and we can store a lot of detail using them. Specifically, we can use the Single size for floating values between -3.4×10^{38} and $+3.4 \times 10^{38}$. Single number field sizes can have up to 7 digits. We can use the double size for floating values between -1.797×10^{308} and $+1.797 \times 10^{308}$. Double number field sizes can have up to 15 digits. Let us go through two examples working with the number 1500345.45349345. Notice this number has 15 digits in total.

If we convert it to a single number, we write:

Code:

SELECT csng(1500345.45349345) as Number_Single

Result:

Notice the resulting number contains only 7 digits, and the decimal has been rounded to one digit.

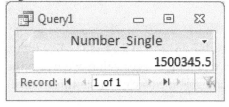

If we convert the same number to a double, we write:

Code:

SELECT cdbl(1500345.45349345) as Number_Double

Result:

As you can see, converting to a double number, we have not lost any of the digits either before or after the decimal since double numbers can hold up to fifteen digits.

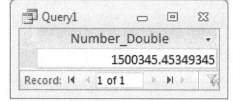

245. The CBool() function

Compare customer first and last name values

Discussion:

The cbool() function will return a true or false value. To demonstrate its usefulness, let us assume that a coworker comes to our office and says that something is wrong with the mailing labels they are producing. On certain occasions, the last and first name fields print the same. Obviously, someone typed in the same value as both first and last name in the database. We can use the cbool() function to find the records for which this occurs.

Code:

SELECT CustomerID, cbool([lastname]=[firstname]) As TrueFalse
FROM customers

Result:

Whenever you see 0 in Access 2010, this means the result is false, or, in other words, the last and first names have different values since you checked for equality. If you see -1, the result is true, which means that the first and last names have identical values. As you scroll through the records, you will notice that you get a -1 for customerid = 19 and an error for 106.

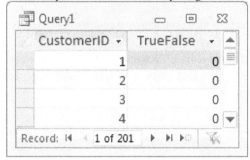

This is cause for investigation. For record 19, last and first names are the same, while for record 106, the first name value is missing! Consequently, with one function, we found two errors that would mess up our coworker's job. Now, we can correct them and send him on his way to produce correct mailing labels.

246. The cCur() function

Convert numbers to currency

Discussion:

If we open the ProductsOrders table in design view, we notice that both the UnitPrice and Quantity fields are of the number data type and specifically long integers. We might want to create a report that shows their multiplication as currency since we want to calculate order subtotals. We can easily accomplish this task by using the ccur() conversion function.

Code:
```
SELECT OrderID, CCur(UnitPrice*Quantity) as OrderSubtotal
FROM ProductsOrders
```

Result:

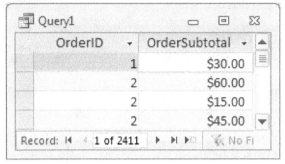

247. The CDate() function
Convert text to a date data type
Discussion:
We might have inherited or imported date data in text format like "November 21 2012" or even "21 November 2012". Since we want to properly store this text data in a date field, we can conveniently use the cdate() function to achieve our goal.

Code:
```
SELECT cdate("November 21 2012") as DateType
```

You will achieve the same result if you use:

```
SELECT cdate("21 November 2012") as DateType
```

Result:

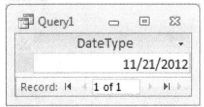

Of course, we can combine the cdate() conversion function with a date function like year() to concurrently extract the year out of our text data. (Check chapter 28 in this book for many tips on dates).

Code:
SELECT year(cdate("November 21 2012")) as FormattedDate

Result:

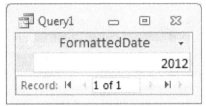

248.   The CStr() function

Convert numeric data to text
Discussion:
Let us assume that the previous DBA used the numeric data type to store zip codes. Zip codes as numbers might behave oddly in situations where we need to concatenate them for example with address numbers. The safest way is to convert them to text before proceeding with any concatenation.

Code:
SELECT cstr(12456) As ZipCode

Result:

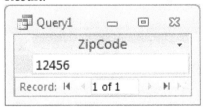

CHAPTER 26
WORKING WITH STRINGS

It is now time to enter the amazing world of text functions and string manipulation. Text functions produce output that is impossible to generate without them. They should be in the toolbox of every database user since lack of such knowledge has direct effects on database and table design. In other words, extra fields might be inserted in tables when not needed. The following are the text functions provided in Access 2010. In this chapter, we will explore a multitude of examples of how to use such functions.

	Function Name	Syntax
1.	Format()	Format(expression [, format] [, firstdayofweek] [, firstweekofyear])
2.	InStr()	InStr([start,] string1, string2 [, compare])
3.	InStrRev()	InstrRev(stringcheck, stringmatch [, start] [, compare])
4.	LCase()	LCase(string)
5.	Left()	Left(string, length)
6.	Len()	Len(string | varname)
7.	LTrim()	LTrim(string)
8.	RTrim()	RTrim(string)
9.	Trim()	Trim(string)
10.	Mid()	Mid(string, start [, length])
11.	Replace()	Replace(expression, find, replace [, start] [, count] [, compare])
12.	Right()	Right(string, length)
13.	Space()	Space(number)
14.	StrComp()	StrComp(string1, string2 [, compare])
15.	StrConv()	StrConv(string, conversion [, LCID])
16.	String()	String(number, character)
17.	StrReverse()	StrReverse(expression)
18.	UCase()	UCase(string)

249. Use the Ucase() function to capitalize field values

Capitalize the first and last names of customers using ucase()

Discussion:

The general syntax of the ucase() function is shown below. It takes just one argument, and it will capitalize the contents of the field on which it is applied. Ucase() will capitalize all of the lowercase characters in the field, leaving the existing capital characters unchanged.

ucase(field name)

In this example, notice the [Last] and [First] field titles in brackets because they are reserved words in Access 2010.

Code:

SELECT UCase(lastname) AS [Last], UCase(firstname) AS [First], city, state, zip
FROM customers

Result:

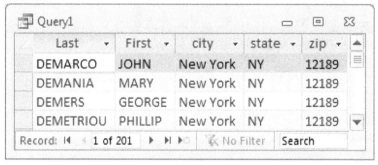

250. Use the strConv() function to capitalize fields

Capitalize the first and last names of customers using strConv()

Discussion:

We can also use the strConv() function to capitalize field values. The strConv() takes two arguments from which the second is a constant. Its general syntax appears below:

strConv (field, constant)

Depending on the value of the constant, the strConv() function will produce different outputs. The table below shows the three possibilities for the constant:

Constant Value	Output Result

1	Converts field value to uppercase characters.
2	Converts field value to lowercase characters.
3	Converts the first letter of every word in the field to uppercase.

As you can see in the code below, the value of the constant is 1, and all of the field contents will be converted to uppercase.

Code:

SELECT strConv(lastname, 1) AS [Last], strConv(firstname, 1) AS [First], city, state, zip
FROM customers

Result:

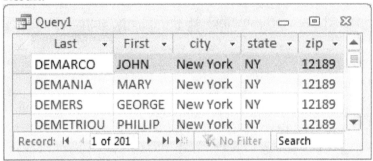

251. Use the format() function to capitalize fields

Capitalize the first and last names of customers using format()

Discussion:

The format() function is the third function we can use to manipulate the case of characters in a field. The general syntax of the format() function with respect to text manipulation appears below. We will use the format() function again and again in date and number fields. For the purposes of string manipulation, however, we will concentrate on this syntax:

Format(field, constant)

Constant Value	Output
<	Force all characters to lowercase.
>	Force all characters to uppercase.

Code:

SELECT format(lastname, '>') AS [Last], format(firstname, '>') AS [First], city, state, zip FROM customers

Result:

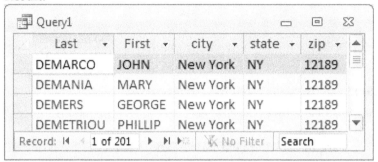

252. Use the strConv() function to capitalize first characters only

Capitalize the first letters of the first and last names of our customers

Discussion:

As we have seen, before the strConv() function takes two arguments, the second is a constant with the possible values of 1,2, or 3. Its general syntax appears below:

strConv (field, constant)

Constant Value	Output Result
1	Converts field value to uppercase characters.
2	Converts field value to lowercase characters.
3	Converts the first letter of every word in the field to uppercase.

In this example, we will use the value 3 for the constant because we want to capitalize only the first character of each word in the last and first name fields.

Code:

SELECT strconv(lastname, 3) AS Last_Name, strConv(firstname, 3) AS First_Name, customers.city, customers.state, customers.zip FROM customers

Result:

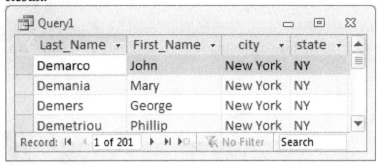

253. Use the Lcase() function to convert field values to lowercase

Convert the first and last names of our customers to lowercase

Discussion:

The lcase() function takes only one argument—the field name—and results in converting all characters of a field value to lowercase. Its general syntax is:

Lcase(field name)

In this particular example, we use it to convert both the first and last names of our customers to lowercase as you can see in the example below:

Code:

```
SELECT Lcase(lastname) AS Last_Name, Lcase(firstname) AS First_Name,
customers.city, customers.state, customers.zip
FROM customers
```

Result:

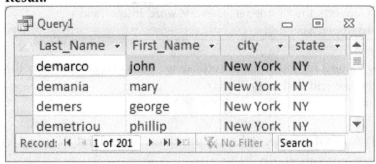

254. Use the strConv() function to convert field values to all lowercase

Convert the first and last names of customers to lowercase

Discussion:

Again, we can use the strConv() function which takes two arguments to convert the characters of a field value to lowercase. We know that the second argument of a strConv() function is a constant with the possible values of 1,2, or 3. Its general syntax appears below:

strConv (field, constant)

Constant Value	Output Result
1	Converts field value to uppercase characters.
2	Converts field value to lowercase characters.
3	Converts the first letter of every word in the field to uppercase.

In this example, we will use the value 2 for the constant because we want to convert the values of the last and first name fields of our customers to lowercase.

Code:

SELECT strconv(lastname, 2) AS Last_Name, strconv(firstname, 2) AS First_Name, customers.city, customers.state, customers.zip
FROM customers

Result:

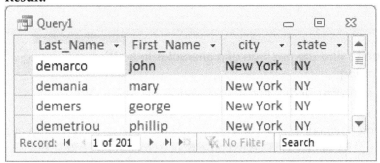

255. Use the len() function to count the number of characters in a field

Count the number of characters in the SKU field

Discussion:

There are occasions in which we like to count the number of characters for a field in every record in the database. This is especially useful when we want to change the data type of a field or when we want to decrease its length. If we work with extraction, transformation, and loading (ETL) tools, this function is particularly useful to know exactly what is happening instead of making guesses and ending up with truncated values. The len() function is especially easy to use, it takes just one argument, and its general syntax appears below:

Len(field name)

In this particular example, we count the number of characters in the product name field of the products table. Notice from the output that the result of the function for each record is different. We can then sort ascending or descending to display the smallest or lengthiest entries first in the output.

Code:
SELECT productid, productname, len(sku) AS CountSKUChars
FROM Products

Result:

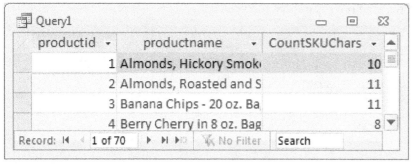

256. Use the instr() function to find the position of a character in a string evaluating from the beginning of a string

Find the number of characters occurring before the "-" character in the SKUs field
Discussion:
In business, we use stock keeping unit codes (SKU) to assign a unique code to products. In our products table, we do have an SKU field. This code consists of some letters and a hyphen followed by some numbers like PDKLS-3483. The letter part of the code before the hyphen signifies some larger category, and we might be required to create a report listing only the letter part of the SKU codes. Our problem is that the number of letters in the SKU code might not always be the same. At least this is what happened in my own experience. So, how can we get the string part of the SKU independent of the number of characters it consists of? To complete this task effectively, we first use the instr() function to determine the position of the hyphen in the string (PDKLS-3483). Its general syntax appears below:

instr(starting character, field, character to find)

In this example, we use inStr(1,sku,"-") to look for the "-" character in the SKU field starting from the first character.

Code:

SELECT productid, productname, sku, InStr(1,sku,"-") AS PartSKU
FROM Products

Result:

productid	productname	sku	PartSKU
1	Almonds, Hickory Smok‹	PDKLS-2332	6
2	Almonds, Roasted and S	PDKLSD-2344	7
3	Banana Chips - 20 oz. Ba	PDKLSD-2347	7
4	Berry Cherry in 8 oz. Bag	PDK-2589	4

Record: 1 of 70   No Filter   Search

257. Use the instr() function to find the position of a blank space evaluating from the beginning of a string

Find the number of characters occurring before a blank space in the SKU field

Discussion:

For this example, I have purposely created an additional problem for us: Some of the hyphens separating the letter code of the SKU from the number code are missing because they were not typed correctly during data entry. We can still use the instr() function to find the position of those blanks. Notice the WHERE clause, which is there so that the result set includes only SKU codes with spaces between letter and number codes and not those with hyphens.

Code:

SELECT productid, productname, sku, InStr(1,sku," ") AS PartSKU
FROM Products
WHERE InStr(1,sku," ") <> 0

Results:

productid	productname	sku	PartSKU
40	Biscuits with cream	ASDT-3456	1
41	Banana Bisquits	ADSE 2345	1
42	Chocolate Bisquits	ADST 2345	1
43	Cocoa and Hazelnut Bisc	ADSD 2345	5

Query1

Record: 1 of 8   No Filter   Search

258. Use the instr() and left() functions to extract a substring from the beginning of a string

Extract the letter part of the SKU field

Discussion:

Now, we are at the essence of the matter, which is how we can dynamically extract a substring from within a string. In other words, how can we extract what we want from part of a field? To do this, we use the left() and instr() functions together. First, we use the instr() function on the SKU field to obtain the numeric value of the exact position of the "hyphen" in the SKU field. Then, we use the left() function, which takes two arguments. The first is the field, and the second is the number of characters to be returned. If we apply the left() function on the string "Hello there" as Left("Hi There", 5), it will return "Hi th".

$$left(sku, InStr(1,sku,"-")-1)$$

What is the -1 doing in the instr() function? When we apply the instr() function alone, it will return the numeric position of the hyphen including the hyphen. Thus, we apply the instr() function minus one character, which, in the end, will result in the string only ("PDKLS")! The cool part of this process is that it happens dynamically. We do not care about the number of letters in the first part of the SKU code. They can be any number, and we will be able to retrieve the string we need.

Code:

```
SELECT productid, productname, sku, left(sku, InStr(1,sku,"-")-1) AS PartSKU
FROM Products
```

Result:

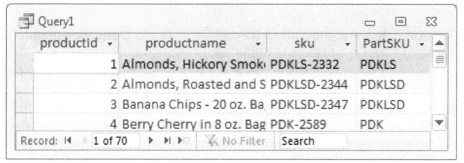

259. Extract a substring before a space in the string evaluating from the beginning of a string

Extract the letter part of the SKU field just before a blank space

Discussion:

This example is the same as the previous one, but this time, we extract the letter code of the SKU before a space.

Code:

```
SELECT productid, productname, sku, left(sku, InStr(1,sku," ")-1) AS PartSKU
FROM Products
WHERE InStr(1,sku," ") <> 0
```

Result:

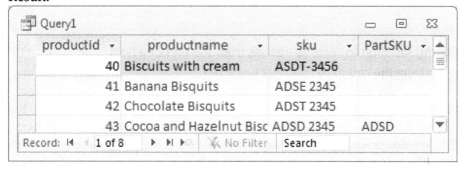

260.   Use the Ltrim() function to remove spaces from the beginning of a field

Remove blank spaces from the beginning of the product name field

Discussion:

The ltrim() function takes only one argument and is extremely easy and useful. It will simply eliminate any blank spaces from the beginning of the values of a field. For instance, in this example, we are not certain if there are blank spaces at the start of the field for some product names. We can simply use the ltrim() function to make certain there are not. The ltrim() function will eliminate any blank spaces if they exist. If there are no blank spaces for this field in some records, it will leave those values unchanged. Besides, blank spaces affect how other functions such as instr() work. We can use the ltrim() function to make sure we count correctly from the beginning of the field.

Code:

SELECT productid, Ltrim(productname) AS LeftTrimmedName, sku
FROM Products

Result:

productid ▾	LeftTrimmedName	▾	sku ▾
1	Almonds, Hickory Smoked - 12 oz. Bag		PDKLS-2332
2	Almonds, Roasted and Salted - 18 oz. Bag		PDKLSD-2344
3	Banana Chips - 20 oz. Bag		PDKLSD-2347
4	Berry Cherry in 8 oz. Bag		PDK-2589

Record: I◄ ◄ 1 of 70 ► ►I ►▷ 🏋 No Filter Search

261.   Use the Rtrim() function to remove spaces from the end of a field

Remove blank spaces from the end of the product name field

Discussion:

The Rtrim() function takes one argument, and its main job is to eliminate blank spaces from the end of a field. Why is this so useful? Let us suppose we are not certain if there are blank spaces at the end of the field for some product names. We can use the Rtrim() function to make certain there are not. The Rtrim() function will eliminate any blank spaces if they exist. If there are no blank spaces, it will leave those field values unchanged. In addition, blank spaces affect how other functions work, for example the right() function. Using the Rtrim() function, we make sure we count correctly from the end of the field.

Code:

SELECT productid, Rtrim(productname) AS RightTrimmedName, sku
FROM Products

Result:

productid	RightTrimmedName	sku
1	Almonds, Hickory Smoked -	PDKLS-2332
2	Almonds, Roasted and Salte	PDKLSD-2344
3	Banana Chips - 20 oz. Bag	PDKLSD-2347
4	Berry Cherry in 8 oz. Bag	PDK-2589

Record: 10 of 70   No Filter   Search

262. Trim blank spaces both at the end and beginning of a string

Remove blank spaces from the beginning and end of the product name field

Discussion:

The role of the trim() function is to eliminate blank spaces from the beginning and end of a field simultaneously. The trim() function takes only one argument as you can see in the example below:

Code:

SELECT productid, trim(productname) AS TrimmedName, sku
FROM Products

Result:

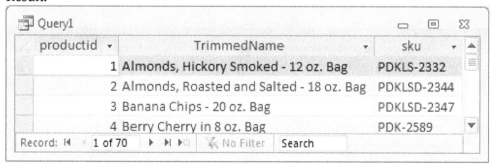

productid	TrimmedName	sku
1	Almonds, Hickory Smoked - 12 oz. Bag	PDKLS-2332
2	Almonds, Roasted and Salted - 18 oz. Bag	PDKLSD-2344
3	Banana Chips - 20 oz. Bag	PDKLSD-2347
4	Berry Cherry in 8 oz. Bag	PDK-2589

Record: 1 of 70   No Filter   Search

263. Insert one space dynamically before or after a field

Insert one blank space in the beginning and end of the product name field

Discussion:

This time, we have the opposite task. Instead of using the ltrim(), rtrim(), or trim() functions to remove blank spaces from the beginning, end, or both ends of a field respectively, we want to add spaces. To achieve this task, we use concatenation characters like '+' to add a space in the beginning and end of the productname field. You can read a whole chapter in this book on concatenation, which you can consult for multiple concatenation techniques (chapter 16).

Code:

```
SELECT productid, (' '+productname + ' ')  AS SpacedName, sku
FROM Products
```

Result:

productid	SpacedName	sku
1	Almonds, Hickory Smoked - 12 oz. Bag	PDKLS-2332
2	Almonds, Roasted and Salted - 18 oz. Bag	PDKLSD-2344
3	Banana Chips - 20 oz. Bag	PDKLSD-2347
4	Berry Cherry in 8 oz. Bag	PDK-2589

Record: 1 of 70 — No Filter — Search

264. Use the space() function to insert any number of spaces dynamically before or after a field

Insert ten blank spaces in the beginning and end of the product name field

Discussion:

In some cases, we might want to add any number of blank spaces in the beginning or at the end of the same field. Using concatenation characters to achieve this task will be a very messy affair. Instead, we can use the space() function to achieve the same outcome as we do in the example below:

Code:

```
SELECT productid, (space(10)+ productname + space(10))  AS SpacedName, sku
FROM Products
```

Result:

productid	SpacedName	sku
1	Almonds, Hickory Smoked - 12 oz. Bag	PDKLS-2332
2	Almonds, Roasted and Salted - 18 oz. B	PDKLSD-2344
3	Banana Chips - 20 oz. Bag	PDKLSD-2347
4	Berry Cherry in 8 oz. Bag	PDK-2589

Record: 1 of 70   No Filter   Search

265. Use the left() function to retrieve any number of characters from the beginning of a field

Retrieve the first four characters of the SKU code

Discussion:

In some situations, the data in our database is well formatted, and we do not have to resort to combinations of functions such as left() and instr() to retrieve a substring from a string in a field. For example, if the letter part of the SKU code in our products table is always of length 4 (PDKS-2345), we can use the left function to retrieve the first four characters in this field. The left() function takes two arguments—the field name and the number of characters we would like to retrieve.

left(fieldname, number of characters to retrieve)

Code:

```
SELECT productid,  productname, left(sku,4) AS 4SKU
FROM Products
```

Result:

productid	productname	4SKU
1	Almonds, Hickory Smoked - 12 oz. Bag	PDKL
2	Almonds, Roasted and Salted - 18 oz. Ba	PDKL
3	Banana Chips - 20 oz. Bag	PDKL
4	Berry Cherry in 8 oz. Bag	PDK-

Record: 1 of 70   No Filter   Search

266.   Use the right() function to retrieve any number of characters from the end of a field

Retrieve the last four characters of the SKU code

Discussion:

In this example, instead of retrieving the first four characters of the SKU code, we would like to get the last four, which, by the way, represent the number part of our SKUs (PDKS-2345). If the SKU field is well formatted, we can use the right() function to achieve this task very easily. By well formatted, we mean the number part of the SKU will always have four digits. Otherwise, we will run into trouble with the right() function. The right() function takes two arguments—the field name and the number of characters we would like to retrieve.

right(fieldname, number of characters to retrieve)

Code:

SELECT productid, productname, right(sku,4) AS SKU4
FROM Products

Result:

productid	productname	SKU4
1	Almonds, Hickory Smoked - 12 oz. Bag	2332
2	Almonds, Roasted and Salted - 18 oz. Bag	2344
3	Banana Chips - 20 oz. Bag	2347
4	Berry Cherry in 8 oz. Bag	2589

Record: 1 of 70   No Filter   Search

267.   Use the mid() function to retrieve any number of characters from any part of a field

Retrieve the first five characters of the product name field starting at character 1

Discussion:

The mid() function is practically an improved left() function, and we can use it instead of left for greater flexibility. The mid() function takes three arguments as they appear below:

Mid(field name, character to start, number of characters to get)

In this example, we use the mid() function to retrieve five characters from the productname field starting at character one or, in other words, at the beginning of the field. We could also have written mid(productname, 5, 5) to retrieve five characters starting with the fifth character in the field.

318

Code:

SELECT productid, mid(productname, 1, 5) As TrimmedName, sku
FROM Products

Result:

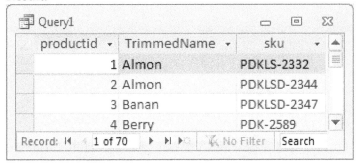

268. Use the string() function to repeat any number of characters from the beginning of a field

Retrieve the first character of the product name field repeated five times

Discussion:

The string() function will return the first character of a field value any number of times we wish. It takes two arguments.

$$\text{String(number of times character repeats, field name)}$$

The string function might look simplistic, and you might wonder about its purpose. Alone, it might not be very useful, but we can always use it in combination with other functions to repeat characters in the middle or at the end of a field. In addition, we can use the string() function in concatenated fields to create categories like AAA, BBB, CCC, etc. In this particular example, we repeat the first letter of the productname field five times.

Code:

SELECT productid, string(5, productname) As Name, sku
FROM Products

Result:

269.   Use the replace() function to update field values

Replace part of supplier's SKU codes dynamically

Discussion:

The replace() function is amazingly useful, and it provides us with great flexibility for doing our work. Let us suppose that one of our suppliers has recently updated the SKU coding they use, and we need to do the same for their products in our own database. From now on, products with the SKU letter codes "PDK" need to be updated to "PDS". Keep in mind that PDKSs and PDKRs need to remain as they are untouched. In addition, the number part of the SKU code needs to remain untouched. So, "PDK-2389" needs to become "PDS-2389". Consequently, we need to isolate the exact letter code "PDK", replace it with PDS, and leave the trailing numbers untouched. This is a job for the replace function. Is basic syntax appears below:

replace(field name, string to search for, string to replace with, at what character to start)

For example the expression

replace(sku, "pdk-", "pds-")

will replace "pdk-" with "pds-". Notice that the fourth argument (at what character to start) is optional, and if we leave it out, the replace function will start the evaluation at the first character of the field. We could start at any character, however.

The way we work when it comes to updates is to isolate the records to be updated first. We write a SELECT SQL statement to isolate the records to be updated. Then, we write the update statement against those records only. This way, just in case something goes sideways, we know which records are affected. This logic is demonstrated below with two consecutive SQL statements:

Code:

SELECT productid, productname, sku

FROM Products

WHERE left(sku, 4) = 'PDK-'

Result:

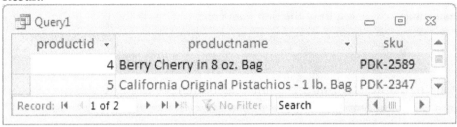

Code:

SELECT productid, productname, replace(sku, "pdk-", "pds-") As skuUpdated

FROM Products

WHERE left(sku, 4) = 'PDK-'

Result:

270.   Use the strComp() function to compare the length of two fields

Compare the length of the first and lastname fields for all customers

Discussion:

Let us suppose that we want to compare the length of two fields in one of our tables. We can accomplish this task by using the Len() function on both fields and then, compare the results. However, there is another quick way to achieve the same task by using the strComp() function. The general syntax of the strComp() function appears below:

$$strComp(field1, field2)$$

The strComp() function will return (-1, 0, 1, or Null) according to the table below:

Comparison Result	Output
field1 is less than field2	-1
field1 is equal to field2	0
field1 is greater than field2	1
field1 or field2 is Null	Null

In this example, we compare the length of the first name and last name fields of the customers table.

Code:
SELECT lastname, firstname, strcomp(firstname, lastname) As CompResult
FROM Customers

Result:

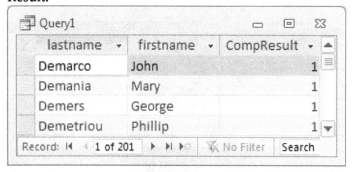

271. Use the strReverse() function to reverse the order of characters in a field
Reverse the order of characters in the SKU field in the products table
Discussion:
The strReverse() function is easy to use, and it takes only one argument as its syntax shows below. It will return a string in which the character order is reversed.

strReverse(field)

In this example, we apply it on the SKU field in the products table, and we see from the output that the number part of the SKU now appears first. Of course, this happens dynamically, and the actual data in the table will not be affected.

Code:

SELECT productid, strReverse(sku) As ReverseSKU
FROM Products

Result:

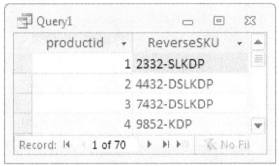

CHAPTER 27
WORKING WITH DATES

Date functions enable us to perform a superior level of work in multiple database tasks. For instance, we can create advanced reports by extracting the year or month out of a date field, and then, you can summarize data based on those years or months. Second, we can extract the quarters out of a date range and create a crosstab query showing our data by quarter. Third, we can create projected order fulfillment cycle times by adding, say, two business days to the order date field and comparing our projections with the actual shipped dates for quality control. Fourth, we can use date functions as default field values to a table field to record the exact date and time a record was inserted. Fifth, with date functions, we can convert numerical date values such as 9/20/2014 to actual named values such as September 20, 2014. Sixth, we can combine date functions with aggregate functions for exceptional data calculations and summaries. Seventh, our level of knowledge on date functions will have a direct effect on the quality of our database design since we can avoid date fields that we can create automatically from other date fields. These examples are just a small part of what we can do with date functions. The main point is that date functions do not just represent additional knowledge; they are required for truly exceptional work. The table below includes the date functions available in Access 2010.

Name	Syntax	Comments
Date()	Date()	Returns a Variant (Date) containing the current system date.
DateAdd()	DateAdd(interval, number, date)	Adds or subtracts a specified time interval from a date
DateDiff()	DateDiff(interval, date1, date2 [, firstdayofweek] [, firstweekofyear])	Returns a Variant (Long) specifying the number of time intervals between two specified dates.
DatePart()	DatePart(interval, date [, firstdayofweek] [, firstweekofyear])	Returns a Variant (Integer) containing the specified part of a given date.
DateSerial()	DateSerial(year, month, day)	Returns a Variant (Date) for a

		specified year, month, and day.
DateValue()	DateValue(date)	Returns a Variant (Date).
Hour()	Hour(time)	Returns a Variant (Integer) specifying a whole number between 0 and 23, inclusive, representing the hour of the day.
Minute()	Minute(time)	Returns a Variant (Integer) specifying a whole number between 0 and 59, inclusive, representing the minute of the hour.
Month()	Month(date)	Returns a Variant (Integer) specifying a whole number between 1 and 12, inclusive, representing the month of the year.
MonthName()	MonthName(month [, abbreviate])	Returns a string indicating the specified month.
Now()	Now()	Returns a Variant (Date) specifying the current date and time according your computer's system date and time.
Second()	Second(Time)	Returns a Variant (Integer) specifying a whole number between 0 and 59, inclusive, representing the second of the minute.
Time()	Time()	Returns a Variant (Date) indicating the current system time.
Timer()	Timer()	Returns a Single representing the number of seconds elapsed since midnight.
TimeSerial()	TimeSerial(hour, minute, second)	Returns a Variant (Date) containing the time for a specific hour, minute, and

		second.
TimeValue()	TimeValue(time)	Returns a Variant (Date) containing the time.
Weekday()	Weekday(date [, firstdayofweek])	Returns a Variant (Integer) containing a whole number representing the day of the week.
WeekdayName ()	WeekdayName(weekday [, abbreviate] [, firstdayofweek])	Returns a String indicating the specified day of the week.
Year()	Year(date)	Returns a Variant (Integer) containing a whole number representing the year.

Table 27-1: Source: http://office.microsoft.com/en-us/access-help/access-functions-by-category-HA010131676.aspx

DateAdd(), DateDiff(), DatePart() interval argument settings.	
Setting	Description
yyyy	Year
q	Quarter
m	Month
y	Day of year
d	Day
w	Weekday
ww	Week
h	Hour
n	Minute
s	Second

Table 27-2 Source: http://office.microsoft.com/en-us/access-help/dateadd-function-HA001228810.aspx?CTT=5&origin=HA010131676

272. Find orders within two dates

Discussion:

In this example we want to produce a list of orders between the dates of 1/1/2014 and 6/30/2014. There are two ways to achieve this task. We can use the inequality and equality predicates or the BETWEEN AND operator. Of course you remember that the BETWEEEN AND operator is inclusive which means the boundary dates will be included in the result set.

Code (using BETWEEN AND):
```
SELECT *
FROM Orders
WHERE OrderDate BETWEEN #1/1/2014# AND #6/30/2014#
ORDER BY OrderDate ASC
```

Code (using inequality and equality predicates):
```
SELECT *
FROM Orders
WHERE OrderDate>=#1/1/2014# AND OrderDate<=#6/30/2014#
ORDER BY OrderDate
```

Result:

OrderID	CustomerID	SalesRepID	ShipperID	OrderDate
581	143	6	2	1/2/2014
431	29	5	1	1/3/2014
473	160	5	2	1/4/2014
146	144	1	3	1/4/2014

Record: I◄ ◄ 1 of 165 ► ►I ►▷ No Filter   Search

273. Find orders outside two dates

Discussion:
To find orders outside two dates we need to use equality and inequality predicates as in the code below. Notice how we use the OR operator when we want to find outside date ranges.

Code:
```
SELECT *
FROM Orders
WHERE OrderDate<=#1/1/2014# OR OrderDate >=#6/30/2014#
ORDER BY OrderDate
```

Result:

The result table shown is:

OrderID	CustomerID	SalesRepID	ShipperID	OrderDate
351	56	4	1	1/14/2012
76	113	1	2	1/15/2012
854	80	9	2	1/15/2012
380	193	4	3	1/15/2012

Record: 1 of 835 — No Filter — Search

274. Use the Now() function for default field values

Discussion:

The now() function takes only one argument, and its general syntax appears below:

$$now()$$

It will output the system date and time, and it is frequently used as the default value for a date field. For example, if we open the SalesReps table, we will notice that there is a field called DateInserted with a default value of now(). This means that every time a record is inserted in this table, the system date and time will be recorded in this field. We can also use now() in a SQL statement or a report to capture the date and time as in the statement below:

Code:

SELECT now() as CurrentTimeAndDate

Result:

CurrentTimeAndDate
3/12/2012 2:25:16 AM

Record: 1 of 1

275. Find the latest order by customer

Discussion:

The sales people are asking for a report that shows the latest order for each customer. Specifically, they want to see a list that contains the last name, first name, and latest order date for each customer. There is a plethora of solutions here but we will go for the simplest one.

Solution 1:

We can quickly identify the latest order by using the max() function and the group by clause but the problem is we will not see the customer first and last names.

Code 1:

```
SELECT customerID, max(orderDate) As LatestOrder
FROM Orders
GROUP BY customerID
```

Result 1:

customerID	LatestOrder
1	1/9/2014
2	6/7/2014
3	6/7/2013
4	9/28/2014

Record: ◄ 1 of 190 ► ►►

Solution 2 (wrong in most cases):

If we need the name of the customer to show we can go with a solution like the one below with the max() function, an INNER JOIN (chapter 30), and the GROUP BY clause. This solution is conceptually correct but practically wrong because in most cases we have multiple customers with the same last name. Even if you concatenate the customers' first and last names and use the group by clause on the concatenated name, you might still get wrong results because some customers will have the same first and last names.

Code 2 (wrong in most cases):

```
SELECT lastname, Max(Orders.OrderDate) AS MaxOfOrderDate
FROM Customers INNER JOIN Orders ON Customers.CustomerID =
Orders.CustomerID
GROUP BY lastname
```

Solution 3 (Simple and correct solution)

In this example we use the group by clause on the first name, last name, and customerid fields combined. There is no way to mess up results since the CustomerID field is the primary key (PK) in the customer table and thus unique for each customer.

Code 3

SELECT Customers.CustomerID, Customers.LastName, Customers.FirstName, Max(Orders.OrderDate) AS LatestOrderDate
FROM Customers INNER JOIN Orders ON Customers.CustomerID = Orders.CustomerID
GROUP BY Customers.CustomerID, Customers.LastName, Customers.FirstName

Result 3

CustomerID	LastName	FirstName	LatestOrderDate
1	Demarco	John	1/9/2014
2	Demania	Mary	6/7/2014
3	Demers	George	6/7/2013
4	Demetriou	Phillip	9/28/2014

Record: 1 of 190   No Filter   Search

276.   Calculate the number of days, months, quarters, or years between two dates.

Discussion:

We can calculate the number of days between two dates using the datediff(interval, date1, date2) function. As you can see from this example, date2 is greater than date1 but Access 2010 does not complain even if it is the other way around; that is to calculate the number of days to a future date. Make sure you enclose the interval argument in quotes.

Code:

Years:

```
SELECT DateDiff("d", #5/15/2012#, #6/3/2013#)  As NumberOfDays
```

Result:

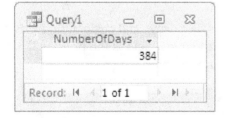

NumberOfDays
384

Record: 1 of 1

The code below will calculate time elapsed in months, quarters, and years.

Code for months:

SELECT DateDiff("m", #5/15/2012#, #6/3/2013#) As NumberOfMonths
Code for quarters:
SELECT DateDiff("q", #5/15/2012#, #6/3/2013#) As NumberOfQuarters
Code for years:
DateDiff("yyyy", #5/15/2012#, #6/3/2013#) As NumberOfYears

277. Count the number of orders by business day of the week and within a specific quarter.

Discussion:

In this example, we calculate the number of orders by business day of the week within a specific quarter. Check how we use the datepart(interval, datefield) function in conjunction with the IN operator in the WHERE clause to isolate the business days only. By default the week in Access starts on Sunday and consequently Monday will be the second (2) day, Tuesday the third (3), and Friday the sixth (6). Also, check how we use the weekday "w" interval argument in the datepart() function in the SELECT statement.

Code:

```
SELECT datepart("w", orderdate) As BusinessDay, Count(OrderID) AS
NumberOfOrders
FROM Orders
WHERE year(orderdate) = 2014 AND datepart("q", orderdate) = 2 AND datepart("w",
orderdate) IN (2,3,4,5,6)
GROUP BY datepart("w", orderdate)
```

Result:

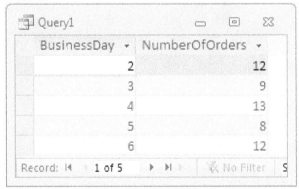

BusinessDay	NumberOfOrders
2	12
3	9
4	13
5	8
6	12

Record: 1 of 5   No Filter

278. Count the number of orders by non-business days of the week and by quarter within a specific year

Discussion:

In this example, we are looking for the number of orders in non-business days of the week, that is, Saturdays and Sundays. However, we also want to present results grouped by quarter within a specific year. Notice in the code below how we use the datepart(interval, datefield) function in the WHERE clause to isolate the non-business days of the week (Saturday and Sunday). Sunday in Access is the first (1) day of the week and thus Saturday is the seventh (7). Notice how we use the datepart() function to group twice by quarter "q" and by weekday "w".

Code:

```
SELECT datepart("q", orderdate) As Quarter, datepart("w", orderdate) As
NonBusinessDay, Count(OrderID) AS NumberOfOrders
FROM Orders
WHERE year(orderdate) = 2014 AND datepart("w", orderdate) IN (1,7)
GROUP BY datepart("q", orderdate), datepart("w", orderdate)
```

Result:

Quarter	NonBusinessDay	NumberOfOrders
1	1	12
1	7	13
2	1	11
2	7	12
3	1	13
3	7	16
4	1	16
4	7	3

Record: 1 of 8   No Filter   Search

279. Use the datepart() function to list orders within a month

Discussion (month):

This time the request is to create a simple list of all orders in June 2012. We can respond to this request by using the datepart(interval, datefield) function to extract the month from the

OrderDate field and the year(datefield) function to extract the year. Notice the usage of "m" for the interval argument in the datepart() function.

Code:
```
SELECT *
FROM Orders
WHERE DatePart("m", [OrderDate]) =6 AND year(Orderdate) = 2012
ORDER BY OrderDate
```

Result:

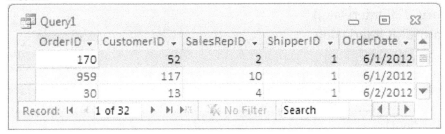

Of course we could obtain the same result by leaving out the functions and just use absolute date intervals which are fine since I learned that what matters is to get the job done.

Code:
```
SELECT *
FROM Orders
WHERE OrderDate BETWEEN #6/1/2012# AND #6/30/2012#
ORDER BY OrderDate
```

Result:

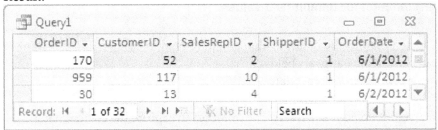

280. Use the datepart() function to count the number of orders by each day of the month

Discussion:

But then, why do we need to learn about functions? Because if our manager asks to count the number of orders by day within June 2012 we will need to use the DatePart(interval, datefield) function to respond as in the example below:

Code:

SELECT DatePart("d",OrderDate) AS Day, Count(OrderID) AS NumberOfOrders
FROM Orders
WHERE Year([OrderDate])=2012 AND DatePart("m",[OrderDate]) = 6
GROUP BY DatePart("d",[OrderDate])
ORDER BY DatePart("d",[OrderDate])

Result:

As you can see from the result set, we obtain the total number of orders for each of the 21 days within June 2012 for which we had orders. Keep in mind that by default in Access the first day of the week is Sunday (day 1).

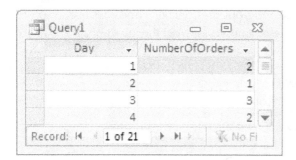

281. Use the Date() function for default field values

Discussion:

The date() function is often used as the default value of a date field in case you do not want to capture the time. Its general syntax appears below:

date()

You can also use it in a SQL statement in a query or in a report to capture the current date:

Code:

SELECT date() as CurrentDate

Result:

282.   Use the datepart() function to count the number of orders by week

Discussion:

In this example we calculate the number of orders within each one of the 52 weeks of the calendar year 2014. Notice from the SQL code that we only have two output fields (Week and NumberofOrders) while we use the year([OrderDate]) field in the WHERE clause to limit the results within the year 2014. This is a quick way to identify order numbers and look for seasonality effects in our sales patterns.

Code:

```
SELECT DatePart("ww",[OrderDate]) AS Week, Count(OrderID) AS NumberOfOrders
FROM Orders
WHERE (((Year([OrderDate]))=2014))
GROUP BY DatePart("ww",[OrderDate])
```

Result:

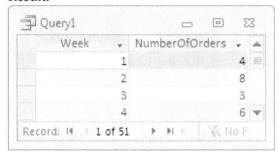

283.   Use the datepart() function to count the number of orders every Monday for the
last three months.

Discussion:

What if we have a request from marketing to count the number of orders for a specific day of the week and for a period of three months? It can be absolutely done and it is much less complicated than it sounds. First we use the DatePart(interval, datefield) function twice to extract the month and the week day from the Orderdate field. Then we use the Year() and Datepart() functions in the WHERE clause to isolate the year to 2014, the quarter to the first quarter of the year, and the weekday to Monday since by default in Access the week starts on Sunday which is day 1. Then, we group the results by month and day to arrive at the desired outcome. This way we can calculate all the orders for any specific day of the week and any period we would like.

Code:
```
SELECT DatePart("m",[OrderDate]) As month, DatePart("w",[OrderDate]) AS Day,
Count(OrderID) AS NumberOfOrders
FROM Orders
WHERE year(OrderDate) = 2014  AND  datepart("q", ([OrderDate])) = 1  AND
datepart("w", ([OrderDate])) = 2
GROUP BY DatePart("m",[OrderDate]), DatePart("w",[OrderDate])
ORDER BY DatePart("m",[OrderDate])
```

Result:

month	Day	NumberOfOrders
1	2	2
2	2	3
3	2	7

Record: 1 of 3   No Filter

284. Use the year() and datepart() functions to calculate order totals for the same week in different years

Discussion:
Management is asking for a report of order totals for the week before Christmas for all the years for which we have data in the database. Practically, we are talking about week 50 out of the 52 weeks for the whole year. For this request we need to group order totals first by year and secondly by week since we also need to show the difference of sales between weeks 50 in each year. Notice in this example that we use the Year(datefield) function to extract the year out of the OrderDate field. Notice as well that we use the Datepart(interval, datefield) function to extract the week since there is no week() function in Access. Finally, notice how we use the DatePart() function in the WHERE clause to make sure we have results only for weeks that equal 50. This results in some very interesting time series analysis.

Code:

SELECT Year([orderdate]) AS [Year], DatePart("ww",[OrderDate]) AS Week,
Sum(unitprice*quantity) AS OrderTotal
FROM Qry_Invoices
WHERE (((DatePart("ww",[OrderDate]))=50))
GROUP BY Year([orderdate]), DatePart("ww",[OrderDate])

Result:

Year	Week	OrderTotal
2012	50	1158
2013	50	1074
2014	50	990

Record: ◄ ‹ 1 of 3 › ►│ No Filter

---

285.   Use the year(), datepart(), or format() functions to calculate order totals by year

Discussion (year function):

On many occasions, we want to extract the year out of a date field to create aggregate summaries of our data. One way to achieve this task is to use the year() function, which takes only one argument. Its general syntax is:

Year(date)

In this example, we want to calculate order totals by year. We use the year() function to extract the year out of the OrderDate field in combination with the sum() aggregate function to calculate order totals.

Code:

SELECT year(OrderDate) AS Year, sum(unitprice*quantity) AS OrderTotal
FROM Qry_Invoices
GROUP BY Year(OrderDate)

Result:

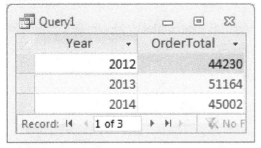

Discussion (datepart function):

We could also extract the year from a date field using the datepart() function. The datepart() function has four arguments, but for practical situations, we can use only two of them. Its simplified syntax appears below:

datepart(interval, datefield)

The interval argument is just a string indicating the date part we want to extract from the date field. For example, we would use "yyyy" to extract the year or "q" to extract the quarter. Do not forget the quotes in the code since without them, it will not work. Check table 1 at the end of this chapter for a list of all possible values for the interval arguments for the datepart() function for amazing flexibility in extracting date parts from years all the way down to seconds.

Code:

```
SELECT datepart("yyyy", OrderDate) AS Year, SUM(unitprice*quantity) AS
OrderTotal
FROM Qry_Invoices
GROUP BY datepart("yyyy", OrderDate)
```

Result:

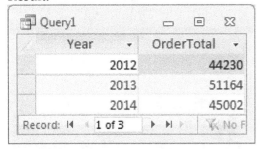

Discussion (format function):

The format function is the most flexible, and it offers more choices than the year() and datepart() functions. Officially, it takes four arguments, but again, for practical purposes, we need only two. Its simplified version appears below:

$$\text{format(datefield, interval)}$$

The interval argument is a string expression like "yyyy" for years or "mmmm" for months. Unlike the datepart() function, however, it will give us a lot more choices for displaying years or months. Using format, we can display the full month name, the month number with or without leading zeros, or the abbreviated month name if we want. Please check table 2 at the end of this chapter for a full list of the available choices with the format() function.

Code:

```
SELECT format(OrderDate, "yyyy") AS Year, sum(unitprice*quantity) AS OrderTotal
FROM Qry_Invoices
GROUP BY format(OrderDate, "yyyy")
```

Result:

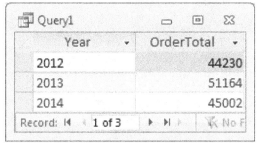

Discussion (format function):

In this example, we use the format function to extract only the last two digits of the years on which we provide summary statistics. Notice that we use the "yy" argument to achieve this task.

Code:

```
SELECT format(OrderDate, "yy") AS Year, sum(unitprice*quantity) AS OrderTotal
FROM Qry_Invoices
GROUP BY format(OrderDate, "yy")
```

Result:

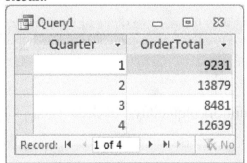

286. Use the datepart() and format() functions to calculate order totals by quarter for a specific year

Discussion (with datepart):

The business goal in this example is to create a quarterly sales report for the year 2012. To achieve this task, we need to use two date functions. First, we will use the year() function to extract the year from the orderdate field and use this expression in the WHERE clause with an equality predicate "=". This way, we make certain that our resulting recordset contains orders only for the year 2012. Then, we can use the datepart() function to group by our order totals by quarter. Of course, we could use the format function to extract quarters, which is demonstrated in the second part of this example.

Code:

```
SELECT datePart("q",[OrderDate])  AS Quarter, sum(unitprice*quantity) AS OrderTotal
FROM Qry_Invoices
WHERE Year(orderdate) = 2012
GROUP BY DatePart("q",[OrderDate])
```

Result:

Discussion (with format):

In this second part of the same example, we use the format() function to extract quarters from a date field. The results will be identical with those of the datepart() function.

Code:

```
SELECT format(OrderDate, "q") AS Quarter, sum(unitprice*quantity) AS OrderTotal
FROM Qry_Invoices
WHERE Year(orderdate) = 2012
GROUP BY format(OrderDate, "q")
```

Result:

Quarter	OrderTotal
1	9231
2	13879
3	8481
4	12639

Record: 1 of 4

287. Use the month(), monthname() datepart(), or format() functions to calculate monthly order and discount totals for a specific year

Discussion (with month):

The business goal in this example is to calculate order and discount totals by month for the year 2010. Management wants to have a look at the numbers to check the discount percentages forwarded by the sales reps. There are four different ways to achieve this result depending on the date function we use. Notice that in all four examples, the rationale is the same. We will use the year() function to isolate the year from the orderdate field and use this expression in the WHERE clause. Then, we need to use a function to isolate the month from the orderdate field so that we can group by month within the year 2012. Finally, notice that we will use two calculated fields (OrderTotal and TotalDiscount) to calculate the order and discount totals for each month.

In this first alternative, we will use the month function to extract the month from the orderdate field. The month() function has only one argument, and its syntax is below:

month(datefield)

Code:

```
SELECT month(OrderDate) AS [Month], Sum(unitprice*quantity) AS OrderTotal,
Sum(([unitprice]*[quantity])*[Discount]) AS TotalDiscount
FROM Qry_Invoices
WHERE year(orderdate) = 2012
GROUP BY month(OrderDate)
```

Result:

Month	OrderTotal	TotalDiscount
1	2792	442.4
2	2944	453.5
3	3495	510.95
4	3872	566.85

Record: 1 of 12   No Filter   Search

Discussion (with monthname):

Suppose the management was not very happy with our first report because the month numbers confused them, and they could not quickly discern the corresponding month name. They now ask us to provide them with another report showing actual month names. We can do this immediately using the monthname() function in conjunction with the month() function. Notice that we cannot use the monthname() function by itself. We have to use it with the month() function to work as it is in the code below. Notice how we use the month(orderdate) function in the ORDER BY clause to have the months appear in the correct order.

Code:

```
SELECT monthname(month(OrderDate)) AS [Month], sum(unitprice*quantity) AS
OrderTotal, sum(([unitprice]*[quantity])*[Discount]) AS TotalDiscount
FROM Qry_Invoices
WHERE year(orderdate) = 2012
GROUP BY monthname(Month(OrderDate)), month([OrderDate])
ORDER BY month([OrderDate])
```

Result:

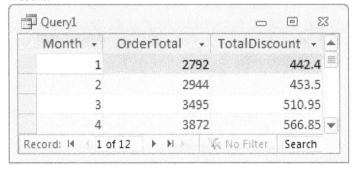

Discussion (with datepart):

We can also use the datepart() function to achieve the same result except that we will get numerals instead of month names. In other words, the result will be identical with that of the month() function. The only real difference is that the month function is much simpler, and we do not need to remember the "m" argument of the datepart() function.

Code:

```
SELECT datepart("m", OrderDate) AS [Month], sum(unitprice*quantity) AS
OrderTotal, Sum(([unitprice]*[quantity])*[Discount]) AS TotalDiscount
FROM Qry_Invoices
WHERE year(orderdate) = 2012
GROUP BY datepart("m", OrderDate), month([OrderDate])
ORDER BY datepart("m", OrderDate)
```

Result:

Month	OrderTotal	TotalDiscount
1	2792	442.4
2	2944	453.5
3	3495	510.95
4	3872	566.85

Record: 1 of 12 — No Filter — Search

Discussion (with format):

Finally, we can use the format() function with the "mm" argument to put a leading zero in front of the month for sorting purposes.

Code:

SELECT format(OrderDate, "mm") AS [Month], sum(unitprice*quantity) AS
OrderTotal, sum((([unitprice]*[quantity])*[Discount]) AS TotalDiscount
FROM Qry_Invoices
WHERE year(orderdate) = 2012
GROUP BY format(OrderDate, "mm")
ORDER BY format(OrderDate, "mm")

Result:

Month	OrderTotal	TotalDiscount
01	2792	442.4
02	2944	453.5
03	3495	510.95
04	3872	566.85

Record: 1 of 12   No Filter   Search

288. Use the datepart() function to count the number of orders by day for the whole year.

Discussion:

The goal here is to count the number of orders by day of the week for the whole year. That is, how many orders we had in total on Mondays, how many on Tuesdays, and how many on Wednesdays etc.   Notice how we use the day of the week argument ("w") in the DatePart(interval, dategield) function to isolate the days of the week and then group by them. Remember that by default in Access the week starts on Sunday = 1.   As you can see from the result set, we obtain some very useful information indeed. For example, that we have the most orders on Wednesday (day 4), followed by Sunday (day 1).

Code:

SELECT DatePart("w",[OrderDate]) AS Day, Count(OrderID) AS NumberOfOrders
FROM Orders
WHERE (((Year([OrderDate]))=2014))
GROUP BY DatePart("w",[OrderDate]);

Result:

Day	NumberOfOrders
1	52
2	44
3	45
4	62
5	47
6	46
7	44

Record: 1 of 7   No F

289. Use the datepart() function to count the number of orders by day of the year

Discussion:

In this example, we calculate the number of orders by day of the year. We have 365 days per year and by using the "y" interval argument we can isolate the number of orders by the day of the year. Very useful data for some time series analysis throughout the year. From the result set, we see that from the 365 days of the year we had orders only on 214 days. In addition, we can see that from the beginning of the year we had our first orders on day 14. If we have a detailed look at the whole recordset, I bet we can make additional conclusions about the timing and volume of our orders.

Code:

```
SELECT DatePart("y",OrderDate) AS Day, Count(OrderID) AS NumberOfOrders
FROM Orders
WHERE Year([OrderDate])=2012
GROUP BY DatePart("y",[OrderDate])
ORDER BY DatePart("y",[OrderDate])
```

Result:

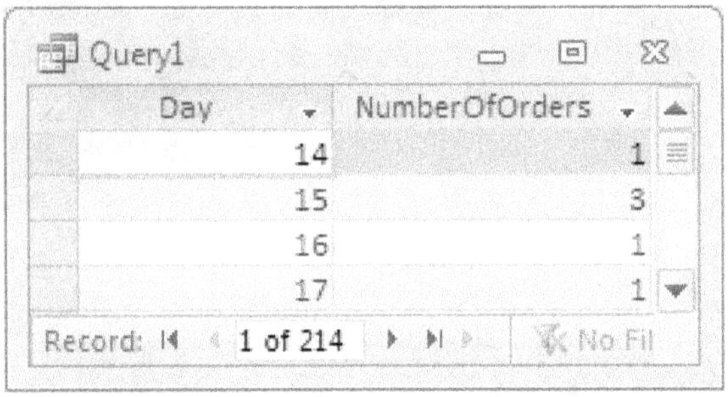
Query1

Day	NumberOfOrders
14	1
15	3
16	1
17	1

Record: 1 of 214   No Fil

290. Use the datepart() or format() functions to create a crosstab report showing product sales by week for a six-month period

Discussion (with datepart):

This time, management wants a report listing product sales by week within a six-month period and within a specific year. To create this crosstab query, we need to use three date functions in combination. First, we will use the month() function to extract the month number from the orderdate field and use this as a criterion in the WHERE clause. Notice how the IN operator is used with the WHERE clause to get the first six months of the year. Since, however, we have multiple years of sales in the database, we need to include a criterion in the WHERE clause to isolate the year we want. We can use the year function on the orderdate field to achieve this task. Finally, in the PIVOT part of the crosstab query, we can use the datepart() function with the "ww" argument to produce a column for each week. (For a detailed overview of crosstab queries, check chapter 19). As you can see from the result set, we can now examine detailed total product sales by week for a period of 27 weeks within the six-month period that we defined in our WHERE clause.

Code:

```
TRANSFORM Sum([unitprice]*[quantity]) AS Ordertotal
SELECT ProductName
FROM Qry_Invoices
WHERE month(orderdate) IN (1,2,3,4,5,6) AND year(orderdate) = 2012
GROUP BY ProductName
PIVOT datePart("ww",[OrderDate])
```

Result:

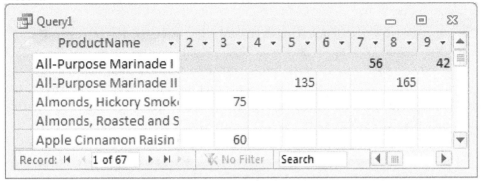

Discussion (with format):

We could use the format function to achieve the same task, but notice in the result set that the weeks are not in order this time.

Code:

```
TRANSFORM Sum([unitprice]*[quantity]) AS Ordertotal
SELECT ProductName
FROM Qry_Invoices
WHERE month(orderdate) IN (1,2,3,4,5,6) AND year(orderdate) = 2012
GROUP BY ProductName
PIVOT format([OrderDate], "ww")
```

Result:

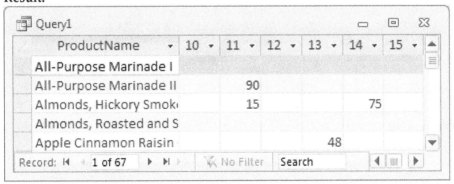

291. Use the day(), datepart(), weekday() and weekdayname() functions to create a crosstab report showing product sales by day within a month.

Discussion (day function):

Management is impressed by our detailed reports, and they now ask for a report of daily product sales for the month of May in the year 2012. Again, we need to use three date functions—two for criteria and one to pivot our results. In this example, we will use the month() and year() functions to isolate the year and the month in the WHERE clause and the day() function to pivot or display product sales by day. Notice that only days with product sales appear as columns in the result set.

Code:

```
TRANSFORM Sum([unitprice]*[quantity]) AS Ordertotal
SELECT ProductName
FROM Qry_Invoices
WHERE month(OrderDate) = 5 AND year(orderdate) = 2012
GROUP BY ProductName
PIVOT day(OrderDate)
```

Result:

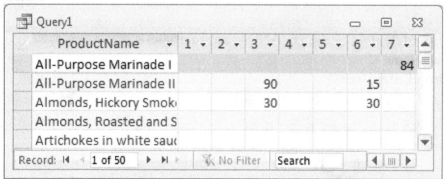

Discussion (datepart function):

We can achieve the same result using the datepart() function with the "d" (day) argument. For a full list of possible arguments for the datepart() function, see table 1 at the end of this chapter.

Code:
```
TRANSFORM Sum([unitprice]*[quantity]) AS Ordertotal
SELECT ProductName
FROM Qry_Invoices
WHERE month(OrderDate) = 5 AND year(orderdate) = 2012
GROUP BY ProductName
PIVOT datepart("d",OrderDate)
```

Result:

ProductName	1	2	3	4	5	6	7
All-Purpose Marinade I							84
All-Purpose Marinade II			90			15	
Almonds, Hickory Smok			30			30	
Almonds, Roasted and S							
Artichokes in white sau							

Record: ◄ ◄ 1 of 50 ► ►► ☒ No Filter   Search

Discussion (weekday function):

In this example, we will create a report of daily product sales within a week. Specifically, management asks for a report of product sales, by day, within the 25th week of the year 2012. This time, we will use the datepart() and year() functions in the WHERE clause to extract the week and the year respectively from the orderdate field. In addition, we will use the weekday() function to display product sales by day within the week. The general syntax of the weekday() function appears below. It takes two arguments, datefield and firstdayofweek, and the second is optional. With the firstdayofweek argument, we can define which day we want to be the first day of the week. We can choose any day between Sunday and Saturday as the table indicates below. In this example, we left the second argument blank, which defaults the first day of the week to Sunday. From the result set, you can see the order totals by product and day of the week.

weekday (datefield, [firstdayofweek])

Argument value	First day of week
1	Sunday (default)
2	Monday
3	Tuesday
4	Wednesday
5	Thursday
6	Friday
7	Saturday

Code:

```
TRANSFORM Sum([unitprice]*[quantity]) AS Ordertotal
SELECT ProductName
FROM Qry_Invoices
WHERE datePart("ww",[OrderDate]) = 25 AND year(orderdate) = 2012
GROUP BY ProductName
PIVOT weekday([OrderDate])
```

Result:

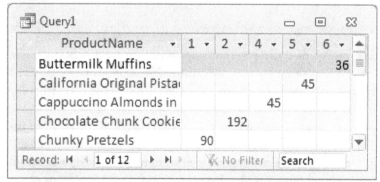

Discussion (weekdayname function)

The previous example is fine, but it will confuse management and anybody else who tries to understand what day of the week corresponds to numbers 6 or 7. To solve this problem, we can use the weekdayname() function to provide the actual day name. Notice that we cannot use the weekday() function alone because we will receive an error from Access 2012. We need to use it in conjunction with the weekday() function to retrieve the day names. As you can see in the result set, the names of the days appear now as column headings.

Code:

```
TRANSFORM Sum([unitprice]*[quantity]) AS Ordertotal
SELECT ProductName
FROM Qry_Invoices
WHERE datePart("ww",[OrderDate]) = 25 AND year(orderdate) = 2012
GROUP BY ProductName
PIVOT weekdayname(weekday([OrderDate]))
```

Result:

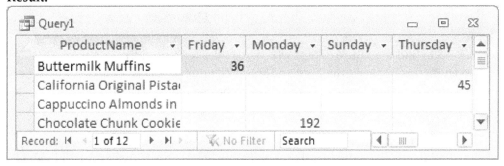

ProductName	Friday	Monday	Sunday	Thursday
Buttermilk Muffins	36			
California Original Pista				45
Cappuccino Almonds in				
Chocolate Chunk Cookie		192		

Record: 1 of 12   No Filter   Search

292.   Anniversaries: Use the LIKE operator to find past anniversaries.

Discussion:

Let us assume we need a list of orders for today's date which is 10/22/2014. Practically, we need to find all orders which occurred on 10/22 of each year in our order history. A very easy and very flexible way to achieve this is by using the LIKE operator as in the code below. As you can see from the result set, we had four past orders the 22nd of October. Notice that we put the asterisk in the year part of the date. Moving the asterisk to the month or day part of the date we can achieve some additional interesting results.

Code:

```
SELECT *
FROM Orders
WHERE OrderDate Like "10/22/*"
```

Result:

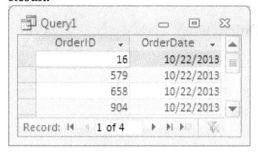

293.   Anniversaries: use the DateAdd() function to find future anniversaries.

Discussion:

In this case we need to find the future date at which our sales representatives complete 20 years of service. We can do this by using the DateAdd(interval, number, date) function. Check how we enclose the yyyy interval in quotes. If you do not enclose the interval argument in quotes the function will not work.

Code:

```
SELECT firstname, lastname, DateAdd("yyyy", 20 , dateofHire) AS 20yrAnniversary
FROM SalesReps
```

Result:

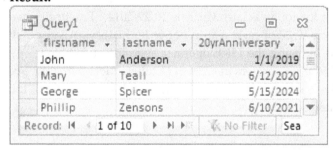

294.   Anniversaries: Finding upcoming anniversaries within a specific period.

Discussion:

We would like to create a list of employees with a birthday within a specific month of the year. We can do this by using the datepart (interval, datefield) function twice; first to show the day of the employee's birthday as you can see in the SELECT statement and second to isolate the month of the year as you can see in the WHERE clause. In this specific example, we are looking for employee birthdays in the month of April. Notice how we use quotes for the interval arguments in both functions ("d" and "m") since without those quotes the datepart() function will not work.

Code:

SELECT firstname, lastname, title, datepart("d", dateofbirth) As DayOfBirth

FROM SalesReps

WHERE datepart("m", dateofbirth) = 4

Result:

firstname	lastname	title	DayOfBirth
John	Anderson	Sales Reppresentative	15
George	Spicer	Assitant Director of Sales	4
Phillip	Zensons	Sales Reppresentative	3
Gerald	Williams	Sales Reppresentative	1

Record: 1 of 4   No Filter   Search

295. Anniversaries: Use the DateDiff() function to calculate time elapsed such as employment length.

Discussion:

We have a request from management to calculate the number of employment years for each of our employees. We can use the DateDiff(interval, date1,date2) function to calculate the elapsed time between the employee's date of hire and today's date. Notice how we use quotes for the interval argument "yyyy" and how we use the date() function to obtain today's date.

Code:

SELECT firstname, lastname, DateDiff("yyyy", DateOfHire, Date()) AS YearsEmployed

FROM SalesReps

Result:

296. Anniversaries: Calculating Employee Age

Discussion:

This time we would like to create a query that lists the ages of our employees. We can do this by using the DateDiff(interval, date1, date2) function which subtracts date1 from date2 and provides the difference in years, months, quarters or in any other period we need. Refer to the beginning of this chapter for all possible interval settings for the DateDiff() function. In this particular example, we would like to see the age in years and that is why we use the "yyyy" setting. Do not forget to include the interval setting in quotes since otherwise the function will not work.

Code:

```
SELECT firstname, lastname, title, DateDiff("yyyy", DateOfBirth, Date())  As Age
FROM SalesReps
```

Result:

297. Use the DateDiff() function to calculate order processing cycle times

Discussion:

Customer service has reported to management that customers are complaining about shipping. Specifically, they complain that it takes a lot of time to receive their orders after they complete the ordering process. Management is trying to determine the cause, and they need our help. They want to know if the problem is internal as a result of packaging and payment processing or if the problem is external as a result of the shipping company. They suspect the problem is internal, and they tell us to produce a report that lists how many days it takes for an order to ship from the time it has been received.

We can do this in no time by using the datediff() function. The datediff() function takes five arguments, but for most practical scenarios, we only need to use the first three. The general syntax of the function appears below. The interval argument is a string that will determine in what interval we want to find the difference between date1 and date2. For instance, we might want to calculate the difference in days, weeks, months, or years. (Please refer to table 3 at the end of this chapter for a full list of values for the interval argument). In addition, date2 should be a later date than date1. Otherwise, the result will be negative. As you can see from the code below, we calculate the difference between orderdate and shippeddate in days. In other words, how many days elapsed between receiving and shipping an order? The results are not good at all. It takes a full five days to get the order out from our factory for the month of September 2012, which is a very long order processing cycle time.

DateDiff(interval, date1, date2[, firstdayofweek[, firstweekofyear]])

Code:

```
SELECT OrderID, datediff("d", orderdate, shippeddate) AS CycleTime
FROM Orders
WHERE year(orderdate) = 2012 AND month(orderdate) = 10
```

Result:

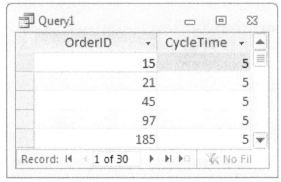

298. Use the DateAdd() function to establish policies on expected shipping dates

Discussion:

Management is not very happy to see that it takes five days to ship an order. This means that customers will receive their orders in about ten to fifteen days total. This is unacceptable because we are in the food industry, and our products need to arrive fresh. So, management asks for our help again to produce a timetable that will list the expected shipping dates for orders. Management has determined that it should take two days at most for any order to ship, and they have established a corporate policy to be strictly enforced. We can produce target shipping dates using the dateadd() function. It takes three arguments, and its general syntax appears below:

dateadd(interval, number, datefield)

The interval argument is a string like "d", "m", or "y" determining the time interval we want to add. For instance, if we want to add days to a date, we use the "d" value. If we want to add years, we use the "y" value for the interval argument. (For a full list of the values for the interval argument, please refer to table 3 at the end of this chapter). The number argument is the actual number of time intervals we want to add. If we want to add 15 days, for example, we use the number 15. Finally, the date argument is the date field to which we want to add a number of days, months, or years. In the code below, we add 2 days to the orderdate field:

Code:

```
SELECT OrderID, dateadd("d", 2, orderdate) AS  PolicyShipmentDate
FROM Orders
WHERE year(orderdate) = 2012 AND month(orderdate) = 7
```

Result:

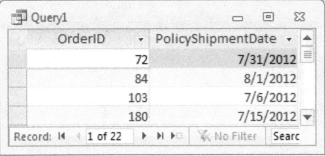

OrderID	PolicyShipmentDate
72	7/31/2012
84	8/1/2012
103	7/6/2012
180	7/15/2012

Record: 1 of 22

Table 1: Datepart() function settings	
Character	**Description**
"yyyy"	Year
"q"	Quarter
"m"	Month
"y"	Day of year
"d"	Day
"w"	Weekday
"ww"	Week
"h"	Hour
"n"	Minute
"s"	Second

Character	Description (The following are tested and working. You might find more settings, but they did not work correctly when tested)
"s"	Returns the second as a number without leading zeros
"ss"	Returns the second as a number with leading zeros
"h"	Returns the hour as a number
"hh"	Returns the hour as a number with leading zeros
"d"	Returns the day without a leading zero
"dd"	Returns the day with a leading zero
"ddd"	Returns the day as an abbreviation
dddd	Returns the full name of the day
"m"	Returns the month without a leading zero
"mm"	Returns the month with a leading zero
"mmm"	Returns the abbreviation of the month
"mmmm"	Returns the full name of the month
"q"	Returns the quarter as a number
"y"	Returns the year as number (0-9) without leading zeros
"yy"	Returns the year as number (0-9) with leading zeros
"yyyy"	Returns the year in four-digit numeric format

Table 3: DateDiff and DateAdd interval argument values	
Value	**Description**
yyyy	Year
q	Quarter
m	Month
y	Day of year
d	Day
w	Weekday
ww	Week
h	Hour
n	Minute
s	Second

CHAPTER 28
UPDATE SQL STATEMENTS

Update statements are powerful tools for the advanced user, administrator, and developer. They provide astonishing flexibility and control to complete a task in minutes for which you would otherwise need hours. For example, suppose we have a database of 100 suppliers and a few thousand products associated with each supplier. Every week, due to promotional campaigns, pricing strategies, or replenishment costs, our suppliers might change their prices and since their products constitute our own raw materials we need to update our own prices. After all, the only constant in business is change. Change will affect your operations, and, in the end, your data. Since this is true, you must be ready for lightning speed changes to your operational data.

Your suppliers will never update their product prices at the same time and at the same percentage rates. This scenario is valid only for theoretical books. What actually happens is that suppliers will send you a price update when their business operations dictate, and this update will most probably be different from everyone else's. So, how do you account for situations like this? Of course, you use flexible update statements that you can reuse effectively. This chapter starts with simple examples and ends up with powerful conditional updates for manipulating your data.

Keep in mind that you cannot undo the results of update statements or update queries. Consequently, my advice and my own policy is to first use a SELECT statement to check the records to be updated and then, run the update itself. This is actually common industry practice. We never run an update statement in the blind.

The general syntax of an update statement is shown below:

UPDATE table
SET fieldvalue1 = value1, fieldvalue2 = value2, fieldvalue3 = value3…
[WHERE condition]

We can also run updates on queries (updateable ones). We might construct a dataset having data from multiple tables and run the update against the query. (I have examples of this in the chapter). In addition, we can update a table based on the values of another table or query. We can easily achieve this by using subqueries. Update statements are highly efficient for operations. Before we delve into examples, let's make sure we understand what cascade updates are and how they work in Access 2010.

299. What are cascade updates, how to use them, and what they mean

There are cases in which we have to update the values of primary keys in your tables. Usually, these changes are mandated by entities external to the organization, such as the government. For example, up until now, we might have used the social security number of an employee as the primary key for the employees table. As a result, SSN functioned as the foreign key to record all related activities for that employee (sales, HR records etc.) Now, the government steps in and says that we cannot do that anymore. This means that we have to change the SSN value for the employee in the employees table, and, most importantly, we need to change all of its occurrences in related tables. So, if this employee worked for us for 10 years, he might have 260 paystub records in the database. We might actually have thousands of references that we need to update for this employee.

Doing so manually is an impossible task, especially if we have several thousand employees. This is where cascade updates come in. Cascade updates will allow us to change the value of the primary key in the primary table, and the database engine will change all of its occurrences automatically, as a foreign key, in related tables. Let's go through a simple graphical example using a customer database to see how cascade updates work.

Customers	
CustID	Name
1	John
2	Mary
3	George
4	Stacy

Orders		
OrderID	CustID	OrderDate
1	2	9/10/2012
2	2	10/10/2012
3	1	11/10/2012
4	3	11/11/2012

Products_Orders		
OrderID	ProductID	Quantity
1	2	2
2	2	5
3	1	3
4	2	4

Products	
ProductID	ProductName
1	A
2	B
3	C
4	D

In the figure above, let's assume that we need to change Mary's primary key value from 2 to 222. First, we need to turn cascade updates on for the relationship between customers and orders. Then, we can simply change the primary key value 2 to the value 222. The database will ask us to confirm the action, and once the updates are completed, this is how the same tables will look:

Customers	
CustomerID	Name
1	John
222	Mary
3	George
4	Stacy

Orders		
OrderID	CustomerID	OrderDate
1	222	9/10/2012
2	222	10/10/2012
3	1	11/10/2012
4	3	11/11/2012

Products_Orders		
OrderID	ProductID	Quantity
1	2	2
222	2	5
3	1	3
4	2	4

Products	
ProductID	ProductName
1	A
2	B
3	C
4	D

Notice how the database automatically changed all of the references of CustomerID=2 to 222 in the Orders and ProductsOrders tables. I strongly recommend having cascade updates turned off except when you actually want to make changes to primary key values. This is a precaution in case an end user changes the value of a primary key by accident. So, how you can use cascade updates in Access 2010?

1. Click on the "Database Tools" tab. Then, in the group "Relationships", click on "Relationships".

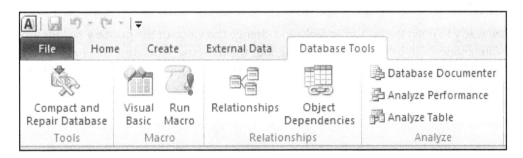

This will open up the relationships window as shown below:

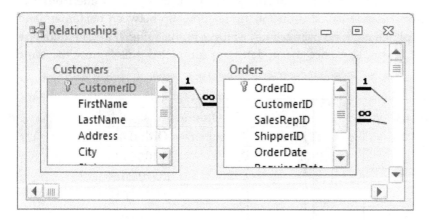

2. Double click on the relationship line between customers and orders. The following screen will appear. Click on "Cascade Update Related Fields", and click "OK".

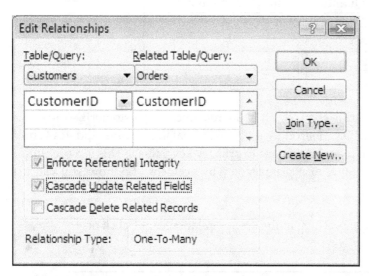

Now, we are ready to open the customer table and change the value of the primary key for any customer. Our change will be propagated throughout the database where the database finds a foreign key value that is equal to the primary key we changed. Remember to edit the relationship again and turn off "Cascade Updates" once the records are updated.

300.   Update a single field value in a single record

Update address information for a single customer

Discussion:

In this example, our goal is to update the address information for one of our customers. Notice the criteria in the query. They need to uniquely identify the customer we want to update. We will use a SELECT statement beforehand just to make sure that we do not have another customer with the same first and last names.

SELECT *
FROM tbls_customers_Upd
WHERE lastname = "Demizio" AND firstname = "Michael"

Code:
UPDATE tbls_Customers_Upd
SET Address = "12 Lark Street"
WHERE lastname = "Demizio" AND firstname = "Michael"

Result:

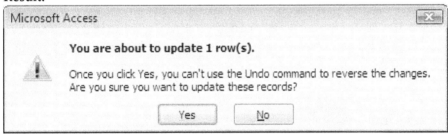

301.   Update multiple field values in a single record

Update address and city information for a single customer

Discussion:

Our job now is to update both the address and city information for a customer. In other words, we will update two fields of the same record. The criteria remain the same, but notice how the two fields that we are updating are separated by a comma in the SET part of the code.

SELECT *
FROM customers
WHERE lastname = "Demizio" AND firstname = "Michael"

Code:

```
UPDATE tbls_Customers_Upd
SET Address = "12 Lark Street", city = "Albany"
WHERE lastname = "Demizio" AND firstname = "Michael"
```

Result:

302.   Update a field value in multiple records

Update zip codes for all customers in a certain city

Discussion:

Our job request is to update zip code values for all of our customers in Denver, Colorado. It might look simple, but we need to pay attention and make sure the city of Denver does not exist in any other States. If it does, we need to add one more criterion in the WHERE clause to identify the state as well. Always run a SQL statement in advance to make sure your operation will affect the correct records.

```
SELECT *
FROM tbls_Customers_Upd
WHERE city = "Denver"
```

Code:

```
UPDATE tbls_Customers_Upd
SET zip = "22215"
WHERE city = "Denver"
```

Result:

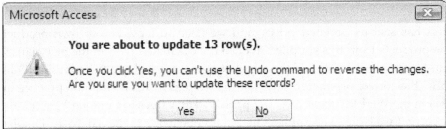

303. Update multiple field values in multiple records

Update city, zip, and address information for all customers in Dallas, Texas

Discussion:

Because of erroneous data entry, customers that show up from Denver, Colorado are actually from Tucson, Arizona. Consequently, we have to update their zip, city, and state information. We need to update multiple field values in multiple records in the database. This is possible by using multiple update values in the SET clause of the update statement. We must always check our criteria in the WHERE clause to make sure they identify the records we want to update.

```
SELECT *
FROM tbls_Customers_Upd
WHERE city = "Denver"
```

Code:

```
UPDATE tbls_Customers_Upd
SET zip = "22730", city = "Tucson", state = "AZ"
WHERE city = "Denver"
```

Result:

365

---

304. Update using calculated values

Update product prices increasing them by a certain percentage

Discussion:

One of our suppliers has sent us updated prices, and we need to increase our own product prices by 5% for the products from this supplier. Notice the calculated field in the SET clause. In the WHERE clause, notice that instead of the supplier name, we will use the supplier ID to make sure we identify the correct product records for this supplier. This is common practice in databases for criteria in the WHERE clause because primary key values are unique. Therefore, we do not need to worry if we have two suppliers with the same name in the database. Finally, notice in this example that we work with the query "Qry_SupplierPrices" which combines the information of suppliers and their products. Running update statements against queries is fine and sometimes desirable because they provide us with just the information we need rather than looking at huge tables. In this particular example, our supplier, "Home of Snacks", has increased prices by 5%, and we will increase our own prices by the same amount.

```
SELECT *
FROM Qry_SupplierPrices
WHERE supplierID = 1
```

Code:

```
UPDATE Qry_SupplierPrices
SET ProductUnitPrice = ProductUnitPrice * (1+0.05)
WHERE supplierID = 1
```

Result:

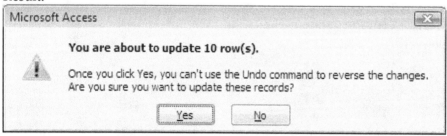

305. Update conditionally using the switch() function

Update product prices using different update conditions for every supplier

Discussion:

As you might expect, in everyday work scenarios, our suppliers, customers, students, or partners do not set up meetings to send us uniform and standardized information just so that we can have a nice time with our operations. Instead, they send us their own percentage increases and not at the same time. So, what can we do to take care of this business fact in minutes instead of making it an operational and administrative nightmare? We can combine the powers of the update statement and the switch() function. As you can see below, our suppliers sent us percentage updates ranging from 2% all the way up to 15%. Using the update statement with the switch() function, we obtain the following: First, using just one statement, we can take care of all of the particular updates in minutes. Second, the statement is so clean that it is reusable the next time we need to do the same job. Third, suppose that some of our suppliers have not sent us any updates. We can leave the statement below as is and update the ProductUnitPrice with itself as is the case with supplierID=5 where nothing is updated.

Code:
```
update Qry_SupplierPrices
SET ProductUnitPrice =
SWITCH (
supplierid=1,    ProductUnitPrice*(1.1) ,
supplierid=2,    ProductUnitPrice*(1.05),
supplierid=3,    ProductUnitPrice*(1.1) ,
supplierid=4,    ProductUnitPrice*(1.05) ,
supplierid=5,    ProductUnitPrice ,
supplierid=6,    ProductUnitPrice*(1.02) ,
supplierid=7,    ProductUnitPrice *(1.03),
supplierid=8,    ProductUnitPrice*(1.05) ,
supplierid=9,    ProductUnitPrice*(1.15) ,
supplierid=10,   ProductUnitPrice*(1.1) ,
)
```

Result:

Microsoft Access

You are about to update 70 row(s).

Once you click Yes, you can't use the Undo command to reverse the changes. Are you sure you want to update these records?

Yes   No

306. Update records in a table using criteria from another table

Update the products table using criteria from the suppliers table

Discussion:

In this example, our goal is to update prices in the tbls_products_Upd table using criteria from the suppliers table. We can achieve this using a subquery. The subquery will retrieve supplier ids from the suppliers table and will update the corresponding product prices in the tbls_products_Upd table. Specifically, the subquery will retrieve supplier ids for suppliers in Boston or Dallas and feed those ids in the WHERE clause of the main update statement.

Let me explain this point a bit more. The business request is to update product prices from suppliers in Boston and Dallas by 20% for everything coming from that direction. Our problem is that the tbls_products_Upd table does not contain any city information. Even so, we can satisfy management by using the subquery below:

Code:
```
UPDATE tbls_Products_Upd
SET ProductUnitPrice = ProductUnitPrice * (1+0.20)
WHERE SupplierID IN
(SELECT SupplierID FROM Suppliers
WHERE city= "Boston" or city = "Denver")
```

Result:

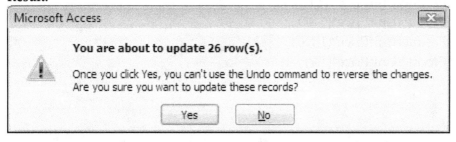

Microsoft Access

You are about to update 26 row(s).

Once you click Yes, you can't use the Undo command to reverse the changes. Are you sure you want to update these records?

[Yes]   [No]

CHAPTER 29
DELETE STATEMENTS

The principal role of delete statements is to remove multiple records in one operation. Instead of deleting table rows manually, we use delete statements to delete many of them with one SQL statement. The general syntax of a delete statement appears below, and while it looks simple, it can become an amazing tool when coupled with criteria and subqueries.

DELETE
FROM table
WHERE criteria

As with update statements, we cannot undo the results of delete statements. Thus, once we delete a set of records, there is no way to get them back. Consequently, we should always backup data or keep the deleted records in a temporary or historical table just in case we made a mistake. In this chapter, we will see how to easily move records to other tables before deleting them. Furthermore, it is professional practice to run a SELECT statement first to determine if its result set contains the records we want to delete and then, run the delete statement. Before we run any code in this chapter, we should learn about the role of cascade deletes. For all of the examples in this chapter, cascade deletes are off, and we should keep them off in our databases as well unless we specifically want to take advantage of their functionality in specific situations. We want cascade deletes off so that we do not accidentally delete a record in a table and then the database deletes all related records in related tables.

307.   What are cascade deletes, how to use them, and what they mean
In order to understand cascade deletes in full, let's work with the record of a customer from five years ago who is no longer in business. We want to delete this customer from the database so that it does not come up in queries and does not take up space.

We could simply go to the customers table and try to delete this record. However, if there are associated orders with this customer, the database will not allow us to delete it since we would then end up with orphaned records in the orders table. Referential integrity rules do not allow this to happen, and we would not be able to delete the customer. For a full explanation of referential integrity, check chapter 4. Understanding referential integrity is a must for all database professionals and users. To delete this customer manually, we should first go to the orders table and delete all of the orders associated with this customer. However, since we also have a many-to-many relationship between Orders and Products, we first need to go to the Products_Orders table and delete the associations (records) of Orders and Products for that customer. If we need to delete the customer Mary from the database, we need to do the following in the order provided:

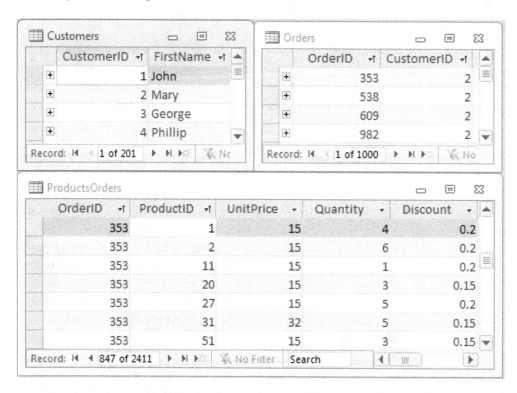

- Delete from the Products_Orders table all of the records with orderid 353, 538, 609, and 982. For example, order 353 contains products 1, 2, 11, 20, 27, 31, and 51.
- Delete from the Orders table the orders with orderid = 353, 538, 609, and 982 since they all belong to Mary.
- Finally, delete Mary's record with CustomerID = 2 from the Customer table.

Even in this simple scenario, deleting a customer is an involved process. Imagine the scenario where you have hundreds of customers with thousands of associated orders. It would be humanly impossible to remove customers manually.

This is where cascade deletes come in. By using cascade deletes, we can delete a customer in the primary table, and the database itself will delete all references to that customer in all related tables. In this example, if cascade deletes are on, when we delete Mary from the customers table, the database will automatically delete all of Mary's references in the Orders and Product_Orders tables reliably and at once. To turn cascade deletes on, follow these steps:

1. Click on the "Database Tools" tab. Then, in the group "Relationships", click on "Relationships".

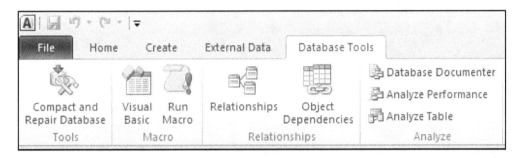

2. This will open up the Relationships window as shown below:

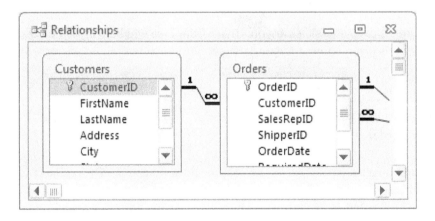

3. Double click on the relationship line between customers and orders. The following screen will appear. Click on "Cascade Delete Related Fields", and click "OK".

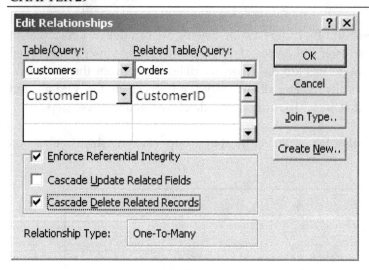

4. Repeat step two for the relationship between the tables Orders and Products_Orders, and enable cascade deletes as well.

5. At this point, if we open the customers table and delete Mary's record, all of Mary's orders will be deleted from the Orders table, and all respective associations between Orders and products will be deleted from the Products_Orders table.

For the purposes of this chapter, cascade deletes are off. In addition, we will be working on the tbls_Orders_DEL table, which is just a copy of the Orders table in which we can delete records at will.

308. Delete a single record in a table
Delete a specific customer's order
Discussion:
The goal in this example is to delete a customer's order. Notice how we use the OrderID as the criterion in the WHERE clause. The OrderID is the primary key of the Orders table, and it will uniquely identify the record for deletion. Try to use primary key values for criteria instead of fields such as customer names, which might have duplicates in the table with the result of deleting records you do not want to delete. In addition, always run a SELECT beforehand or a SELECT INTO so that you can identify or backup your data respectively. I will show you how you can use the SELECT INTO to make a temporary table for deleted data. For this example, you need to follow four steps:

Step 1: Run a SELECT statement to uniquely identify and verify records for deletion. Never run a delete statement directly.

SELECT *
FROM tbls_Orders_Del
WHERE orderid = 20

Step 2: Turn on cascade deletes for the relationship between the tables Orders and ProductsOrders.

Step 3: Run the DELETE statement
DELETE
FROM tbls_Orders_Del
WHERE orderid = 20

Result:

Step 4: Turn off cascade deletes for the relationship between the tables Orders and ProductsOrders so that nobody can delete any orders by mistake. If they are off, the database will give a referential integrity warning. We can open the Orders table and try to delete any record to have a look at the referential integrity message. Check chapter 4 for a full explanation of referential integrity consequences.

309. Delete multiple records in a table
Delete all orders for a specific customer
Discussion:
In this example, we want to delete all orders for customerid= 2, i.e. Mary. To achieve this task, we will use the CustomerID field in the WHERE clause, which is the primary key for the customers table and the foreign key in the orders table. Our task involves four steps as they appear below:

Step 1: Run a SELECT statement to uniquely identify and verify records for deletion.
SELECT *
FROM tbls_Orders_Del
WHERE customerid = 2

Step 2: Turn on cascade deletes for the relationship between the tables Orders and ProductsOrders. We do not need to turn cascade deletes on for the relationship between the tables customers and orders since we are not deleting the customer herself in this case—just her orders.

Step 3: Run the DELETE statement
DELETE
FROM tbls_Orders_Del
WHERE customerid = 2

Result:

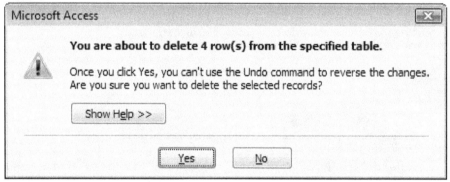

Step 4: Turn off cascade deletes for the relationship between the tables Orders and ProductsOrders so that nobody can delete any orders by mistake.

310. Delete records in a certain date range
Delete multiple orders from multiple customers within a date range
Discussion:
This is an example of how we can use date criteria to delete orders within a specified date range. In this date range, we might have multiple orders from multiple customers.

Our four steps to delete all orders for a specific date range appear below:

Step 1: Run a SELECT statement to uniquely identify and verify records for deletion.

SELECT *
FROM tbls_Orders_Del
WHERE orderdate BETWEEN #10/15/2012# AND #10/17/2012#

Step 2: Turn on cascade deletes for the relationship between tables Orders and ProductsOrders.

Step 3: Run the DELETE statement
DELETE
FROM tbls_Orders_Del
WHERE orderdate BETWEEN #10/15/2012# AND #10/17/2012#

Result:

Step 4: Turn off cascade deletes for the relationship between tables Orders and ProductsOrders so that no one can delete any orders by mistake.

311. Delete duplicate records while controlling if you want to delete the earliest or the latest ones

Delete earliest or latest duplicate customer orders
Discussion:
Let's discuss the setup of this example so that you can understand it in detail. First, in the table tbls_Orders_DEL, records with orderid 1001, 1002, and 1003 are duplicates. Specifically, the record with orderid = 1 is identical to 1001, the record with orderid = 988 is identical to 1002, and the record with orderid = 990 is identical to 1003. Keep in mind that these records have identical field values but different primary keys values.

The burning question is which records we should delete; the earliest ones or the latest ones? We know that a record with a lesser orderid value was entered before a record with a higher orderid value since the primary key is an autonumber. In the following example, we discuss both alternatives in detail. In any case, the four steps to follow appear below:

Step 1: Run a SELECT statement to uniquely identify and verify records for deletion.
The SQL statement below will SELECT the records with smaller orderid values. Notice we use a subquery to obtain what we need. In the main SELECT statement, we select all orders from the tbls_Orders_Del table that do not belong in the subquery. Consequently, we need to check what the subquery will fetch. The subquery itself will fetch the duplicate records with the maximum orderid values in the tbls_Orders_Del table. From the six duplicated records, it will select the three with the maximum orderID values (1001, 1002, and 1003). The main SELECT statement will fetch what is left from the six duplicated records, i.e. 1, 988, and 990. We can also use the NOT IN operator instead of the "<>" inequality predicate to obtain the same results. I know it is counter intuitive to use max() to get the earliest records, but max() is used in the subquery to identify duplicates with maximum primary key values. Then, the main SELECT statement will fetch all duplicates not in the subquery. The logic is the same the other way around for the next example:

SELECT *
FROM tbls_Orders_Del AS T2
WHERE OrderID <>
(SELECT Max(OrderID)
FROM tbls_Orders_Del AS T1
WHERE T2.CustomerID = T1.CustomerID AND T2.SalesRepID = T1.SalesRepID AND T2.ShipperID = T1.ShipperID AND T2.OrderDate = T1.OrderDate)

Query1				
OrderID ▾	CustomerID ▾	SalesRepID ▾	ShipperID ▾	OrderDate ▾
1	139	2	2	11/6/2013
988	145	10	1	3/21/2014
990	160	10	1	5/17/2012

Record: I◀ ◀ 1 of 3 ▶ ▶I ▶▦ ▓ No Filter Search

This SQL statement will select the latest duplicate records:

SELECT *
FROM tbls_Orders_Del AS T2
WHERE OrderID <>
(SELECT Min(OrderID)
FROM tbls_Orders_Del AS T1
WHERE T2.CustomerID = T1.CustomerID AND T2.SalesRepID = T1.SalesRepID AND
T2.ShipperID = T1.ShipperID AND T2.OrderDate = T1.OrderDate)

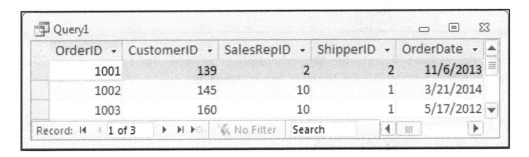

Step 2: Turn on cascade deletes for the relationship between the tables Orders and
ProductsOrders

Step 3: Run the DELETE statement
DELETE
FROM tbls_Orders_Del AS T2
WHERE OrderID <>
(SELECT Min(OrderID)
FROM tbls_Orders_Del AS T1
WHERE T2.CustomerID = T1.CustomerID AND T2.SalesRepID = T1.SalesRepID AND
T2.ShipperID = T1.ShipperID AND T2.OrderDate = T1.OrderDate)

Result:

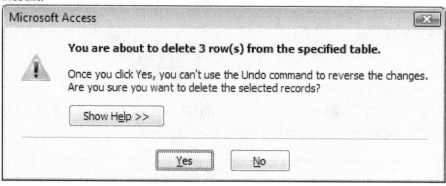

Step 4: Turn off cascade deletes for the relationship between the tables Orders and ProductsOrders so that nobody can delete any orders by mistake.

312. Delete ALL duplicate records (originals plus duplicates) that have the same field values and same primary key values

Delete all duplicate customer orders including original and duplicate orders

Discussion:

In this example, our goal is to delete all duplicate orders, including the original orders. We are working on a scenario where six records are identical such as records with orderids 1, 3, and 5. The records with orderid = 2 and 4 are unique and should not be touched. Notice that for this example, I have created a new table named tbls_Orders_Del2.

OrderID	CustomerID	SalesRepID	ShipperID	OrderDate
5	123	2	2	11/14/2012
5	123	2	2	11/14/2012
3	137	2	2	6/29/2013
3	137	2	2	6/29/2013
2	184	2	1	7/25/2013
1	139	2	2	11/6/2013
1	139	2	2	11/6/2013
4	165	2	1	12/14/2014

Record: 1 of 8 — No Filter — Search

The four steps to run in a real situation are the following:

Step 1: Run a SELECT statement to uniquely identify and verify records for deletion.
SELECT *
FROM tbls_Orders_DEL2
WHERE orderid IN(
SELECT OrderID
FROM tbls_Orders_DEL2
GROUP BY OrderID, CustomerID, ShipperID, OrderDate
HAVING count(*)>1)

Step 2: Turn on cascade deletes for the relationship between the tables Orders and ProductsOrders.

Step 3: Run the DELETE statement
DELETE
FROM tbls_Orders_DEL2
WHERE OrderID IN(
SELECT OrderID
FROM tbls_Orders_DEL2
GROUP BY OrderID, CustomerID, ShipperID, OrderDate
HAVING count(*)>1)

Result:

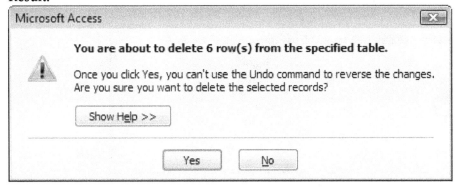

Step 4: Turn off cascade deletes for the relationship between the tables Orders and ProductsOrders.

313. Use SELECT INTO to back up records before deleting them

Create a temp table to back up customers' orders before deleting them

Discussion:

In this example, we delete records from the tbls_Orders_DEL table but just in case we need these records later on, we back them up on the fly in a new table using a SELECT INTO statement. In addition, if we want to append the deleted records in a historical table, we can easily do so by using the INSERT INTO statement, which has the functionality of an append query. The bottom line is that the code of both SQL statements for SELECT INTO or INSERT INTO will be exactly the same with the code of the DELETE statement changing only its first line.

Code:

```
SELECT * INTO TempTable
FROM tbls_Orders_Del
WHERE orderdate
BETWEEN #10/15/2012# AND #10/17/2012#
```

```
DELETE
FROM tbls_Orders_Del
WHERE orderdate
BETWEEN #10/15/2012# AND #10/17/2012#
```

Result:

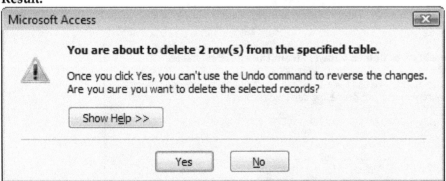

314. Delete records in a table based on values in a different table using a subquery

Delete records from the orders table using criteria from the customers table

Discussion:

This time, we have a request from management to delete all orders from Los Angeles for a customer with a last name Orlando. The problem is we do not have a state field and a last name field in the orders table. This is ok since we can use a subquery to easily delete records in one table based on criteria from a different table. In a production environment, follow the steps below:

Step 1: Run a SELECT statement to uniquely identify and verify records for deletion.

SELECT *
FROM tbls_Orders_DEL
WHERE CustomerID IN
(SELECT CustomerID FROM Customers
WHERE city= "Los Angeles" AND lastname = "Orlando")

Step 2: Turn on cascade deletes for the relationship between the tables Orders and ProductsOrders.

Step 3: Run the DELETE statement
DELETE
FROM tbls_Orders_DEL
WHERE CustomerID IN
(SELECT CustomerID FROM Customers
WHERE city= "Los Angeles" AND lastname = "Orlando")

Result:

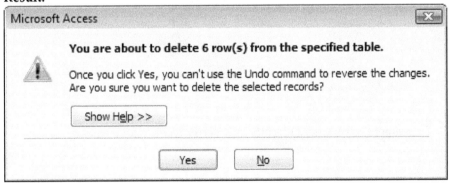

Step 4: Turn off cascade deletes for the relationship between the tables Orders and ProductsOrders.

315. Delete records in a table based on calculations in a different table

Update address information for a single customer

Discussion:

This time, the request from management is to delete all orders with a grand total of more than $500. We need to resort to the Products_Orders table for criteria, make calculations on this table, and use the calculated fields as criteria. It sounds like a big deal, but it is not.

A sample dataset from the ProductsOrders table appears below. Notice the pairs of OrderIDs and ProductIDs so that you know what product is included in what order. For example, order 2 contains products 32 and 70. Order 3 contains products 26, 27, 43, and 51.

To be able to comply with the request of management, we first need to calculate order subtotals or, in other words, total amounts for each product. To put it yet another way, we multiply unitprice*quantity. Once we have the order subtotals, we need to calculate order totals. To do this, we use the SUM() function and the GROUP BY clause. Finally, since we only want order totals which exceed $500, we insert the criterion ">500" in the HAVING clause. Please note that we use HAVING instead of WHERE since HAVING is applied after the records are grouped while WHERE is applied before they are grouped.

OrderID	ProductID	UnitPrice	Quantity	Discount
2	23	15	4	0.15
2	24	15	1	0.2
2	32	15	3	0
2	70	15	6	0.15
3	26	22	3	0.2
3	27	15	2	0.15
3	43	15	5	0.15
3	51	15	4	0.2

Record: 1 of 2411 · No Filter · Search

Step 1: Run a SELECT statement to uniquely identify and verify records for deletion.

```
SELECT
FROM tbls_Orders_DEL
WHERE OrderID IN(
SELECT Sum([unitprice]*[quantity]) AS totalOrder
FROM ProductsOrders
GROUP BY OrderID
HAVING (((Sum([unitprice]*[quantity]))>500)))
```

Step 2: Turn on cascade deletes for the relationship between the tables Orders and ProductsOrders.

Step 3: Run the DELETE statement
```
DELETE
FROM tbls_Orders_DEL
WHERE OrderID IN(
SELECT Sum([unitprice]*[quantity]) AS totalOrder
FROM ProductsOrders
GROUP BY OrderID
HAVING (((Sum([unitprice]*[quantity]))>500)))
```

Result:

Step 4: Turn off cascade deletes for the relationship between the tables Orders and ProductsOrders.

CHAPTER 30
WORKING WITH JOINS

The power of joins is a bit of a hidden jewel in the world of databases and data analysis. Developers and power users alike stay away from a good understanding of joins, mostly because they perceive them as complicated and impractical concepts. Both beliefs are false. You must understand joins to understand databases, and they are actually easy to use. They just look complicated. Devoting some time to understanding the remarkable muscle of joins will transform the way you work and give you amazing flexibility in your everyday work tasks. In this chapter, we will look at practical applications of joins through realistic scenarios. In fact, this is the only way someone could convince me to use joins: Show me what they can actually do in practice.

In relational databases, we keep data in separate tables. We keep supplier information in the suppliers table, customers in the customer table, and orders in an orders table. This is what we call the physical structure or design of the database. This is done so that normalization rules apply in the database where we keep our business transactions (orders, quotations, invoices). What we are interested in, however, are the conceptual invocations from a relational database. We would like to generate and send out information, such as invoices, in a way that makes sense for our customers and for us. In this respect, joins are links that we establish between or among tables with the goal of retrieving related information.

In this chapter, we will explore the use of inner, left, and right joins. Among these three, inner joins are the most commonly used in practical applications. Left joins are useful in certain business scenarios, while right joins can be used to check the integrity of the database and identify any orphaned records.

316. Inner Joins
Find customers who actually have some orders
Discussion:
Let us assume our supervisor has a very simple request: She wants a report of customers who actually ordered something from us. The customers table might include people who asked for quotations, leads, or it might include customers who have not ordered anything for some time.

How can we answer this request? We can go back to the chapter about duplicate, orphaned, and related records and use a subquery such as:

Code:
```
SELECT *
FROM Customers
WHERE CustomerID
IN (SELECT CustomerID from tbls_Orders)
```

Result:
Notice the number of customers returned is only 190. However, in the customers table, there are 201 customers. So, 11 customers have not had any orders at all for the historical data we have.

We can achieve the same result using a join. Let's create a new query in design view and add the customers and orders tables. There is a one-to-many relationship between customers and orders. For one customer, there might be multiple orders, but each order definitely belongs to one customer.

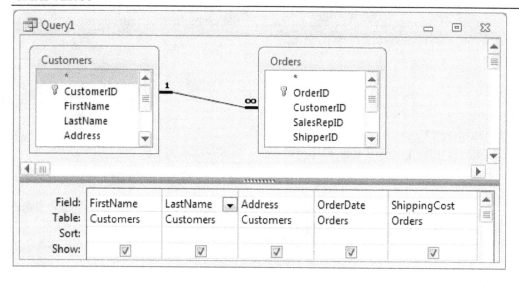

Double-click on the relationship line between customers and orders. The following dialog box comes up. By default, Access 2010 will join two tables through an inner join or, in other words, include records from each table where there is a common CustomerID value. By the way, CustomerID is the primary key (PK) in the customers table and the foreign key (FK) in the orders table.

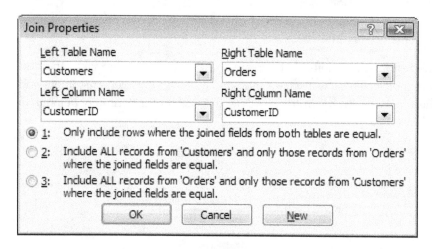

This is the case of an inner join. Notice that an inner join will give us the customers who have orders. If there are any customers without orders, they will not appear in the result set. In addition, if there are any orders without associated customers, they will not appear either. Only where the two tables match on the CustomerID will records be returned. The SQL code for the inner join appears below. Notice that the database returned 1000 records. This is because there are 1000 cases in which the CustomerID in the customers table has an associated

CustomerID in the orders table. The eleven customers without a CustomerID in the orders table will not appear in the result set of this inner join.

Code:

```
SELECT FirstName, LastName, Address, OrderDate, ShippingCost
FROM Customers
INNER JOIN Orders ON Customers.CustomerID = Orders.CustomerID
```

Result:

Discussion:

The initial request, however, was to present a list of unique customers who have orders. We do not need any repeated customer names in the result set. To achieve this, we need an inner join and a GROUP BY clause by last name, first name, and address fields. Notice how the number of customers returned is the same as that returned by the subquery we used in the beginning of this example.

Code:

```
SELECT FirstName, LastName, Address
FROM Customers
INNER JOIN Orders ON Customers.CustomerID = Orders.CustomerID
GROUP BY FirstName, LastName, Address
```

Result:

317. Left Joins

List all customers whether they have orders or not

Discussion:

There are cases in which we do not want to retrieve only the matching records from two related tables. For instance, we might want to list all customers from the customers table and their associated orders where they exist. In this case, the output of our query will list all records from the customers table and their associated orders in the orders table. For customers without orders, it will return blank values for fields from the orders table such as the OrderDate and ShippingCost fields.

The figure below shows the query design for an inner join, which is the default join type when we create a query in Access 2010.

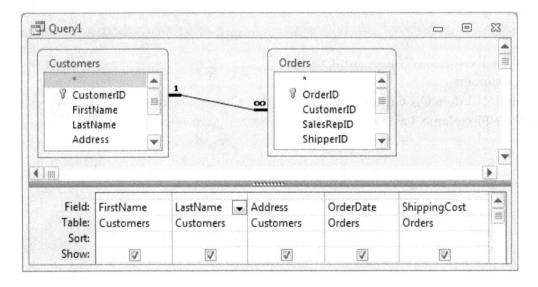

Double-click on the relationship line between customers and orders. The Joins dialog box comes up. Change the join type to number 2: "Include ALL records from Customers and only those records from Orders where the joined fields are equal".

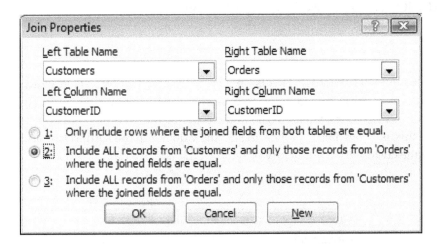

The query design now changes to:

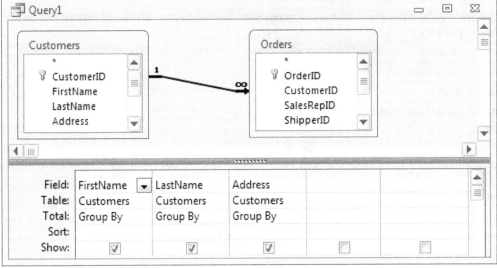

A left join will output all of customers from the customers table and any related fields from the orders table based on matches on the CustomerID field. If there are any customers without orders, they will still appear in the result set. If there are any orders without associated customers, they will not appear in the result set. Notice the relationship arrow that now has a point toward the Orders table. This is the visual sign that there is a left join relationship between these two tables.

Code:

SELECT lastname, firstname, Address, OrderDate, ShippingCost
FROM Customers LEFT JOIN Orders ON Customers.CustomerID =
Orders.CustomerID;

Result:

Note that the database returned 1011 records. This is because there are 1000 records in which the CustomerID in the customers table has an associated CustomerID in the orders table. In addition, we have 11 customers without a CustomerID in the orders table, but they will appear in the result set because this is a left join. Notice the blank values for the OrderDate and ShippingCost for some of the customers without any orders.

lastname	firstname	Address	OrderDate	ShippingCost
Demarco	John	11 Lark Street	6/10/2012	34
Demarco	John	11 Lark Street	6/9/2013	40
Demarco	John	11 Lark Street	11/7/2012	34
Demarco	John	11 Lark Street	3/23/2012	49

Query1

Record: 1 of 1011 — No Filter — Search

318. Right Joins

List all orders including those without customers

Discussion:

In this scenario, we want to produce a list of all orders from the orders table whether or not they have any matching records in the customers table. If a record from the orders table has a matching record in the customers table, this is fine and should actually be the case for all orders. If our query returns any records in which the fields from the customers table are blank, these are orphaned records. This means that we have orders without customers, and the integrity of our database is compromised. Let's start with a normal query and see how we can change it to a right join query.

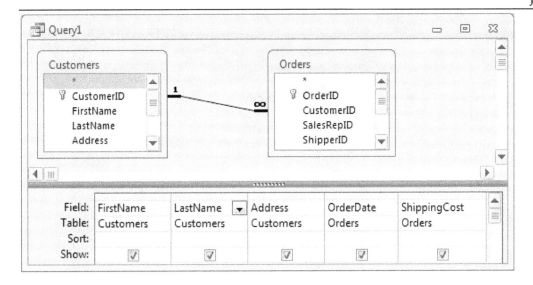

Double-click on the relationship line between customers and orders. The Joins dialog box comes up. Change the join type to number 3: "Include ALL records from Orders and only those records from Customers where the joined fields are equal".

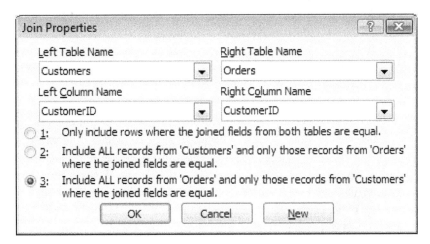

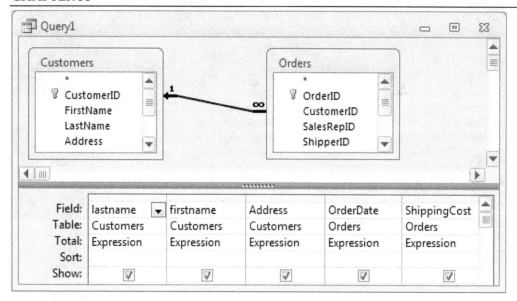

A right join will output all of the orders from the orders table and any related customers from the customers table based on matches on the CustomerID field. If there are any orders without customers, they will still appear in the result set. If this is the case, these orders are considered orphaned records, and they need to be investigated very closely and eliminated from the database. In addition, we need to have a look at the database design to see how it is possible that these orders are there in the first place. This can happen only if referential integrity is off. If it is off, turn it on.

Then, we need to deal with the orphaned records. We cannot have orders without customers because first, it does not make sense and second, because our database integrity is compromised. Maybe these were orders belonging to existing customers and entered with the wrong CustomerID as the foreign key while referential integrity was not on. If this is the case, change the value of the CustomerID field in the orders table to associate them with existing customers in the customers table. If we cannot find any customers to associate the orphaned orders, we must delete them from the database. Notice the relationship arrow that now has a point toward the customers table. This is the visual sign that there is a relationship with a right join between these two tables.

Code:

SELECT lastname, firstname, Address, OrderDate, ShippingCost
FROM Customers
RIGHT JOIN Orders ON Customers.CustomerID = Orders.CustomerID;

Result:

Notice that the database returned 1000 records. This is because there are 1000 records in which the CustomerID in the orders table has an associated CustomerID in the customers table. As you know, there are 11 customers without a CustomerID in the orders table, but they will not appear in the result set because this is a right join listing ALL records in the orders table and only associated customers in the customers table. Notice that we do not have any blank values for the lastname, firstname, and address fields from the customers table, which means we have no orphaned records in the orders table.

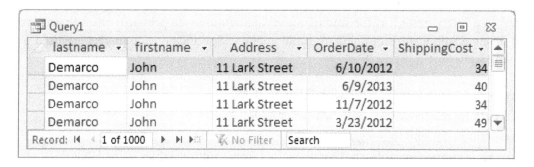

CHAPTER 31
WORKING WITH SUB-QUERIES

A subquery is a query nested within another query. Subqueries are primarily used to achieve results in a single step instead of using multiple queries. Specifically, subqueries are used in the following scenarios:

1. To create dynamic search lists with IN or NOT IN
2. To perform existence tests with EXISTS or NOT EXISTS
3. To perform dynamic aggregations with aggregate functions
4. To create temporary tables that combine data from multiple tables using UNION
5. To update records in update statements
6. To delete records in delete statements
7. To find duplicate records
8. To find related records in another table
9. To return a single value
10. To create dynamic and customized data categories using the switch() function

Let us explore the scenarios above through practical examples.

319. Use a subquery with the IN predicate to find non-discounted products
Find orders for which you extended no discounts for at least one of the products included in the order (solution 1)

Discussion:
Our business goal in this example is to retrieve orders for which we provided no discount for at least one of the products contained in the order. That is, for at least one of the products contained in these orders, the discount rate was 0. Keep in mind that there might be multiple products in each order. In addition, notice that the ProductsOrders table is the table in between that establishes the many-to-many relationship between the Orders and Products tables. Consequently, the logic should be to first look in the ProductsOrders table for all of the products with zero discounts. Using the OrderID from this result (the subquery) you will be

able to find the corresponding orders in the Orders table. From the result, we can see that out of the 1000 orders in the Orders table, we provided at least one non-discounted product for 136 orders.

Code:
SELECT *
FROM orders
WHERE orderid
IN (SELECT orderid FROM ProductsOrders WHERE (Discount) =0)

Main Query Result:

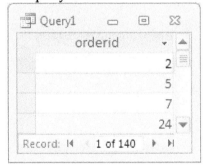

Subquery Result:

Notice that we have a discrepancy: The subquery returned a list of 140 orders, while the main query returned a list of only 136 orders. What happened? As you can see in the picture below, there are some orders like OrderID=390 which contain two products, and we provided no discounts for either of them Order 390 appears twice in the subquery but only once in the main query, which means that the final count of 136 is correct.

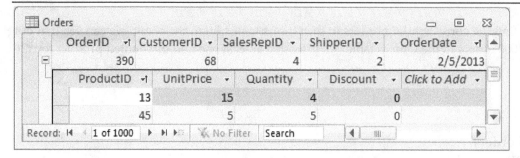

320. Use a subquery with EXISTS to find non-discounted products

Find orders for which we extended no discounts for at least one of the products included (solution 2)

Discussion:

A more effective and faster solution than using the IN predicate is to use EXISTS. By using EXISTS, we expect the subquery to return some values. In this example, we are again looking for non-discounted products in orders, and we will obtain the exact same result as in the previous example. O and P are simply abbreviated names for the Orders and ProductsOrders tables respectively.

Code:
```
SELECT *
FROM Orders O
WHERE EXISTS (SELECT OrderID FROM ProductsOrders P WHERE O.OrderID = P.OrderID AND discount = 0);
```

Result:

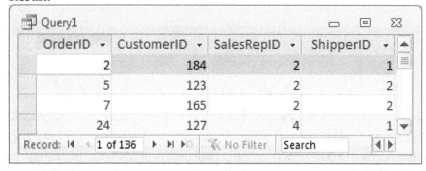

321. Use a subquery with the IN predicate to find customers with orders in a specific quarter

Find customers with orders in the fourth quarter of the year 2012 (solution 1)

Discussion:

In this example, we will use the IN predicate with two date functions to retrieve customers with orders in the fourth quarter of 2012. Keep in mind we are looking for customer names and not orders placed in that period.

Code:

SELECT *
FROM Customers
WHERE CustomerID IN
(Select CustomerID FROM Orders WHERE
((((DatePart("q",[OrderDate]))=4) AND ((Year([orderdate]))=2012)))

Result:

322. Use a subquery with EXISTS to find customers with orders in a specific quarter

Find customers with orders in the fourth quarter of the year 20102(solution 2)

Discussion:

We can obtain the same output with the previous example by using EXISTS.

Code:

SELECT *
FROM Customers C
WHERE EXISTS
(Select CustomerID FROM Orders O WHERE C.CustomerID = O.CustomerID AND
((((DatePart("q",[OrderDate]))=4) AND ((Year([orderdate]))=2012)))

Result:

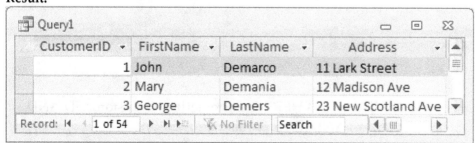

323. Use a subquery with EXISTS to relate two tables on fields other than the primary keys

Find customers who reside in the same city as that of sales representatives

Discussion:

Our supervisor asks for a list of customers who live in the same city as our sales representatives. So, if we have a sales representative in Orlando, Florida, our supervisor wants us to identify all of the customers living in that city. We need to create a relationship between the Customers and SalesReps tables based on the city field. We can accomplish this task using the following SQL statement. As you can see from the result set, we have 58 customers living in the same cities as our salespeople.

Code:

```
SELECT *
FROM customers
WHERE exists
(SELECT *
FROM salesreps
WHERE customers.city = salesreps.city)
```

Result:

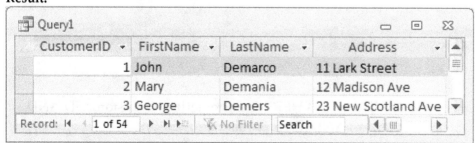

324. Use a subquery with the NOT IN predicate to find orphaned records

Find orders without customers

Discussion:

We can easily retrieve orphaned records using a subquery. In this example, we are looking for orders without customers. If we find any orders without customers, you need to delete them from the database and check the referential integrity setting for the one-to-many relationship between the tables Customers and Orders. In this example, we use the table tbls_orders where I put some orphaned records for demonstration purposes. As you can see from the result set, three orphaned records are found.

Code:

```
SELECT *
FROM tbls_orders
WHERE CustomerID
NOT IN (SELECT CustomerID FROM Customers)
```

Result:

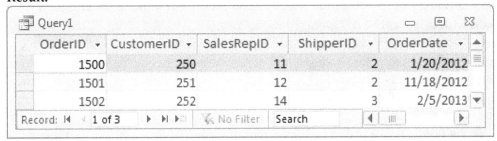

OrderID	CustomerID	SalesRepID	ShipperID	OrderDate
1500	250	11	2	1/20/2012
1501	251	12	2	11/18/2012
1502	252	14	3	2/5/2013

Record: 1 of 3 — No Filter — Search

325. Use a subquery with NOT EXISTS to find unrelated records

Find customers without any orders

Discussion:

This time, we will use NOT EXISTS to find customers who have not submitted any orders at all. Thus, we are trying to find customers without any related orders in the orders table. This is not a problem when it comes to database integrity. It is just a business fact. We might want to initiate a promotional campaign for these customers, for example.

Code:
```
SELECT *
FROM Customers C
WHERE NOT EXISTS (SELECT CustomerID FROM Orders O WHERE C.CustomerID
= O.CustomerID)
```

Result:

CustomerID ▾	FirstName ▾	LastName ▾	Address ▾
19	Erin	Erin	28 Karrie Terrace
37	Allan	Cimo	24 Crestwood CT
40	Kelly	Costa	45 Sixth Ave
66	Arnold	Webster	53 Southern Blvd

Record: I◄ ◄ 1 of 11 ► ►I ►※ 🏷 No Filter Search ◄ IIII ►

326. Use a subquery to find above average priced products (working on one table)

Find products with prices above the average product price

Discussion:

In this example, we are looking for products with above average prices. We want the database to calculate the average price per product, compare every product price to the average price, and display only those products which exceed the average price. It looks like a lot for a single SQL statement, but it is possible. The essence of this SQL statement is in the WHERE clause where we ask the ProductUnitPrice to be bigger than the average ProductUnitPrice using the inequality predicate ">" and the aggregate function avg().

Code:
```
SELECT productname, ProductUnitPrice
FROM Products
WHERE (ProductUnitPrice) > (SELECT avg(ProductUnitPrice) FROM Products)
ORDER BY ProductUnitPrice DESC
```

Result:

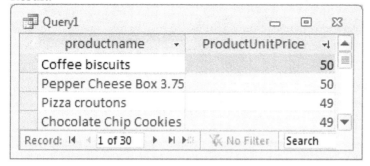

327. Use a subquery, EXISTS, GROUP BY, HAVING, and the sum() function to isolate bigger orders (working with two tables)

List order information with shipped invoices above $500

Discussion:

This time, we need to retrieve orders with a total of over $500. Our problem is that we need to list order information from the Orders table while making calculations on the ProductsOrders table where we keep product prices and quantities. We can achieve this task using a subquery with EXISTS and GROUP BY, which will run very fast as well.

The crucial part of this piece of code is in the GROUP BY clause. We need to group by OrderID in the subquery since in the ProductsOrders table, the same OrderID appears multiple times because there might be multiple products in the same order. (Check the GROUP BY chapter for details). However, we want our subquery to produce only one OrderID per order. In addition, we use the HAVING clause because we do not know beforehand what orders have a total of $500 or more. By using the HAVING clause, we are telling the database to first calculate the order totals through the sum() function, group the results by order, and then, apply the filter (Sum([unitprice]*[quantity]))>500).

Code:

```
SELECT *
FROM orders O
WHERE EXISTS
(SELECT orderid, Sum([unitprice]*[quantity])
FROM ProductsOrders P
WHERE O.OrderID = P.OrderID
GROUP BY orderid
HAVING (((Sum([unitprice]*[quantity]))>500)))
```

Result:

OrderID	CustomerID	SalesRepID	ShipperID	OrderDate
308	196	3	3	10/20/2013
354	3	4	1	4/28/2012
404	101	4	2	11/23/2013
609	2	6	2	5/9/2014

Record: 1 of 5 — No Filter — Search

328. Create temporary tables using a subquery and UNION

Retrieve person information from customers and suppliers and create a temp table with the combined results

Discussion:

Let's assume that a fellow employee asks us for a combined list of names and addresses of our customers and suppliers because she wants to send out a common greeting postcard to all of them. We can create a temporary table with the combination of names using the SELECT INTO and UNION statements in combination. Notice how single quotes (") are used in the SQL statement for suppliers since in that table, there are no first and last name fields.

Code:

```
SELECT lastname, firstname, address, city, state, zip INTO tempPeopleTable
FROM
(SELECT lastname, firstname, address, city, state, zip
FROM customers
UNION
SELECT ContactName, '' , address, city, state, zip
FROM suppliers)
```

Result:

Microsoft Access

You are about to paste 211 row(s) into a new table.

Once you click Yes, you can't use the Undo command to reverse the changes. Are you sure you want to create a new table with the selected records?

Yes   No

329. Update records in one table using criteria from another using a subquery

Update product prices in the products table using criteria from the suppliers table

Discussion:

Management has decided to increase the prices of products from suppliers from Boston and Dallas. This is because transportation costs from those cities have increased considerably lately. We need to update prices in the products table using criteria from the suppliers table. This time, we also need to use filtering criteria within the subquery statement. The subquery in this example needs to retrieve the SupplierIDs of suppliers in Boston and Dallas. The resulting SupplierIDs will be used by the main query to update product prices in the products table. Notice that in the products table, every record contains a SupplierID value.

Code:

```
UPDATE tbls_Products_Upd
SET ProductUnitPrice = ProductUnitPrice * (1+0.20)
WHERE SupplierID IN
(SELECT SupplierID FROM Suppliers
WHERE city= "Boston" or city = "Dallas")
```

Result:

330. Delete records in one table using criteria in another table

Delete order information in the orders table using criteria from the customers table

Discussion:

This time, our task is to delete orders from customers in Los Angeles and Orlando. These orders will be processed by another distribution center, and we do not want them to clutter our database and affect our reports. In essence, the subquery will retrieve the CustomerIDs of these customers from the Customers table. Then, the main query will use these CustomerIDs to delete the orders that contain them in the tbls_Orders_DEEL table. Always remember to run a SELECT statement first before deleting records. (Check chapter 29 for a full overview of DELETE statements).

Code:

```
DELETE
FROM tbls_Orders_DEL
WHERE CustomerID IN
(SELECT CustomerID FROM Customers
WHERE city= "Los Angeles" AND lastname = "Orlando")
```

Result:

331. Find duplicate records using a subquery

Find all duplicate records in a table

Discussion:

Our goal in this example is to use a subquery to find all duplicate records in the tbls_Orders table. Keep in mind that these records have identical field values and identical primary keys values. So, they are exact duplicates. If you need to find duplicate records based on the values of one or multiple fields but with different primary key values, consult chapter 23 where I list various scenarios for duplicate records. As you can see from the result set in this example, there are 11 duplicate records in this table.

Code:

```
SELECT *
FROM tbls_Orders WHERE OrderID IN(
SELECT OrderID
FROM tbls_Orders
GROUP BY OrderID
HAVING count(*)>1)
ORDER BY OrderID
```

Result:

OrderID	CustomerID	SalesRepID	ShipperID	OrderDate
8	71	3	1	4/1/2014
8	71	3	1	4/1/2014
45	93	1	3	10/23/2012
45	93	1	3	10/23/2012
254	198	3	2	7/15/2012
254	198	3	2	7/15/2012
820	46	8	1	9/4/2014
820	46	8	1	9/4/2014
993	99	10	2	10/14/2012
993	99	10	2	10/14/2012
993	99	10	2	10/14/2012

Record: 1 of 11   No Filter   Search

332.   Use the max() function to return a single value in the subquery

Find the latest shipped order from the orders table

Discussion:

Let's assume we need to present the details of the latest order we shipped. We can find the maximum (latest) shipped date in the orders table and use this date as a criterion to list the details of our latest order. This way, however, we need to create two queries. In addition, if we need to use it again, we need to remember the names of the two queries and their association. Instead, with a subquery, we can perform both steps in one SQL statement as follows:

Code:

```
SELECT *
FROM Orders
WHERE shippeddate = (SELECT max(ShippedDate) FROM Orders)
```

Result:

OrderID	CustomerID	SalesRepID	ShipperID	OrderDate
4	165	2	1	12/19/2014
* (New)				

Record: 1 of 1   No Filter   Search

333.   Create a crosstab report with a subquery

Create a crosstab report that shows the number of products in every discount percentage category

Discussion:

In this example, we have a request from management to present a report that will list all orders, the number of products in each order, and the discount category each product belongs to. For each order, management wants to know how many products were given a 0 discount, how many a 15% discount, and how many a 20% discount. This is a crosstab query, but we can actually use subqueries to create this report. As you can see from the code below, we can use a subquery to create the discount category we want. We can include any discount categories we want and leave out the ones that we do not want to appear.

Code:
```
SELECT OrderID,

(SELECT Count(*) FROM ProductsOrders P
WHERE O.OrderID=P.OrderID AND (discount = 0) ) AS '0%',

(SELECT Count(*) FROM ProductsOrders P
WHERE O.OrderID=P.OrderID AND (discount = 0.15) ) AS '15%',

(SELECT Count(*) FROM ProductsOrders P
WHERE O.OrderID=P.OrderID AND (discount = 0.20) ) AS '20%'

FROM Orders AS O
```

Result:

OrderID	'0%'	'15%'	'20%'
1	0	0	1
2	1	2	1
3	0	2	2
4	0	1	0
5	1	3	1

Record: 1 of 998   No Filter   Search

The above SQL example will work in any relational database, and it represents a way to create crosstab reports. However, in Access 2010, we have the option to create the exact same report by taking advantage of the TRANSFORM and PIVOT statements for crosstab queries to obtain the same results in a faster and easier way without the need to write multiple subqueries. In addition, if we had 15 different discount levels, we would have to write 15 subqueries. Instead, by using crosstab queries, we can always write the same code below. However, in case we needed to present only a few specific discount categories, subqueries give us tremendous and unique flexibility for it.

Code:
TRANSFORM Count(ProductsOrders.[Discount]) AS CountDiscount
SELECT OrderID
FROM ProductsOrders
GROUP BY OrderID
PIVOT Discount

Notice that 1000 orders returned using subqueries, while only 919 returned using TRANSFORM. This is because TRANSFORM left out orders that contained no products, while the subqueries code returned all orders—even those without any products displaying 0s for all three discount categories of "0", "15%", and "20%". This is not a problem of the crosstab or subqueries code. It is simply a business fact that there are some orders in the database that are not processed yet. This fact makes things a bit more complicated, but it happens. So, I want you to know how crosstab queries and subqueries fare under these circumstances.

Result:

OrderID	0	0_15	0_2
1			1
2	1	2	1
3		2	2
4		1	
5	1	3	1

Record: 1 of 919 — No Filter — Search

APPENDIX I
THE SAMPLE DATABASE

You can download the sample database from:
http://databasechannel.com/Products/default.html by clicking on the book you have.

The Entity Relationship Diagram (ERD) of the database is shown below:

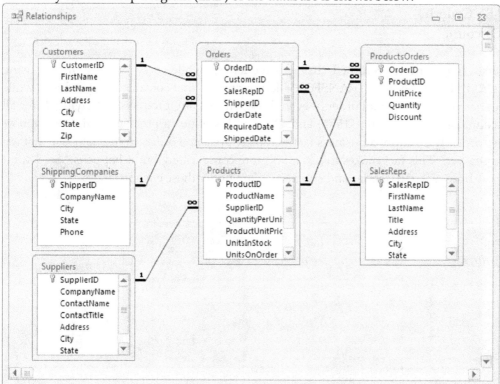

1. There is a one-to-many relationship between Customers and Orders.
2. There is a many-to-many relationship between Orders and Products with the table ProductsOrders functioning as the join table. The table ProductsOrders holds all of the details about each particular order and what products it contains. Its primary key is the combination of the primary keys of the Orders and Products tables.

3. As you can see from the ERD, there are also one-to-many relationships between the ShippingCompanies and Orders tables, Suppliers and Products, and SalesReps and Orders. The SalesReps table is our employees table, i.e. our salespeople.

The tables you see in the ERD diagram are the main tables in the database. However, I have created copies of the main tables so that you can work on examples without affecting the main tables. All of the secondary tables have the prefix "tbls", and you can work on them at will, deleting or updating data without affecting the main tables of the database. Just in case something goes wrong, however, you can download the database again as you please.

INDEX OF TERMS

www.ingramcontent.com/pod-product-compliance
Lightning Source LLC
Chambersburg PA
CBHW082109070326
40689CB00052B/3858

* 9 7 8 0 9 8 8 3 3 0 0 2 3 *